CW00806948

FIGURED WORLDS:
ONTOLOGICAL OBSTACLES IN
INTERCULTURAL RELATIONS

ANTHROPOLOGICAL HORIZONS
Editor: Michael Lambek, University of Toronto

This series, begun in 1991, focuses on theoretically informed ethnographic works addressing issues of mind and body, knowledge and power, equality and inequality, the individual and the collective. Interdisciplinary in its perspective, the series makes a unique contribution in several other academic disciplines: women's studies, history, philosophy, psychology, political science, and sociology.

For a list of the books published in this series see p. 301.

Figured Worlds

Ontological Obstacles in Intercultural Relations

Edited by John Clammer, Sylvie Poirier,
and Eric Schwimmer

UNIVERSITY OF TORONTO PRESS
Toronto Buffalo London

© University of Toronto Press Incorporated 2004
Toronto Buffalo London
Printed in Canada

ISBN 0-8020-8749-3

Printed on acid-free paper

National Library of Canada Cataloguing in Publication

Figured worlds : ontological obstacles in intercultural relations / John
Clammer, Sylvie Poirier, Eric Schwimmer, editors.

(Anthropological horizons)
Includes bibliographical references and index.
ISBN 0-8020-8749-3

1. Ethnic conflict.   2. Culture conflict.   3. Ontology.   I. Clammer, John
II. Poirier, Sylvie, 1953–   III. Schwimmer, Eric   IV. Series.

GN496.F44 2004   305.8   C2003-906042-X

This book has been published with the help of a grant from the Canadian
Federation for the Humanities and Social Sciences through the Aid to
Scholarly Publishing program, using funds provided by the Social Sciences
and Humanities Research Council of Canada.

University of Toronto Press acknowledges the financial assistance to its
publishing program of the Canada Council for the Arts and the Ontario
Arts Council.

University of Toronto Press acknowledges the financial support for its
publishing activities of the Government of Canada through the Book
Publishing Industry Development Program (BPIDP).

Contents

Acknowledgments

This volume was conceived in October 1996 at a conference at Université Laval in Quebec, 'Ontological Obstacles in Intercultural Relations.' The papers that were originally presented and selected for this volume have since been rewritten and extensively revised and supplemented by additional essays from Tim Ingold, David Parkin, and Colin Samson, who were not able to attend the original meeting. The editors wish to gratefully acknowledge the financial support of the Social Sciences and Humanities Research Council of Canada through its program Aid to Occasional Research Conferences and International Congresses in Canada. We also thank the Faculty of Social Sciences and the Department of Anthropology at Université Laval and its graduate student assistants, who greatly facilitated the organization of the workshop. Our deepest thanks go to the university itself for generously offering the Forêt Montmorency field station, its wooded lakeside setting highly appropriate given the theme of the meeting. The editors would also like to express warm gratitude to the Indigenous Canadian participants, namely Mary Coon (Cree-Atikamekw), Clifford Moar (Innu), and Curtis Nelson and Charly Patton (Mohawk), whose passionate contributions, while not embodied in written papers, either here or at the original workshop, added a profound dimension to an academic conference. In respect for their struggles we sincerely hope that their insights have found their way into the essays that constitute this book, and we dedicate it to their efforts to bring nature back into culture.

Some of the chapters in the book have been previously published. A revised version of Tim Ingold's article appeared in *The Perception of the Environment* (Routledge, 2000); Sylvie Vincent's was published in French in the journal *Recherches amérindiennes au Québec* 32, no. 2 (2002): 99–106.

The editors wish to thank Donald Kellough for the translation and linguistic revision of some of the chapters. This book has been published with the help of a grant from the Humanities and Social Sciences Federation of Canada, using funds provided by the Social Sciences and Humanities Research Council of Canada. We gratefully acknowledge its support.

Preface: The Nature of Nature

ERIC SCHWIMMER

> World visions can conceive of everything, except alternative world visions.
>
> Umberto Eco, *Semiotics and the Philosophy of Language*

Umberto Eco's challenging philosophical postulate has not yet been fully digested in the social sciences. The present volume offers approaches in social science for the study of alternative ontologies. Though many studies have been made about difference, these mostly focus on intermediate-level concepts: ethnic groups, values, power discrepancy, material resources, colonialism, traditional beliefs, ritual, artistic languages. Yet when inquiry starts by defining an 'observable datum' and a 'correct (or true) observation,' it posits philosophical categories from the outset that are part of a particular ontology or world vision.

Each of the four parts of this book presents one necessary part of the study of an ontology or 'way of being in the world.' Part I describes how knowledge is obtained about such a figured world, made up of sensation, affirmation and will, prophecy, revelations, myths, dreams, and metamorphoses. Part II sets out how the different figured worlds within a given social space are related, either in a network of exchange and complementarity, or as a set of unbridged conflicting solitudes. In Parts III and IV, we turn to the dynamics of these conflicting solitudes, mostly from the viewpoint of subordinated minorities. This may take the form of movement from bondage to freedom, perceived in both its existential, ontological, and practical and material aspects. Such a movement may arise either on the transitory level of the person (Part III) or in more perpetual institutional structural forms (Part IV).

Our field areas – Canadian First Nations, Australian Aborigines, New Zealand Mâori, Japanese, Zanzibari – were chosen because they all share one ontological complex that has caused much confusion and strife in many parts of the world: an 'animist' attitude to nature, as expressed in ritual, myth, and general values. Though other ontological issues could have been chosen, this one has worldwide distribution and local relevance to Canada as well as being a core preoccupation of Western thought about nature. A Western philosopher who has profoundly explored the implications of postulating the equivalence of God and nature is Spinoza. A study by the philosopher Richard Mason (1997) shows this postulate lays a heavy burden on modern investigators. The immanent God of Spinoza, like immanent spirituality in cultural objects we studied, 'becomes naturalised, but nature also becomes divine ... While we can hardly forget that he identified God with nature, it may be easier to forget that this implied an identification of nature with God ... A recognition or acceptance of God and religion as natural is one of the hardest thoughts to keep in focus, because it can only be seen at the same time as an acceptance of nature as divine' (Mason 1997, 113, 170, 259).

Ingold's paper sets the tone by distinguishing explicitly between 'science' (in the Cartesian sense) and the kind of knowledge obtained through the experiences of the 'poetics of dwelling.' While Ingold follows a Lévi-Straussian pattern in describing the technical side of the 'transformations' (dreams, metamorphoses, etc.), he shows the essence of their religious struggle to be an exorcism of bondage and self-liberation. The conditions of an investigator's apprenticeship are fully shown in Poirier's paper, which illustrates the implications of the immanent spirituality of nature by the example of the divine as well as material geometry of Kukatja territory-mapping operations.

In contrast, Clammer's treatment of Shintô shows that such a vision of the world may not always be intelligible as a thing in itself, but may become a 'clear and distinct idea' only if the investigator broadens his or her analytic range to include the world visions of Buddhism, Confucianism, and Japan's military-political system. Even then, a postulate that veneration of nature is an 'essence' of contemporary Japanese culture remains a mere conjecture unless its ubiquity can be established by wide-ranging tests. If the postulate is confirmed, it leads to the further question: by what historical process was a complementarity between disparate world visions achieved in this case, when it proved to be very difficult in the other cases we examined?

In contrast, this volume presents two studies (Part II) showing the kinds of crises that can occur when incompatible world visions coexist within the same state for a prolonged historical period. Here, oral traditions of an alternative ontology and mainstream historical sources from the same territorial space set up two world visions that remain wholly opaque to one another. Parkin and Vincent both found that their minority group continues to emit signals of deep crisis and suffering, in an ontological idiom that remains meaningless to the mainstream. The mainstream has never taken the ontological dimension of the minorities' stories seriously. For the reasons given by Mason, this may be very hard to bring about, as mainstream historiography is deeply embedded in the culture's ontological systems.

The rest of the volume considers the practical consequences of the presence of plural ontologies within the same state. In Part III, the distinction between positional and ontological identity is clarified, and it is shown, in two papers on Algonquian illness and health, that an ontological problem arises here. Sedentarization made the Innu subject to rules that were incompatible with their ontology. This experience left many unable to take charge of themselves, which led to social disasters, signalled by numerous suicides. As the political system left no room for the negotiation of ontologies, they attempted to comply. Their resistance was limited to forms of withdrawal. Samson analyses these forms, as practised within the settlement, while Tanner studies withdrawal to other places, to another, older form of obedience, in Innu healing rites. As bands acted in concert, older ritual performances, based on rules that only a few individuals could accept, were replaced by practices that maintained the essence of old ritual in a new form. Intolerable conditions of bondage thus gave rise to a process of self-liberation, reflectivity, and authoring of new selves. Tanner usefully shows that healing rites involving spiritually charged objects are the essence of a project of practical thinking in the field of mental health.

Part IV studies the possibilities of negotiating pluralistic social systems that admit a plurality of ontologies as legitimate. We did not include armed resistance and terrorism, but restricted ourselves to peaceful forms of resistance. Indigenous people everywhere are struggling for self-determination. Modern states make concessions while ensuring that state power will continue to depend on mainstream ontology. What minorities seek is the political legitimacy of multiple ontologies. The success of negotiations depends on the willingness of controlling institutions to allow the autonomous expression of an ontology whose essence lies in the 'poetics of dwelling.' It also depends on the skill and knowledge of minority leaders and their mediating institutions in presenting the rudiments of that ontology to outsiders, in forms that can be shared by both sides.

Although most of the essays deal with Indigenous Peoples, the pattern of divinizing nature is by no means confined to them. Therefore, we are also addressing a wider audience, the carriers of newly generated concepts of 'nature,' often with a connotation of immanent spirituality, and so formulated that individuals adopting them can attune them to their own reflections. Movements institute forms of apprenticeship to help members to develop skills relevant to the lives of 'New Men' (in the sense of Appadurai 1996, 5), who will, individually and collectively, share in the burden of ontological negotiation. These New Men create new rules to live by, which may in time create their own bondage. But we are, at present, witnessing a flourishing of immanent spirituality within movements that reflect upon and transform 'nature' concepts, offering their own joys, their own healing, as well as their own solidarity and mobilization.

REFERENCES

Appadurai, A. 1996. *Modernity at Large.* Minneapolis: University of Minnesota Press.
Eco, U. 1984. *Semiotics and the Philosophy of Language.* Bloomington: University of Indiana Press.
Mason, R. 1997. *The God of Spinoza.* Cambridge: Cambridge University Press.
Spinoza, B. 1992 [1677]. *Ethics.* Indianapolis: Hackett.

FIGURED WORLDS:
ONTOLOGICAL OBSTACLES IN
INTERCULTURAL RELATIONS

Introduction: The Relevance of Ontologies in Anthropology – Reflections on a New Anthropological Field

JOHN CLAMMER, SYLVIE POIRIER,
AND ERIC SCHWIMMER

Conflict between cultures is endemic in the modern world. It surfaces in examples as diverse as ethnic cleansing in the former Yugoslavia, religious or sectarian war in Northern Ireland and parts of the former Soviet Union, separatism in the Basque country, and the independence movement in East Timor. Many of these disputes are large in scale and may threaten the stability of regions or even, potentially, the world. Closer to many anthropologists, with their characteristic interest in the local and its expression in the life of small-scale communities and of relations between such communities (despite growing disciplinary concern with globalization and large-scale structures), are the conflicts that arise between Indigenous Peoples and the nation states in which almost without exception they are now embedded. Where such conflicts are identified at all, whether between indigenes and the state or between competing groups within pluralistic state-based societies, they are often explained in terms of what are actually lower-level concepts, such as ethnicity or identity (Eriksen 1998), rather than through a more fundamental archaeology of uncovering what we are here calling, following the phrase introduced into anthropological discourse by Holland et al. (1998), 'figured worlds' – the cosmologies or ontological conceptions upon which culture is ultimately based, and in the friction between which, in a pluralistic world, conflict is generated.

Older traditions of legal anthropology tended to emphasize dispute resolution as its foundational practice and veered largely towards a materialist model of the obviously prior question of how conflict was generated – one based, that is, on competition for resources. But even more basic is the question of what those resources themselves mean and how they come to be resources in the first place. For one society this may be land, for another game, for yet another the sacred places and paths that particular spaces contain and, indeed, embody. To address these issues, other questions must be asked, involving the highest-level conceptions available to a culture, questions that involve its under-standings of human identity and selfhood and the relationship of people to the physical world within which their actions are necessarily con-tained. In short, the ontologies – the figured worlds in which practice is shaped – constitute the largest or most fundamental frame out of which culture is shaped. It is currently fashionable in anthropology to regard the basic role of the discipline, in a postcolonial world, to be the recov-ery of Indigenous knowledge. But no ontology is simply a system of knowledge; it is equally, as the term itself implies, an account of a way of being in the world and a definition through practice (and not only through cognition) of what that world is and how it is constituted. If ontologies are basic to the construction of culture, then it is reasonable to assume that differing conceptions of being-in-the-world necessarily enter into conflicts between systems (societies or cultures) based on different ontological premises. How one figures one's own world greatly determines how one will relate to other possible and perhaps conflict-ing configurations that one might encounter.

It is precisely this issue which is hidden, or insufficiently explicated, in disputes between Indigenous Peoples and modern nation states over land, hunting, fishing, and the extraction of natural resources. Conven-tional anthropological approaches to dispute resolution have tended to concentrate on disputes within a single culture in which the disputants share the same basic ontological assumptions, or on conflicts between members of contiguous cultures where large cosmological common-alities exist regardless of any political differences between them. In neither of these cases are ontological conceptions as such at issue; the disputes are taking place within a common framework. But in cases in which the ontologies are at radical variance, the disputes move to an altogether different level, one involving far more than simply questions of property rights and similar factors.

There are large political issues here, ones that stand in acute need of anthropological intervention. In the contemporary globalized world of late modernity, few if any cultures exist in isolation, and, indeed, the notion of culture itself in this environment has, as we are aware, come under acute critical scrutiny (Clifford 1994; Wright 1998). A rather oc-cluded aspect of this revaluation, however, has been the recognition that the actual dynamics of relationships between cultures are not necessarily benign. Whatever peaceful contact occurs through trade, intermarriage, and travel, less peaceful encounters occur through war, conquest, economic domination, the unrestrained expansion of the consumer economy, and what for many Indigenous Peoples amounts to the sum of all of these – the expropriation of their ancestral land and hunting territories by states or corporations for mining, forestry, hydro-electric plants, agri-business, tourism, military usage, or urban expansion. A large body of anthropological literature now attests to the fact that the loss of land is not simply the loss of property, but something closer to the loss of soul, of the material mediator between humans and the universe.

Anthropology, and not simply what is sometimes dubbed applied anthropology, turns out to be of central practical importance, bearing directly on the concrete and contemporary crises that many indigenes face in Canada, India, Malaysia, New Zealand, Brazil, Venezuela, Australia, and many other locations around the globe, and also bears on theoretical and strategic debates within development studies. When conflicts between indigenes and states are closely examined from an anthropological perspective, at their root lie not only material factors but also ontological conceptions – cosmocentric as opposed to anthropocentric understandings of peoples' place in the universe, images of nature, ideas of the self, of the body, of gender, and of mind-body relationships, to name some of the most significant. These in turn prove to be linked in profound ways to ideas of health, healing, religion, identity, food, aesthetics, symbolism, and architecture. In the final analysis, the explication of culture cannot ignore the question of ontologies.

This also applies to the explication of the relationship between cultures. Much of the existing work on multiculturalism (e.g., Jordan and Weedon 1995) confines itself largely to issues of race and ethnicity and, to a lesser extent, to gender, without either connecting these to the underlying ontologies at work (e.g., particular conceptions of nature and the place of human beings within it) or, if ethnicity and gender are to be so privileged, without understanding them as implicated in wider networks of meaning and signification – networks containing, for example, ideas of embodiment, selfhood, and the nature of relationships. This is not only true of multiculturalism; disputes over, for example, sociobiological interpretations of human nature and behaviour are subject to the same considerations. Ontologies – the figured worlds upon which cultures are founded and through which they performatively reproduce themselves – are foundational to the understanding of intercultural relations. They are the practical reason that, as both practice and reason, frames knowledge (in constituting an epistemology) and provides the matrix of relationships.

Ontologies are consequently political in the widest sense (body politics, cultural politics) and are the key to the phenomenological forms that order actual everyday life – gender, sexuality, understandings of health and illness, relationships to nature, the expression of emotions, attitudes towards religion and religious conversion. A methodology for their explication, the taking seriously of the cultural data that they reveal and the exploration of their place in politics, and hence in disputes, constitute, we suggest, one of the most important projects for anthropology if it is to both theoretically evolve and to establish its relevance as a discipline of practical implications in a highly complex multicultural world.

Forêt Montmorency

This collection of papers arose directly out of a colloquium held in Forêt Montmorency, Quebec. Three papers were added afterwards but the author of one of these (Ingold) had been invited before the conference was held, while another (Samson) was related to the same data and in the same spirit. Parkin's paper added a new dimension, still focused on the precise problem of the colloquium. Thematically, this collection is homogeneous. Its theme is the ontological obstacles in intercultural relations. Anthropologists have always been repositories of multiple ontologies. On the other hand, they have used a wide range of devices (not enumerated here) to avoid having to consider these ontologies as a serious account of the universal and necessary characteristics of existence. In the period when universities seriously taught the Popperian approach, field activity and experience were viewed as a 'learning period,' an 'apprenticeship' without scientific value in itself. Papers in the present collection view them much more as an 'initiation,' implying the truth value of what is being learnt. Such are the boons of postcolonialism. The ethnographer 'initiand' is being defined as a *person* among persons, human and non-human. His or her task is to decipher the 'poetics of dwelling' of figured worlds. This task thus becomes *in part* involved with literary theory.

The fact that Quebec was the conference site helped to focus the new field, not necessarily on Quebec Autochthons, but on a bundle of contexts that may have become forcefully, even obsessively, present in that locality which thus becomes a good place to conceptualize our field theoretically. Our starting point was undoubtedly the situation of many Indigenous Peoples, which we perceived as being critical, materially and culturally. Viewing their obstacles holistically, we began to study ontology and saw that the labour of understanding goes beyond cognitive, intellectual analysis. It requires also a sort of initiation adding to the researcher's own apprehension of reality, when dealing with bodily nature and non-human *persons* that Westerners tend to regard as *things*.

Philosophy of nature and of animism became its general focus, irrespective of the site of research or the provenance of authors. So, for example, although Parkin wrote about Zanzibar, his problem of 'suffering bodies and disaster zones and landscapes' was welcomed for the new light it shed on perceptions of nature we had already noted among Autochthons in Canada and Papua New Guinea (see Schwimmer 1972, 1977).

Perhaps a historical anecdote about how the colloquium came about will serve to illuminate how this new field of anthropology is constituted. The history goes back to an encounter between Clammer and Schwimmer at the ASA Decennial Conference at Oxford in 1993. On that occasion Clammer gave a paper titled 'Sustaining Otherness: Self, Nature and Ancestralism among Contemporary Japanese Christians,' in which he notably suggested that

> the Japanese conception, and indeed experience, of the interpenetration of nature and society expresses itself both in the belief in a special relationship between the Japanese and nature and, more fundamentally, in the way in which understandings of the self are constructed ... The web of relationships that define and encompass the individual are seen as greater than just society ... Freedom is not just emancipation from society, but the pure experience of nature. From this point of view the Christian approach to self and to nature is distinctly odd. Nature in conventional Christianity is regarded as external to man (and to God) and the self is regarded as incomplete. Both are considered as 'fallen' and salvation as ... entirely unmediated by nature. Some commentators on Christianity in Japan have recognized this problem. Lee (1967), for instance, sees the Japanese attitude to nature (and through it to the body) as being one of the biggest barriers to the spread of that religion. (Clammer 1997, 182)

Similar ontological barriers arise between mainstream Christians in Canada and Autochthons who, like the Japanese, construct their self-identity in a special relationship with nature, a Japanese form of animism. In the Canadian case, however, this ontological obstacle to mutual comprehension has caused immeasurably more damage to the Autochthons, especially in spheres like health, education, mental well-being, crime, economic development, political autonomy, and juridical negotiation. Underlying the many failures of this cohabitation is the fact of radical ontological misunderstanding, as the cognitive and affective worlds of dominant and dominated remain unknown to one another. It therefore appears as though many practical problems cannot be solved without a serious concern with ontological history of figured worlds. The word 'serious' plays a key role as our first reaction to alien ontologies is to regard them as simply untrue. Faced with people who hold untrue beliefs, our first reaction is to correct their errors. Yet this may lead only to further error, for we know since Wittgenstein that the cognitive worlds of Indigenous Peoples are not really in error, yet we proceed, often even in anthropology, as though there are errors to be corrected in the figured worlds of some peoples.

Roughly, this explains the historical genesis of the Forêt Montmorency colloquium. Clammer's modelling of Japanese Christianity was transformed to apply to Indigenous Peoples in Quebec, but also among Australian Aborigines and New Zealand Mâori, eventually also in Zanzibar. It is relevant to note that most participants of this colloquium, including the Cree, Mohawk, Innu, and Atikamekw intellectuals present, were deeply involved in applied anthropology, but that all were convinced of the ontological nature of some of their basic problems.

The themes of this volume are still those of the colloquium. Clammer's holistic paper 'The Politics of Animism' served as the keynote address. At the time of the colloquium, the question that concerned us most was why differences in conceptualizing the human/nature relationship gave rise to such deep, refractory problems. Now that all the papers are in, we can see that we had wandered into one of the best-kept secrets that divide the world into non-communicating fragments. If animism, supposedly the most primitive form of religion, really survived in contemporary Japan (and many other highly modern societies), we need to call into question what has long been thought about humanity's relation to land, animals, plants, and the cosmos in general. It may have been a mistake to define the concept as a type of religion. The key question that divides the world is perhaps rather, Where does knowledge come from? Does it come from a soul inside us, or from relations we entertain with human and non-human persons in the outside world?

The second answer to this question has often, in the West, been regarded as inferior to the first. Bird-David (1999) called it a 'relational epistemology' – 'The object of this animistic knowledge is understanding relatedness from a related point of view within the shifting horizons of the related viewer' (S77). This is true for all models in this volume. On the theme of identity, Schweder and Bourne (1984) show that the Western concept of identity tends to be acontextual, abstract, and independent, while the non-Western notion is context dependent, concrete, and socially defined. Without necessarily following this radical division between 'East' and 'West,' all our participants are involved with the second of these two notions of identity. They situate it in historical, collectively defined, socially produced, culturally constructed activities, with a meaningful, holistic intent toward their surroundings. This is what Holland et al. (1998) call 'figured worlds.'

Figured Worlds

'Figured worlds' is another term that, while not explicitly launched at the colloquium, seems to reflect a common orientation of this essay collection. It stands for a viewpoint that may reconcile the apparent contradiction between 'culturalism' (which holds that truth is relative to culture) and 'constructionism' (which finds truth only in the management of social capital). Few anthropologists fully adhere to either of these viewpoints, but they are invoked in many debates. Figured worlds are discourses built up by relational logic, linking people, cultural forms, and social positions by facts of experience in specific historical worlds. The notion of 'relational logic,' developed in the works of Peirce, Lévi-Strauss, Bateson, and Bakhtin, is pervasive in this volume. Unlike naturalistic anthropology, it does not derive its findings from postulates but from a notion of *system* in which no element can change without precipitating change in all the others; it is made up of 'differences that make a difference.' The human and non-human 'persons' involved in such systems have experiences in different contexts, interpret them in a plurality of 'voices' (heteroglossia) from which they create a multi-layered 'identity.' This kind of anthropology does not study the internal structure of the 'individual person' but rather her or his environmental context. Bateson poses the question, How we can know anything? 'In the pronoun *we*, I of course included the starfish and the redwood forest, the segmenting egg and the Senate of the United States' (1979, 4).

Indigenous Peoples caught between strongly contrasting ontologies construct their figured worlds as a global system within which they usually include imaginative responses to the positional constraints. Thus, Poirier's landscape of the Kukatja figured world contains a bullock, representing Western ontology. On this point, Parkin's paper in this volume is exemplary. Constructionist theory readily explains the imagined alliance with the Oman sultanate as part of the Pemba figured world, but would reduce Popobawa, the bat-wing spirit, to an insignificant essentialist survival. Again, culturalist theory could not explain the rationale of Popobawa's comings and goings.

Parkin resolves the apparent theorical impasse by fusing constructionist and culturalist perspectives. 'A proliferation of unexplained sufferings, rooted in the past' (Parkin, below, p. 129) is part of the figured world on a deep ontological level. It explains fear of Popobawa as a constraint due to historical experience of the Zanzibari political environment, temporarily immobilizing the Oman-oriented figured world without annihilating it. Parkin's model of the Pemba imagination subordinates current political constructions to a perennial view of man-in-nature, linking the vicissitudes of nature to those of the human condition.

Although it has always been an objective of our trade to describe local worlds as meaningful wholes, we have only recently become aware of the awesome implications of the ontological dimension of figured worlds. Culturalism is one way of escaping the dilemma, as it does not assign a truth value to alien ontologies. Constructionism likewise evades this dilemma, as it minimizes differences between ontologies. Meanwhile, the prospect of Western scientists studying Indigenous ontologies is not welcomed by all Indigenous researchers: 'The arguments of different indigenous peoples based on spiritual relationships to the universe, to the landscape and to stones, rocks, insects and other things, seen and unseen, have been difficult arguments for Western systems of knowledge to deal with and accept. These arguments give a partial indication of the different world views and alternative ways of coming to know, and of being, that still endure within the indigenous world ... It is one of the few parts of ourselves which the West cannot decipher, cannot understand and cannot control ... yet' (Smith 1999, 74). This volume shows, however, that Western ignorance of the incompatible figured world of Autochthon hunters is far from an unmixed blessing. It is a major problem, even for hunter-gatherers 'well integrated into their respective states who live by such diverse means as state benefits or jobs in the state bureaucracies' (Bird-David 1999, S73; see also Samson and Tanner in this volume).

Ingold's paper opens up ontological questions in which anthropology, more than a century after E.B. Tylor, is just beginning to take a serious interest: What is a 'person'? Do animals and inanimate things have speech, sentience, volition, memory? Can a human being be turned into a bear prowling in the forest? How do 'persons' acquire knowledge? What is experience? Ingold's paper (conjointly with his 1999 'Comment') argues that authors such as Hallowell, Humphrey, Guthrie, Goody, and Descola all leave room for maintaining that the trees, animals, and stones with which hunters communicate are *really non-human* and that they all fit 'squarely within a naturalist ontology.'

Instead, Ingold – like other contributors to this volume – holds that the borders between the human and non-human realms are permeable, that human and non-human forms are subject to metamorphosis, and that figured worlds are perpetuated through commitment, participation, and performance by human and non-human persons. Ingold describes the ontology of this system as the 'poetics of dwelling' (a hunter-gatherer ontology explicated in Ingold 1998) and treats it on an equal level with the ontology of Western science. In some systems the self is autonomous, in others it is relational, and the twain may never meet. These ontologies all give meaning to the universe as a whole. People who view their selves as relational are well aware of the incomprehension and ill-treatment their ideas provoke on the part of dominant powers.

It is perhaps in Poirier's essay that we come closest to a practical solution to this problem. She presents the image of a foreign apprentice who goes to an Aboriginal community to seek experience and knowledge of plants and animals. Her story of Tjuppurula's painting helps us to understand the initiatory performances by which Kukatja knowledge is constituted and perpetuated. She does not claim she will ever equal Kukatja's depth of knowledge, but she keeps on trying, with the community as willing guide. She is not seeking 'control' (as Linda Smith fears), but a kind of initiation, enabling her, as a novice, to see the world both as a Kukatja landscape and as the landscape with which she grew up. This viable approach is rooted in a relational logic. By the same token, this researcher learnt to regard her own self as not necessarily autonomous but open to several relational perspectives, of which the Kukatja perspective is one. This procedure resembles Bakhtin's model of the 'dialogic' character in a novel, speaking in several 'voices,' each of which comes from its own figured world.

The contradiction with which this volume is specifically concerned is that the science of anthropology developed within a Western ontology, flawed by symbolic colonialism. If this flaw is mostly unconscious, so much worse for our credibility. Since the 1980s, when Bakhtin's work became better known, a new approach developed, which Appadurai has approvingly dubbed 'the hijack of culture by literary studies' and 'the basis for a cosmopolitan ethnography' (1996, 51). Ingold's remarkable notion of Ojibwa ontology (a poetics of dwelling) is a case in point. This term not only tells us that the local scene contains many (non-human and human) persons sending messages full of 'meaning,' but also that the 'codes' are never constant or sure; the relations are 'poetic.' They seem like a blend of Bakhtinian dialogism and Batesonian mapping.

This is not a relativist model, because, as Bird-David says, '*As* and *when* and *because* [persons] engage in and maintain relationships with other [i.e., non-human] beings, they constitute them as kinds of person: they make them relatives by sharing with them' (1999, S73). Initiation into such a figured world is an experience that commits the novice absolutely. Nor can novices easily simulate commitment, for they are under close surveillance. These local figured worlds do not have universal relevance in the manner of literature or theatre, by suspending disbelief, but as relations entered into, such as work activities, outcomes, and values. The learners of a new imaged world can apply their knowledge in other landscapes and correct errors they have previously lived by. This has become the stuff of postcolonial fieldwork. Maybe the refinements of Bakhtinian dialogism will soon become part of the standard training of the fieldworker.

Positional Identities

Figured worlds are not relevant only to hunter-gatherers and other Indigenous Peoples, but also to historically circumscribed, though never closed, venues of social activity in industrialized societies. Holland et al. (1998) tell of romance at two universities, of drinking and not drinking in a chapter on Alcoholics Anonymous, and of the diagnosis of mental illness, all in the United States. The more complex the local world, the greater the weight of the symbolic capital of prestigious actors. For this reason, Bourdieu's constructivist analysis of power relations is a powerful tool in many contexts. At the same time, there are events, such as Popobawa, whose meaning remains obscure unless we look beyond praxis and analyse the ontological foundation of Pemba's positional identity.

The same is true for networks of Indigenous political, social, and religious agents who mediate between their people and government or non-government organizations in contemporary states. These are analysed in some detail in the chapters by Samson, Schwimmer, and Tanner. Such persons are often referred to as bicultural, because they are bilingual and have positions within both the Indigenous and the mainstream communities. In the Indigenous communities they are strongly identified, often as leaders, with local imagined worlds. It is in their dealings with the mainstream that their discourse becomes many-voiced in the way of Bakhtin's novelistic characters. For in discourse with mainstream organizations, it is not enough for the bicultural to be familiar with mainstream language; they must also be able to press the claim of their Indigenous people, which often requires reference to ancient rights, customs, and social principles. In the manner of the quotation from Linda Tuhiwai Smith above, they switch codes several times in the same paragraph, from epistemological critique to animism, with a hint of Indigenous activism thrown in.

This raises the general question of how bicultural agents live in situations where practices derived from naturalistic ontology are incompatible with principles of relational logic. Certainly, if such situations arise in democratic states, negotiation may lead to peaceable outcomes. Such outcomes do, however, have ontological consequences: they lead to new constructions of cultural identity. Though mainstream power favours assimilation, this is the most precarious of possible choices for Indigenous Peoples. Many prefer to create new figured worlds and identities invoking some historical core elements, derived from a relational ontology. On the other hand, the range of relations absorbed in the identity of 'New Men' ('survivors of the damage of colonialism' [Potiki 1993, 319]) is very wide, transforming relational and mainstream essences to newly created concepts ascribed to a universal category of Indigenous, oppressed, Third World, dark-skinned peoples with whom 'New Men' identify *in general*. But most peoples described in this book (e.g., by Tanner, Poirier, Schwimmer) do not differentiate clearly between the *positional* identity of the 'New Man' within an ethnically ordered mainstream society and his *ontological* identity as a universal category.

Clammer's study, however, opens wider perspectives as Shintô animism and shamanism are shown to coexist with Buddhism and Confucianism in such a way that the typical Japanese person in some measure adheres to several ontological systems. Though all these maintain their own logical boundaries, these need not coincide with ethnic or social boundaries. To some extent, the same might be said of Zanzibar, where identities are shown to be linked to a plurality of ethnic and other collective commitments. Both Clammer's and Parkin's studies show that persons may adhere to a set of nationally available ontologies, none of which are reserved for a particular ethnic group, caste, or class. This is also observable in New Zealand, where the Pâkehâ (White) population has for some years been exposed to and 'consumes' many 'products' of Mâori 'culture' – novels, stories, songs, dances, visual arts, lifestyle – which are beginning to offer vistas of an alternative ontology to the whole country. Such categories are treated here as positional constraints on figured worlds, but not as logically prior to figured worlds.

Nonetheless, many ontological issues (e.g., history, law, health care) are inseparable from the 'ethnic' terms in which they are usually treated. Vincent shows that mainstream Canadian and Innu historiography operate on incompatible ontological foundations, that histories are part of figured worlds, and that a history cannot be understood outside the figured world that is represented in it. Is it possible, in principle, to write a history confronting two ontologies, two identity constructs, and tell the story of their symbiosis over time? Vincent cites no examples, but there are some in New Zealand, recognized as such by intellectuals on both sides of the fence (Judith Binney, Ann Salmond, Ranginui Walker). If Innu or mainstream scholars construct an image of Quebec history consonant with the perspectives of both sides, this might facilitate symbiosis between the two peoples; but Vincent is describing the state of bicultural historiography in Canada, which seems hardly more advanced than in the days of Herodotus.

The contradictions in historiography, for which Vincent provides evidence, have a major impact on the jurisprudence of rights of Indigenous minorities. Melkevik's analysis in this volume confirms Appadurai's dictum that 'States are everywhere seeking to monopolize the moral resources of community, either by flatly claiming perfect coevality, or by systematically museumizing and representing all the groups within them in a variety of heritage politics that seems remarkably uniform throughout the world' (1996, 39). This is what the Supreme Court of Canada appears to have been doing, but as a Norwegian philosopher of law, Melkevik knows that some other judicial systems (e.g., in Norway and New Zealand) recognize partnership obligations with present-day Indigenous Peoples, without giving weight to dubious projections of pre-contact legal systems.

Melkevik's model is favourable to a jurisprudence based on the present figured worlds and ontologies of Sami, Mâori, Canadian, and Australian Autochthons. Such a principle has effects that are less radical than one might imagine, as the dominant Whites in all these countries can claim their own very considerable rights by their own jurisprudence and ontology, but his model is useful because of its recognition of Indigenous Peoples' cultural autonomy and of the legitimacy of their ontologies.

Samson's and Tanner's studies of Innu health place this issue on the more practical footing of physical survival. On the basis of their experience with White medicine and social services, Innu concluded that if they did not preserve their own ontology, they would die out. Their movement may not seem economically 'rational,' but they have reason to think their survival depends on it. Again, even if Indigenous ontology can become a life-or-death issue in certain mismanaged local cases, one wonders whether a more enlightened administration could not construct devices for the two ontological systems to operate side by side, without blocking effective access to services in health, education, and other social agencies. Certainly, this much has been achieved in countries like New Zealand and Norway without high unit costs. If other systems seem to cost less to maintain, this is because they remain effectively inaccessible. Ontological obstacles may create communicational barriers that block access to the social services that are ostensibly offered.

Authoring Selves and Making New Worlds

This volume nowhere suggests that the recognition of alien ontologies suffices to resolve the very complex problems of Indigenous Peoples. Its purpose is more limited. We favour the symbiosis, within the same state, of radically different ontologies. We believe that the symbiosis of naturalistic ontologies and a poetics of dwelling in the same state is not only possible but can be culturally beneficial. The form of symbiosis, known as 'procedural liberalism,' and favoured by American theorists like Rawls, is thoroughly naturalistic, giving no weight to concepts rooted in specific cultural traditions, but only to universal values concerning individual rights. Such a theory can have some positive outcomes, for instance, for New Zealand Mâori. Schwimmer's paper shows that it is possible to design professional procedures overstepping facts of ontological contradiction. Indigenous ontologies need not be penalized. It remains an open question, however, whether their 'truth value' is recognized by the mainstream. This is, indeed, the inquiry to which the present collection of essays is directed.

Taylor (1992, 1994) compares two models, designated as pluralism and dualism. He advocates that both models should give deep-level respect and recognition to national minorities, including their ontologies. He argues that a fusion of horizons operates through our developing new vocabularies of comparison, through transforming our standards. 'We owe all cultures a presumption of this kind' (Taylor 1992, 67). On this presumption, naturalism and the poetics of dwelling would be of equal worth. Yet this reasoning has theoretical as well as practical drawbacks. It goes counter to the poetics of dwelling, which offers no basis for owing anyone a presumption. Moreover, relational logic is incompatible with universalist proceduralism – a body of fixed rules anyone can learn to fit in with strangers. On a practical level, we may need to distinguish between 'pluralist' systems (where phenomenological inquiry into their often most elusive ontological systems may be impracticable) and 'dualist' systems (where a state is host to nation-like formations with ancient links to part or all of its territory). It is only in the latter type that Charles Taylor's method could effectively be pursued with some hope of arriving at profound mutual comprehension.

Two points emerge from our discussion. First, it confirms Tanner's argument that ontologies are not just metaphysical and theoretical, but also have important practical implications. Tanner discusses a sequence of three modes of Innu settlement. The traditional mode was semi-nomadic, with summer camp as a communal residential base. The second was sedentarized, in a mainstream Canadian environment, but as Samson also shows, this settlement mode is close to suicidal. The third mode is bi-residential: it offers a choice between living in modern-style settlements or in old-style hunting lodges where healing movements operate. This sequence of residence modes is at the same time a sequence of constructions of identity. In the third mode, identity and the figured world are defined in terms of a plurality of ontologies. These form a culturally heteroglossic system. The same might be said of

Schwimmer's analysis of contemporary Mâori. Second, the papers in this book and a few other recent sources (Bird-David 1999; Holland et al. 1998) propose a new subdiscipline, called ontological anthropology, with four branches, two of which study the authoring of selves. Many papers in this collection fall into more than one of these branches:

1 The construction of figured worlds: This method, illustrated by several cases in Holland et al. (1998), is based on three principles of relational epistemology: (i) persons are constitutive of relationships ('dividual'); (ii) 'environment' includes relations with family, plants, animals, ancestors, landscape, foods, but also with external power foci and the researcher; (iii) and performances of various kinds – 'religious,' 'magical,' 'entertainment,' etc. – are all viewed as social experiences, nested within socio-economic practice, serving to educate the attention and reproducing 'superpersons' as 'dividual' persons (Bird-David 1999). This volume shows instances of all these elements, including performances (e.g., Ingold, Poirier, Clammer, but also Parkin and Tanner). It also refers to actors' cultural knowledge and symbolic capital, and to learning situations, shared experiences, and events during the research period. Ontological data accumulate as the researcher participates in activities, thus learning the deeper meanings of what is done and not done.

2 Positional identities: Holland (1998) analyses how, in Nepal, one identifies one's caste position relative to others. This has to do with day-to-day and on-the-ground lived experience, relations of power, deference, and entitlement, social affiliation, and distance. Indigenous Peoples may occupy positions analogous to caste, except that many of the rules have become objects of negotiation. People are demanding recognition of their identity. Samson likewise opens up identity questions in this volume, in virtue of Innu-Akaneshau relations in Labrador. When he argues that 'alcohol is expressive of Innu existence,' he is showing how, due to context and history, Innu create their analogue of Popobawa. As Parkin, Vincent, and Tanner show, this aspect of positional identity calls for an ontological dimension. Some of the crucial facts fall outside Bourdieu's type of analysis.

3 Authoring selves: For Lévi-Strauss, whose 'work provided the first modern explanation that accepted indigenous knowledge of the

world' (Bird-David 1999, S70), the creation of new knowledge was
a 'bricolage' of elements of myth, a collective long-term process.
Bakhtin's concepts of 'heteroglossia' and 'dialogism' are likewise
models for the creation of knowledge,[1] but creators are persons and
action is instantaneous. Though few texts in this collection mention
Bakhtin, most of them use heteroglossia extensively as an epistemological mode. Ingold and Poirier bring out the heteroglossia arising
in the regular activities of hunting-gathering groups, whereas
Samson and Tanner (but also Clammer and Schwimmer) focus on
cultural heteroglossia arising from ontological diversity in large-
scale societies. Vincent presents Innu discourse as culturally mono-
glossic, but still mentions a key myth where White persons are
given a key role. In these papers, heteroglossia is a device for
authoring selves and correlating, within each utterance or action,
different voices of ontological anthropology: (i) principles of relational epistemology; (ii) negotiated positional identities; and (iii)
new sources of trans-national information (*rap speech/music*) about
the world.

4 Making worlds: New worlds and new identities emerge as a result
of a 'kind of dynamic uniting the intimate and the social sites of
cultural production' (Holland et al. 1998, 235). Our symposium
gives examples of new worlds, some splendid ones that remain on
the level of private imagination (Edward Piwas *apud* Samson), some
failed ones (Parkin), some in gestation (Te Whânau o Hoani Waititi
Marae), some based on the principle of legal pluralism (Melkevik),
and, finally, some that open up questions about the very concepts
of the New Man and New Worlds. We publish two accounts of the
Innu Health Movement, both reliable, but differing in perspective.
Tanner focuses on the figured world of isolated 'culture camp'
communities, where a New Man identity appears to be viable. Samson looks at the government-sponsored settlements and presents a
very different figured world, in a 'context of utter domination,'
where Innu cannot control the social sites of cultural production.
This would be a major obstacle to setting up New Man identities.

How to explain our interest in these ontologies? Does the West, in
some way, seek to appropriate the New Man? Is Linda T. Smith right in
distrusting our motives? Perhaps the time has come for the West to take
each of these voices of ontological anthropology seriously as we be-

come aware of disturbances in our cosmic equilibrium. Centralized, globalized institutions have become so strong that relational networks have shrunk and fragilized. Humanity's apparently absolute mastery of nature has led to rapid degeneration of our environment. After inventing a body/spirit dichotomy, humankind depends less on the evidence of the senses and more on the constructions of the *cogito*. If a rival construct such as the poetics of dwelling entered our awareness, would there be more equilibrium in our lives, while our institutions, economy, and rationality still survive?

Can relational epistemologies survive side by side with high-tech ways of living? The only answer an anthropologist can give is that not only are many Indigenous Peoples trying to bring this about, but also some ultra-modern states, notably in East Asia. Should such attempts be dismissed as ethnic identity ideologies? At any moment in time, this might seem to be the case, but ethnic ideologies have not, in the past, been confined to particular parts of the world. When they were invoked in the West, as by Spinoza, they were marginalized by cognitive schools of thought for centuries (Mason 1997),[2] but relational epistemology is apt to be remembered sooner or later in a different form, being perhaps an ineradicable part of humankind.

The Negotiation of Ontologies

If this is indeed the case, as we believe the papers in this collection to conclusively demonstrate, a whole subterranean history of intercultural relations waits to be recovered. Elements of this can already be seen scattered around the current intellectual landscape – the rediscovery of the body by contemporary sociology, the spilling over of ideas from ecology into wider social movements, the concern of postmodernist theory with localism and spatiality, attention even within anthropology to issues of risk and the uncertainties of life in the modern world (Douglas 1994), New Age forms of spirituality drawing not only on Asian but equally on American Indian traditions, the new alliances between formerly disparate liberatory movements (Marxism, ecology, feminism), and the rediscovery of previously marginal anthropological writers such as Gregory Bateson. A number of implications flow from this for the immediate development of anthropological theory. If conflict or contact between cultures is seen in terms of the negotiation of ontologies, any theory of social and cultural change is bound to be transformed, and the concept of 'multiculturalism' is enriched as its concerns with ethnicity and gender are deepened. Furthermore, interconnections prove to be established between apparently unrelated areas – land, zoosemiotics, kinship, ritual, the body, health, the self. This, as we have suggested above, transforms and provides the tools for transcending the apparently ineradicable tensions and incompatibilities between culturalist, constructivist, and relativist paradigms.

Finally, it forces us again to reconsider the perennial issue of cultural comparison. To consider animism for example as something *sui generis* and as a useful and empirically valid term, and not as something to be explained away in functionalist terms or in evolutionary ones, raises profound questions for the intentions, methodology, and practical consequences of anthropology. At one level we are in agreement with trends that have already emerged in anthropology, geography, and historical studies. For example, in studying the negotiation of ontologies, we are largely in accord with Marcus and Fischer's (1986) view of anthropology as cultural critique, and we are also in accord with Thomas (1994) on the ontological differences between the various historical forms of colonialism. Yet, at the same time, we see from the cases presented in this volume that anthropology still faces formidable problems in finding a mutually acceptable language that can describe the disagreements between cultures in a way that clarifies rather than intensifies the true nature of those disagreements.

While all such issues are political in some sense, we are also suggesting here that they are equally profoundly ontological. Once this is recognized a clearer basis for negotiation between cultures can be established not on the basis of difference as such, but on the recognition of the nature of those disputes as having their roots in ontological and hence existential and cosmological configurations of being-in-the-world.

If these concerns are indeed valid, then the whole basis of Western science and the political and cultural expansionism that has been based upon it is called deeply into question. Since this Western world view is an ontology in its own right, it is subject to the same consideration as all other ontologies. But at the very least it is radically relativized and forced to confront its claims to superiority. This act of relativizing forces the admission of alternative ways of being and alternative forms of knowledge, forms which have for centuries provided the basis for harmonious living on the common earth, and are proving again to be the resource upon which all may be forced to draw to ensure the possibility of sustainable life, biodiversity, and genuine cultural respect in the dawning new century.

NOTES

1 'At any given time, in any given place, there will be a set of conditions – social, historical, meteorological, physiological – that will ensure that a word uttered in that place and at that time will have a meaning different than it would have under any other conditions.' 'Dialogism is the characteristic epistemological mode of a world dominated by heteroglossia. Everything means, is understood as part of a greater whole – there is a constant interaction between meanings, all of which have the potential of conditioning others' (Bakhtin 1981, 426, 428).

2 'In current terminology we could say it was because he refused to accept the possibility of unconnected, discontinuous forms of description' (Mason 1997, 259).

REFERENCES

Appadurai, A. 1996. *Modernity at Large.* Minneapolis: University of Minnesota Press.

Bakhtin, M. 1981. *The Dialogical Imagination: Four Essays by M. Bakhtin.* Edited by M. Holquist. Austin: University of Texas Press.

Bateson, G. 1979. *Man and Nature.* New York: Bantam Books.

Bird-David, N. 1999. '"Animism" Revisited.' *Current Anthropology* 40 (Supplement): S67–S91.

Clammer, J. 1997. 'Sustaining Otherness.' *Japan Forum II*, 9 (2): 177–94.

Clifford, J. 1994. *The Predicament of Culture.* Cambridge: Harvard University Press.

Douglas, M. 1994. *Risk and Blame: Essays in Cultural Theory.* London: Routledge.

Eriksen, T.H. 1998. *Common Denominators: Ethnicity, Nation Building and Compromise in Mauritius.* Oxford: Berg.

Holland, D., W. Lachicotte, D. Skinner, and C. Cain. 1998. *Identity and Agency in Cultural Worlds.* Cambridge: Harvard University Press.

Ingold, T. 1998. 'Culture, Nature, Environment.' In B. Cartledge, ed., *Mind, Brain and the Environment*, 158–80. Oxford: Oxford University Press.

– 1999. 'Comment,' in Bird-David 1999.

Jordan, G., and C. Weedon. 1995. *Cultural Politics: Class, Gender, Race and the Post-modern World.* Oxford: Blackwell.

Marcus, G.E., and M.J.J. Fischer. 1986. *Anthropology as Cultural Critique.* Chicago: Chicago University Press.

Mason, R. 1997. *The God of Spinoza: A Philosophical Study.* Cambridge: Cambridge University Press.

Potiki, R. 1993. 'The Journey from Anxiety to Confidence.' In W. Ihimaera, ed., *Te Ao Mârama* 2, 314–19. Auckland: Reed.

Schweder, R.A., and E.J. Bourne. 1984. 'Does the Concept of Person Vary Cross-culturally?' In R.A Schweder and R. LeVine, eds., *Culture Theory: Essays on Mind, Self and Emotion,* 158–99. Cambridge: Cambridge University Press.

Schwimmer, E.G. 1972. 'Symbolic Competition.' *Anthropologica* 14 (2): 117–55.

– 1977. 'What Did the Eruption Mean?' In M.D. Lieber, ed., *Exiles and Migrants in Oceania,* 296–341. Honolulu: University Press of Hawaii.

Smith, L.T. 1999. *Decolonising Methodologies.* London: Zed Books.

Taylor, C. 1992. *Multiculturalism and the Politics of Recognition.* Princeton: Princeton University Press.

– 1994. 'Le pluralisme et le dualisme.' In A.-G. Gagnon, ed., *Québec, État et société,* 61–84. Montréal: Québec/Amérique.

Thomas, N. 1994. *Colonialism's Culture.* Cambridge: Polity Press.

Wright, S. 1998. 'The Politicization of "culture."' *Anthropology Today* 14 (1): 7–15.

PART I

The Reconstruction of Figured Worlds

Chapter 1, by Tim Ingold, is a theoretical critique of anthropological approaches to Indigenous ontologies. It shows how the anthropologist, in applying his culture's own philosophical categories in his conversations with informants, is thereby introducing logical contradictions that are absent from Indigenous philosophy. Ingold shows that our understanding of those cognitive systems will remain inadequate unless we learn and apply philosophical categories our informants actually depend on. Their systems are not an alternative science of nature, based on Cartesian logical deduction, but a 'poetics of dwelling,' a system of proximate causes and effects.

In chapter 2, Sylvie Poirier shows the methods by which alien philosophical categories can be learnt and applied in ethnographic investigation by a new kind of analysis of field observations, including the social appropriation of dreams, showing time and history emerging from the process of being-in-the-world. The texts analysed are not all verbal; an Aboriginal painting is interpreted in detail with the aid of informants in the field.

John Clammer widens the ontological approach in chapter 3 by studying the coexistence of several ontologies and figured worlds in a complex society (Japan). Shintô becomes fully intelligible only if we revise classical theories about animism. Far from being at the bottom of an evolutionary chain, Shintô animism has relations of mutual dependence and interpenetration with both Buddhism and Confucianism. Clammer identifies three distinct ontologies that coexist and are largely mutually intelligible in Japan.

Chapter One

A Circumpolar Night's Dream

TIM INGOLD

Sometime a horse I'll be, sometime a hound,
A hog, a headless bear, sometime a fire;
And neigh, and bark, and grunt, and roar, and burn,
Like horse, hound, hog, bear, fire, at every turn.
William Shakespeare, A Midsummer Night's Dream

Introduction

In the course of compiling his *Systema Naturae* of 1735, the great Swedish naturalist Carolus Linnaeus was confronted with the problem of how to select the distinguishing characteristics of the genus he had christened *Homo*. With the limited factual evidence available to him, he found it rather difficult to discover any anatomical features that would reliably separate humans from apes. The distinction, he surmised, was of a different order, to be grasped through introspection rather than observation. Do you ask how a human being differs from an ape? The answer, said Linnaeus, lies in the very fact that you ask the question. It is not one that apes ask of themselves. Apes and humans may look alike, but only humans are able to reflect upon the kind of beings they are. This is because they have been endowed, by their Creator, not only with a functioning body but also with the gift of intellect or reason, thanks to which humankind is equipped to exercise control and dominion over the rest of nature.

Nowadays, of course, we are in a much better position to specify the precise anatomical differences between humans and apes; moreover, God has been replaced, in the overall scheme of things, by the evolutionary force of natural selection. Yet in other respects the eighteenth-century dualism between reason and nature has come down to us more or less intact. Thus it is one thing to ask what a human being is, as a particular kind of natural object; quite another to ask what it means to be human, to exist as a rational subject. The first question can be tackled empirically, but only when we already have an answer to the second, which is a question of ontology. Taken together, however, these two questions set up a paradox that lies at the heart of Western scientific thought.

Science aims to produce an objective, value-free account of the natural world; in other words, it claims to study nature as it really is. Yet this claim of science, to provide an authoritative account of the workings of nature, is founded on the premise that the world is accessible to human reason in a way that it is not for any other creature. Not all humans, of course, are scientists; however, we have a strong moral and ethical commitment to the view that all humans have the capacity to be scientists, a capacity that is supposed to lie in the liberation of reason from the compulsions of nature, or of intelligence from instinct. At some point in the past, it is argued, our ancestors must have broken through the bounds of nature and set upon the path of history, leading ultimately to modern science and civilization. And it was in doing so, in coming to reflect upon the conditions of their own existence in the world, that they realized their essential humanity. Thus, the ontological question of what it means to be human is answered by taking ourselves out of the natural world, from which point we launch into our empirical description of human beings as objects of detached scientific scrutiny whose existence is confined within that very world.

Here, then, is the paradox. Surely, as science insists, humans are part of nature. That is to say, they are biological organisms, composed of the same stuff, and having evolved according to the same principles, as organisms of every other kind. Like other creatures, they are born, grow old, and die; they must eat to live, protect themselves to survive, and mate to reproduce. But if that were all there is to it, how could there be science? It would seem that the very possibility of a scientific account of humankind as a species of nature is only open to a creature for whom *being is knowing*, one that can so detach its consciousness from the traffic of its bodily interactions in the environment as to treat the latter as the object of its concern. To be human in this sense – to exist as a knowing subject – is, we commonly say, to be a *person*. So is the scientist a person rather than an organism? Is there no way of comprehending human existence within nature save by taking ourselves out of it? How can we exist both inside the world of nature and outside of it, as organisms and persons, at one and the same time?

To resolve this paradox, we need to find an alternative mode of human understanding that starts from the premise of our engagement with the world, rather than our detachment from it. We have to show, in other words, that the work of reason is not confined to an interior mental space delineated by the scope of its formal deliberations, as distinct from the external world of nature upon which it reflects, but is immanent in the actual life of the organism-person in its environment. This is what I take to be the central task of anthropology, and what makes anthropologists especially qualified to carry it out is their familiarity with the kinds of knowledge and understanding – often and rather problematically called 'non-Western'[1] – which stem from people's everyday, pragmatic involvements with their environments or 'lived worlds.' In this chapter I want to draw on one particular anthropological study of how people in a non-Western society perceive themselves and the world around them. This is the account by A. Irving Hallowell of what it means to be a person among the northern Ojibwa, Indigenous hunters and trappers of the forests to the east of Lake Winnipeg and north of Lake Superior in Canada.[2]

Hallowell's article 'Ojibwa Ontology, Behavior and World View,' first published in 1960, is in my estimation one of the great classics of northern circumpolar ethnography.[3] I have turned to it over and over again for inspiration, and every reading has yielded some new insight. I must emphasize, however, that what follows is not intended as a contribution to Ojibwa ethnography. I have not carried out fieldwork in the region, nor do I have the deep familiarity with the literature on these people that would qualify me for such a task. Rather, I offer some reflections that, though stimulated by a reading of Hallowell's work, are primarily motivated by the goal of resolving the paradox set out above – that is, of finding a way to restore human beings to the continuum of organic life that does not, at the same time, reduce them to mere objects of nature. These reflections are not, however, entirely without ethnographic substance, for they resonate both with themes that crop up with remarkable regularity in the literature on northern circumpolar societies[4] and with my own outlook, which has undoubtedly been shaped by the experience of working in this region.

Animals as Persons

It is customary, in the West, to assume that to speak of persons is to tell of the thoughts, intentions, and actions of human beings. 'Person' and 'human' are all but synonyms, to the extent that to ask whether non-human animals can be persons seems almost perverse. Nevertheless, people in Western societies do very often treat animals, or speak of them, as if they were persons. Let me briefly present two examples of this tendency. The first lies in attitudes towards household pets. Many people who are convinced that, as a general rule, animals cannot be persons are quick to make an exception of their pets. But if you ask them why pets are persons, or at least rather like persons, whereas other animals are not, they will probably say that on account of having been raised in human households, virtually as members of the family, these particular animals have become almost human themselves. They are credited with human feelings and responses, spoken to and expected to understand, given names, put through life-cycle rituals, and sometimes even dressed in clothing. Thus, far from softening or obscuring the boundary between humanity and animality, the special treatment of pets constitutes the exception that proves the rule: namely that, in the West, to be a person is to be human. Animals can only be persons to the extent that some of our humanity has, so to speak, 'rubbed off' on them through close contact with human members of the household. And just as the animal can never become fully human, its personhood, too, can never be more than partially developed. That is why pets are often treated as somehow retarded, locked in perpetual childhood. However old they are, they are never allowed to grow up, but are rather treated as cases of arrested development.

The second example of the Western tendency to liken animals to persons concerns fables, especially those composed for children. Our storybooks are full of tales in which human characters are turned, or turn themselves, into wolves, bears, mice, frogs, birds, fish, and a host of other creatures. Some of these stories are of great antiquity. But whatever they may have meant for people in the distant past, for contemporary audiences and readers there is never any suggestion that they are anything but stories. The animal characters, often depicted in strikingly human form, stand in metaphorically for human ones, and serve to illustrate distinctively human dispositions and foibles: the cunning fox, the innocent deer, the conceited toad, the noble lion, and so on. In short, the animal characters are used to deliver a commentary on the nature of human society. Moreover, no child raised in contemporary Western society would make the mistake of confusing such animal stories with natural history books, of supposing that 'The Frog Prince' is an observer's account of the behaviour of amphibians, or that 'Little Red Riding Hood' is an account of the habits of the wolf. Children are taught, at a very early age, to distinguish between telling stories and recounting the 'facts.'

Both these examples, of pet-keeping and fables, illustrate a propensity, technically known as anthropomorphism, to ascribe human qualities to non-human beings. In the first example, the ascription is metonymic (the animal is an extension of the human), while in the second it is metaphoric (the animal substitutes for the human). Either way, so long as we continue to assume that only humans can truly be persons, the attribution of personhood to animals is bound to be anthropomorphic. The Ojibwa, however, do not make this assumption. Persons, in the Ojibwa world, can take a great variety of forms, of which the human is just one. They can also appear in diverse animal guises, as meteorological phenomena such as thunder or the winds, as heavenly bodies such as the sun, and even as tangible objects such as stones, which we would have no hesitation in regarding as inanimate. None of these manifold forms in which persons appear is any more basic, or 'literal,' than the others. Moreover, as we shall see, persons can be encountered not only in waking life but also, and equally palpably, in dreams and in the telling of myths. And most importantly, they can change their form. Indeed, for the Ojibwa this capacity for metamorphosis is one of the key aspects of being a person and is a critical index of power: the more powerful the person, the more readily a change of form may be effected.

Though persons may appear in animal form, not all animals are persons. One can usually tell if an animal is a person, because its behaviour will be out of the ordinary. But some animals are always extraordinary. One such is the bear. The hunter, on encountering a bear, will act towards it as a person who can understand what is being said and will respond according to its own volition (OO 36). There is nothing in the least anthropomorphic about this. The hunter is not regarding the bear as if it were human. To the contrary, it is perceived to be unequivocally ursine. Unlike the pet in Western society, the personhood of the bear does not depend upon its previous contacts with humans – indeed, it need not have had any such contacts at all. For the same reason, the bear is just as much a 'full person' as is the human hunter.

The Ojibwa relate to persons in animal form as grown-ups, not as children. And whereas anthropomorphized animal-persons in the West are treated as beings that need to be looked after and controlled by their human guardians, the animal-persons in the environment of the Ojibwa are considered to be on the same level as, if not more powerful than, human beings themselves.

Likewise, the animals that figure as persons in the traditional narratives of the Ojibwa are not anthropomorphic characters. Their tales, like our own, are replete with incidents in which humans turn into animals, or marry animals, or give birth to animals, and vice versa. But these are not fables, nor are they intended to deliver an allegorical commentary on the human condition. They are tales about events that really took place, in the histories of real persons, and in the same world that people ordinarily experience in the course of their quotidian lives. What they recount is based on detailed, accurate observation of the landscape, of weather conditions, and of the behaviour of animals. The mythological figure of the Thunder Bird, for example, can make itself manifest in the form of a peal of thunder or a kind of hawk. There is a striking correspondence between the normal seasonal occurrence of thunderstorms and the period during which migratory birds wintering in the south appear in Ojibwa country. In one myth, a man who marries a Thunder Bird woman and goes off to live with his in-laws (the mythic 'masters' of various species of hawk) finds himself having to eat what they call 'beaver,' but what to him are frogs and snakes – which are, indeed, the principal foods of the sparrow hawk.[5] And the nests of the Thunder Birds can be physically identified in the landscape as collections of stones in high, inaccessible locations (OO 32–3).

In short, what distinguishes the Thunder Bird from any ordinary hawk is nothing like what, for us, distinguishes the Wolf of Little Red Riding Hood from the wolf of the forest. The distinction is not between animals of fantasy and of fact, but rather between animals that are persons and animals that are not. Animal-persons are no more fantastic than human ones. The Ojibwa do, nevertheless, differentiate between narratives of past experience of these two sorts of person. Hallowell calls them 'myths' and 'stories' respectively (OO 26–7). Stories recount events in the lives of human beings, from the anecdotal to the legendary. Myths, by contrast, tell of the lives of non-human persons – or, to be more precise, the myths *are* these persons, who, in the telling, are not merely commemorated but actually made present for the assembled audience, as though they had been brought to life and invited in. For this reason, the narration of myth is a ritualized event, and there are restrictions on who can tell it and when it can be told. But despite these formalities, myths are no less true, or more phantasmagoric, than stories. The difference is simply that in myths, the protagonists are persons of the 'other-than-human' class, otherwise known and addressed by the inclusive kinship term, 'grandfathers.'

Other-than-Human Grandfathers

All persons, whether human or not, share the same fundamental structure. This structure consists, in Hallowell's words, of 'an inner vital part that is enduring and an outward form which can change' (OO 42). The inner essence, or soul, holds the attributes of sentience, volition, memory, and speech. Any being that possesses these attributes is a person, irrespective of the intrinsically unstable form in which it appears. While human persons and other-than-human grandfathers are alike in this regard, such that no absolute division in kind can be drawn between them, they do differ in degree – that is, in the amount of power persons possess and hence in their capacity for metamorphosis. Grandfathers are more powerful than living humans. Most powerful are the Sun, the Four Winds, the Thunder Birds, and the spirit 'masters' of all the different species of animals. These beings are immortal but can change their form with relative ease, appearing now as a human, now as an animal, now perhaps as some meteorological phenomenon, as we have seen with the Thunder Bird. In myth the Thunder Bird can figure as a man or a woman, in dreams it shows up as a hawk, in waking life it announces its presence as a thunderclap. By contrast, only the most powerful human persons, such as sorcerers and shamans, can change into a non-human form and make it back again – and then only with some danger and difficulty. Sorcerers, for example, can transform themselves into bears in order better to pursue their nefarious activities.

However, for most humans, metamorphosis means death; indeed, the only change of form that all humans undergo is brought about upon their demise. As with any metamorphosis, death involves an alteration of manifest appearance, while the vital essence of the person continues its existence in some other form. Spirits of the dead are that much more powerful, and can manifest themselves in the guise of either ghosts (which may be seen or heard) or animals, often birds.[6] But whereas the power of human persons always increases when they die, there is only one way in which they can grow in power during their lifetimes, and that is through the guardianship or tutelage of one or more grandfathers. For men in particular, grandfatherly assistance is considered crucial for coping with the vicissitudes of life. In the past, every boy, on reaching puberty, would embark upon a prolonged period of fasting. Alone in the forest, he would hope to dream of his future guardian, from whom he would receive blessings that would see him through all kinds of difficulties in later life, so long as he met certain necessary obligations towards the grandfather concerned. In one account, for example, a boy encountered a human-like figure in his dream, who then turned into a golden eagle. This person was the 'master' of the eagles. The boy, too, was transformed into an eagle in his dream. Thus winged and feathered, he flew to the south with his new protector, before returning to the point whence he originally departed (CE 178).

The idea that a human being can be turned into a bear prowling in the forest, or an eagle soaring in the sky, is simply inconceivable within the normal canons of Western thought. Any creature born of human parents, it is supposed, is bound within the limitations of the human bodily frame, whatever environmental circumstances may be encountered during its lifetime. It is these bodily specifications that are fixed and enduring, whereas ways of thinking, feeling, speaking, and behaving – adding up to what is conventionally known as 'culture' – are variable, even within the life-history of a single individual. This seems to be the precise inverse of the Ojibwa model of the person, according to which it is the variable body that clothes a constant spiritual essence comprising the powers of self-awareness, intentionality, sentience, and speech. In their encounter with Euro-Americans, Ojibwa were evidently troubled by the incompatibility between these different ontologies of personal being. John Tanner, a White man who grew up among the Ojibwa people during the early nineteenth century and subsequently wrote of his experiences, claimed that the ursine sorcerer, prowling around at night, was actually a man dressed up in a bear skin (CE 177). This, and other similar statements by both native and non-native informants, may be understood, according to Hallowell, as 'rationalizations advanced by individuals who are attempting to reconcile Ojibwa beliefs and observation with the disbelief encountered in their relations with whites' (OO 37).

Rendering metamorphosis as a kind of dressing up is certainly one way of explaining it – or, rather, explaining it away – in terms that Westerners would understand. The person's bodily form does not actually change, it is merely concealed beneath an outer clothing, a disguise. Among themselves, however, the Ojibwa have no need to resort to explanatory contrivances of this kind. The potential of persons to change their form, to reveal themselves in different guises to different people on different occasions, is, for them, simply self-evident (CE 177). But by the same token, the purpose of the outward bodily form is not to conceal. It has nothing to hide. Nor does it enclose the vital essence of the person like a container, insulating it from immediate contact with the environment. To the contrary, the body enables rather than constrains; it furnishes the distinctive equipment, including skills and dispositions as well as anatomical devices, by which a person can carry on a particular kind of life in the world. Viveiros de Castro (1998), commenting on very similar principles in Amazonian Indian cosmology, likens the adoption of a specific bodily form to the diver's donning of a wet-suit, the purpose of which is not to disguise the wearer as a fish, but to enable him to swim like one. Thus, metamorphosis is not a covering up, but an opening up, of the person to the world. A person who can take on many forms can turn up in all kinds of situations, now in one form, now in another, each one affording a different perspective. The greater the person's powers of metamorphosis, the wider the range of their practical possibilities of being, and hence the more extensive the breadth of their experience and the scope of their phenomenal presence.

All of this leaves us with a problem of the following kind. We may accept that a person can change their form at will, like Puck in Shakespeare's *Midsummer Night's Dream* (whose lines head this chapter), knowing all the while that the character in question exists only as a *dramatis persona* in a masque or play, who is actually being impersonated by an ordinary human actor. But if I were to report, in all sincerity, having encountered such a character in real life, I doubt whether much credence would be given to my claims. People would say that if I was not actually lying, then I must be suffering from delusions, leaving me incapable of telling fact from fantasy, or reality from dreams. Yet these are precisely the sorts of claims that the Ojibwa make. Are they, then, lying or deluded? Accusations of both kinds have been levelled often enough, against the Ojibwa people and others who think like them, reinforcing the stereotype of the primitive Indian who can neither think logically nor be trusted. Anthropologists, who by temperament and training are more sympathetic to native accounts, generally adopt an expository strategy not unlike that of the theatre-goer attending a performance of Shakespeare's *Dream*, amounting to a willing suspension of disbelief. This strategy makes it possible to get on with the job of understanding what people are telling us, without our having to worry about whether there is any foundation in reality for what they have to say.[7]

Hallowell himself does just this, when he argues that what, for the Ojibwa, are attributes of personhood form part of a comprehensive 'world view' that is projected onto reality-as-we-know-it. His concern is to understand the world view, not the fundamental nature of reality. Yet he goes on to stress that Ojibwa do not, themselves, 'personify' natural objects (OO 29). For example, the sun is perceived as a person of the 'other-than-human' class; it is not perceived initially as a natural object onto which 'person' attributes are subsequently projected. It is not, in other words, made into a person; it is a person, period. There is more than a hint of duplicity here. It would be a mistake, says Hallowell, to suppose that the Ojibwa personify objects, yet from his standpoint as an anthropological observer, this appears to be precisely what they are doing. Evidently what Hallowell takes to be a particular cultural construction of an external reality is, in Ojibwa eyes, the only reality they know. For the Ojibwa, the sun is a person because it is experienced as such; for Hallowell the sun is not *really* a person but is constructed as such in the minds of the Ojibwa. And if it is not really a person, then it cannot really undergo metamorphosis. By this move, Ojibwa metaphysics appear to pose no challenge to our own ontological certainties. Turning our backs on what Ojibwa people say, we continue to insist that 'real' reality is given independently of human experience, and that understanding its nature is a problem for science. Must we then conclude that the anthropological study of Indigenous understandings, whatever its intrinsic interest, can tell us nothing about what the world is really like, and that it therefore has no bearing on natural scientific inquiry?

Living Things and Being Alive

This question returns us to the paradox I raised in the introduction. The notion that persons, as beings in the world, can appear in both human and other-than-human forms may sound strange, but it is not half as strange as the notion that to become a person – to be in a position to know and reflect upon the nature of existence – means taking oneself *out* of the world. And if Native people, caught up in their own reflections, are one step removed from the world, the anthropologist-cum-scientist, recognizing these reflections for what they are – alternative images or 'views' of a naturally given reality – must be two steps removed. The challenge for us now is to bring these persons, as it were, back 'down to earth,' to restore them to the primary context of their active, perceptual engagement within an environment. Taking this condition of engagement as our point of departure, can we find some way of making sense of Ojibwa understandings concerning such matters as metamorphosis? Can we, in other words, ground these understandings in the real experience of persons in a lifeworld rather than attributing them to some overarching cosmological schema for its imaginative reconstruction? To begin to address this challenge, we need to go back to a question that is even more fundamental than that of what makes a person: What makes something alive, or animate?

Hallowell recounts a fascinating anecdote concerning the nature of stones:

> I once asked an old man: Are *all* the stones we see about us here alive? He reflected a long while and then replied, 'No! But *some* are.' This qualified answer made a lasting impression on me. (OO 24)

Hallowell had been led to ask this question on account of a peculiarity in the grammatical structure of the Ojibwa language. As with other languages in the Algonkian family, to which it belongs, a formal distinction is supposed to be made in Ojibwa between 'animate' and 'inanimate' nouns. Stones are grammatically animate, and Hallowell was keen to know why. The answer he received, however, was puzzling in two respects. First, there is the general question of how something as apparently inert as a stone can possibly be alive. But secondly, why should some stones be animate and others not? As Hallowell recognizes (OO 23), the categorical distinction between animate and inanimate is not one that originated with Ojibwa themselves, but rather was imposed by Western linguists who brought with them their own conventional understanding of what these terms mean. Before attempting to resolve the puzzle of the stones, we have, therefore, to pause to consider the meaning of the animate as a category of Western thought.

Ever since Plato and Aristotle, it has been customary in the West to envisage the world of nature as made up of a multitude of discrete objects, or things, each with its own integrity and essential properties. These things may be grouped into classes of varying degrees of inclusiveness on the basis of selected properties that they are perceived to possess in common. One major class, known as 'animate,' comprises all those things that are said to possess the property of life. All remaining things, which do not possess this property, are 'inanimate.' There has been much debate about what it takes for something to be alive: vitalists argued for the existence of some mysterious life force that they thought was infused into all organisms; mechanists dismissed the idea as unscientific hocus-pocus, but in their enthusiasm to reduce organisms to clockwork they virtually dissolved the animate into the category of the inanimate. The problem was only resolved, after a fashion, by the discovery of the DNA molecule, popularly hailed as the 'secret of life,' which seemed to offer a basis for distinguishing living things that satisfied the objective canons of natural science. Throughout all this debate, however, one fundamental idea has remained unquestioned, namely, that life is a qualifying attribute of objects. We look for it in a world that already consists of things-in-themselves, whose essential nature is given without regard to their positioning and involvement within wider fields of relations.

These are the kinds of things – stones, trees, birds, and so on – that are denoted by words of the class grammarians call nouns. Thus, to place the Ojibwa word for stone in the grammatical category 'animate noun' is to assume that so far as the language is concerned, all stones are things with the essential attribute of life. The same would go for trees, the sun and moon, thunder, and artefacts like kettles and pipes, the words for which are likewise placed in the 'animate' class (OO 23). Judging from his qualified response, this is something that even the old man whom Hallowell questioned on the matter would have found hard to accept. Reflecting on his answer, Hallowell concludes that 'the Ojibwa do not perceive stones, in general, as animate, any more than we do. The crucial test is experience. Is there any personal testimony available?' (OO 25). And indeed, such testimony can be adduced: Hallowell heard tell of an instance in which, during a ceremony, a stone was observed to roll over and over, following the master of the ceremony around the tent, another in which a boulder with contours like a mouth would actually open its 'mouth' when tapped by its owner with a knife, and yet another where a man asked a particular stone whether it belonged to him and received a negative response!

The critical feature of all these examples is that the liveliness of stones emerges in the context of their close involvement with certain persons, and relatively powerful ones at that. Animacy, in other words, is a property not of stones as such, but of their positioning within a relational field that includes persons as foci of power. Or to put in another way, the power concentrated in persons enlivens that which falls within its sphere of influence. This immediately makes sense of the old man's remark, for whether a stone is alive or not will depend upon the context in which it is placed and experienced. It also explains why animacy is attributed to artefacts that are closely bound up with the lives of persons. But by the same token, it makes a nonsense of the categorical distinction between living and non-living things. The animate stone is not so much a living thing as a 'being alive.' A study conducted among the Ojibwa in the 1960s by Mary Black lends weight to this conclusion. Black notes that the Ojibwa term *bema.diziwa.d*, which comes closest to 'living things,' literally translates as 'those who continue in the state of being alive.' Yet the term might be more accurately glossed, she suggests, as 'those who have power.' Significant, too, is the fact that Black's informants were agreed in dismissing the tidy classifications of formal linguistic analysis. They did not regard classes such as animate and inanimate as mutually exclusive, and objects could freely shift from one class to the other, depending on the context (Black 1977, 143).

Hallowell tells us that the Ojibwa word for life 'in the fullest sense,' including health, longevity, and good fortune, is *pimädäziwim*. As such, it is something that every person strives to achieve (OO 45). But life in this sense is not given, ready-made, as an attribute of being that may then be expressed in one way or another. It is rather a project that has continually to be worked at. Life is a task. The Cree people, neighbours of the Ojibwa who speak a closely related Algonkian language, have a virtually identical word meaning 'life,' *pimaatisiiwin*. Colin Scott (1989, 195) reports that one Cree man translated the word as 'continuous birth.' This translation seems to resonate perfectly with Ojibwa notions. As an ongoing process of renewal, life is not merely expressive of the way things are, but is the very *generation* of being. And power, in effect, is the potential of the life process to generate beings of manifold forms. Thus conceived, it is a property not of individuals in isolation but of the total field of relations in which they are situated. Only within such a field can a person strive for *pimädäziwim* (OO 48).

Let me return, for a moment, to the case of the rolling stone that followed its master around the ceremonial tent. On what grounds was it judged to be alive? Clearly, the critical criterion was that it had been observed to move. It did not move of its own volition, since it was controlled by the power of the master; nevertheless, the stone acted, and it was not acted upon, for example, by being pushed or pulled. But once again, in coming to terms with this phenomenon, we must be wary of the characteristically Western assumption that the world is full of things that may or may not move of their own accord, depending on whether they are of the animate or inanimate class. As we have seen, it would make no more sense to the Ojibwa than it does to us to suppose that the stone exists as a living thing, as though the property of life were an aspect of its substantive nature, of its 'thingness,' as distinct from its movement in the world. The movement is not an outward expression of life, but is the very process of the stone's staying alive, its 'continuous birth.' The same could be said of trees, which are included in Hallowell's list of things formally classified in Ojibwa grammar as 'animate' (OO 23). The Western biologist would doubtless be more inclined to regard the tree than the stone as a 'living thing,' by appeal to some aspect of its substantive nature such as DNA or carbon chemistry. For the hunter in the woods, however, what makes a tree alive are its distinctive movements as they are registered in experience: the swaying of its boughs in the wind, the audible fluttering of leaves, the orientation of branches to the sun. Recall that the winds and the sun are persons for the Ojibwa, and can move trees much as powerful humans can move stones.

Different beings, whether or not they qualify as persons, have characteristic patterns of movement – ways of being alive – that reveal them for what they are. The sun, for example, has its own regular pattern of rising and setting, a regularity that, in Hallowell's words, 'is of the same order as the habitual activities of human beings' (OO 29). If we were to consider the sun in abstraction from its observed movement across the sky, then it would indeed appear to be a mere physical body, and its movement a mechanical displacement. But this is not how it is presented to us in immediate experience. Rather, the movement is as much a part of the way the sun is as my own habitual movements are of the way I am. And these movements, of the sun in the heavens, of trees in the wind, of animals and human beings as they go about their everyday tasks, do not take place against the backdrop of a nature that is fixed, with its locations and distances all laid out in advance. For they are part and parcel of that total life process, of continuous birth, through which the world itself is forever coming into being. In short, living beings do not move upon the world, but move along with it (Ingold 1993, 164).[8]

The Meaning of Experience

At this point I would like to return to Hallowell's observation, apropos the vitality of stones, that 'the crucial test is experience' (OO 25). What

means of common sense or common humanity, without taking the trouble of an ethnographic investigation' (163). With others, he stresses some of the limitations of a system of thought dominant among Western cultures, based in particular on a dubious but no less absolute notion of 'objectivity,' i.e., the certitude of a world-in-itself underlying this notion, and the correlated view of a world devoid of spirit and subjectivity.

Ontologies are not only thought out, they are also lived out. They open on to different forms of knowledge and practice, indeed to varieties of 'true' experience. As an example of what I mean, I would like to relate a personal experience with Nungarryi, an Aboriginal woman from the Western Desert of Australia. We are walking over the desert land. A wind is blowing. I feel the dryness of the wind on my skin. I hear the wind whistling about me. All my senses and thoughts are actively participating in the experience, for the wind is very strong. On the basis of a dominant Western ontology, I experience the wind as an object external to my physical being and my sense of self. For a moment, I am completely oblivious to the countryside around me. I seem somehow to be walking 'against' it, feeling it to be rather intrusive. My Aboriginal friend experiences the wind differently, at least as I have come to understand this experience over the years. She seems to be walking 'with' the wind. First of all, the country (or landscape) we are walking in is personified, steeped in memories and actions, both human and ancestral. Secondly, in Kukatja ontology, the wind necessarily has both material and spiritual dimensions to it, which are intrinsically linked. In local representations of the body, when the wind penetrates any one of the human body's openings, it becomes breath; as breath, the wind could not possibly be considered intrusive. Indeed, in Kukatja thought and sensory perceptions, there is 'a total interaction between the wind, the breath and the spirit ... The wind protects and nourishes the spirit and the breath inhabiting the human body, and constitutes a permanent link with the ancestral realm' (Peile 1985, 81; see also Peile 1997, 100). The wind is thus consubstantial with humans: they share the same ancestral essence. Furthermore, partly on the basis of this consubstantiality, the wind is a non-human agency. Indeed, what I hear as (intrusive) whistling might be for my friend an ancestral voice, an agency wishing to reveal a message.[1] The experience, in other words, contains a potential communicative value.

While both types of experience and sensory perception are received as true on the basis of our respective cultural objectivity and value-

are we to understand by this key word, 'experience'? And what, precisely, is being tested? One approach to answering these questions might be to argue as follows. There exists, on the one hand, a real world 'out there,' customarily called nature, whose forms and composition are given quite independently of the human presence, and on the other hand, a world of ideas or mental representations, which bears a relation of only partial correspondence to this external reality. Some things in the world are not represented in the mind, but some images in the mind have no counterpart in the real world. It is experience that mediates between the two worlds, providing both the raw material – in the form of sensory data – from which ideas are constructed, and the opportunities to test them by empirical observation. Thus, at first glance we might form the impression that a certain stone actually moved; this could then be checked by further examination, which would either confirm or refute the initial hypothesis.

For the Ojibwa, however, knowledge does not lie in the accumulation of mental content. It is not by representing the world in the mind that they get to know it, but rather by moving around in their environment, whether in dreams or waking life, and by watching, listening, and feeling, actively seeking out the signs by which it is revealed. Experience, here, amounts to a kind of sensory participation, a coupling of the movement of one's own awareness to the movement of aspects of the world. And the kind of knowledge it yields is not propositional, in the form of hypothetical statements or 'beliefs' about the nature of reality, but personal, consisting of an intimate sensitivity to other ways of being, to the particular movements, habits, and temperaments that reveal each being for what it is. Indeed, such knowledge, closely analogous to that which the skilled craftsman has of his raw material, is not easily articulated in propositional form, and would seem to be devalued by any attempt to do so, to disembed it from its grounding in the context of the knower's personal involvement with the known. This is probably the reason why a young man who, through a dream encounter, has secured the blessing of an other-than-human 'grandfather,' is forbidden under normal circumstances to speak of his experience in any detail (OO 46). You keep such things to yourself – although others can tell, from your subsequent attitudes and behaviour, that you have a new person in your life.

'The concept of the "natural,"' Hallowell tells us, 'is not present in Ojibwa thought' (OO 28). Experience, therefore, cannot mediate between mind and nature, since these are not separated in the first place.

It is rather intrinsic to the ongoing process of *being alive to the world*, of the person's total sensory involvement in an environment. What, then, does experience put to the test? Let me try to answer this question by way of another example. Visual sightings of the Thunder Bird in its hawk-like manifestation are exceedingly rare, yet one boy's report of such a sighting, although initially greeted with some scepticism, was finally accepted when his description was found to match precisely that offered by another man who had encountered the same bird in a dream (OO 32). People can lie about their encounters with other-than-human persons, sometimes with dire consequences, but in this case the boy must have been telling the truth. How, otherwise, could he have described the bird so accurately? However, the conditions of truth, in this case, lie not in the correspondence between an external reality and its ideal representation, but in the authenticity of the experience itself. Rather than confirming the factual existence of the Thunder Bird as a datum of nature that is independent of experience, the boy's vision was proof of his exceptional powers of perception. It is these powers that are being constantly tested by experience.

Moreover, experiences of this kind are formative. They contribute to the shaping of a person's own sense of self, and of their attitudes and orientations towards the world. Or, in short, experience is intrinsic to the process of continuous birth wherein persons – both human and other-than-human – come into being and pursue the goal of life, each within the field of their relations with the others. And as Hallowell pointed out in his classic article 'The Self and Its Behavioral Environment' (Hallowell 1955, 75–110), the process is a mutual one. The formation of the self is, at one and the same time, the formation of an environment for that self, and both emerge out of a common process of maturation and personal experience. Through this process, 'an intelligible behavioral environment has been constituted for the individual that bears an intimate relation to the kind of being he knows himself to be and it is in this behavioral environment that he is motivated to act' (CE 85–6). The self, in this view, is not the captive subject of the standard Western model, enclosed within the confines of a body, and entertaining its own conjectures about what the outside world might be like on the basis of the limited information available to it. On the contrary, for Hallowell – as indeed for the Ojibwa who have exercised such an obvious and profound influence on his thought – the self exists in its ongoing engagement with the environment: it is open to the world, not closed in.

At first glance, however, this view of the self seems inconsistent with the structure of personhood that Hallowell attributes to the Ojibwa. Recall that this structure consists of an inner part that endures and an outward appearance that is susceptible to transformation. Does this not imply that the self is enclosed within its bodily garb? And if so, how can it be open to the external world? To deal with this objection we have to abandon the metaphors, implicit in so much Western philosophical speculation on mind and body, of container and content. What Hallowell, in his characterization of the Ojibwa person, calls the inner essence is not enclosed by the outward form but rather lies behind it – behind the superficial world of appearances. To penetrate beneath the surface of the person is not, then, to go inside into the mind rather than outside into the world. It is, rather, to dissolve the very boundary that separates mind from world, and ultimately to reach a level where they are one and the same. Nothing better illustrates this point than the difference between Western and Ojibwa interpretations of dreaming.

Dreaming and Metamorphosis

People in the West are encouraged to think of dreams as hallucinations, comprising a stream of free-floating images that exist only in the interiority of the unconscious mind, a mind that is freed during sleep from its bodily bearings in the real world. Thus, we consider the dream world to be the very opposite of the solid, physical world 'out there,' just as illusion is opposed to reality, fantasy to fact. For the Ojibwa, by contrast, the world of dreams, like that of myth, is continuous with that of one's waking life. Just as myths are understood as the past experiences of other-than-human persons, so dreams are among the past experiences of human selves (CE 181). In their dreams, humans meet the grandfatherly protagonists of myth, and carry on activities with them in a familiar landscape, albeit viewed from an unfamiliar perspective, revealing secrets of the environment that one may not have noticed before but whose presence is invariably confirmed by subsequent inspection. This is not to say that the Ojibwa confuse dream experiences with those they have while wide awake. The difference is that in dreams, the vital essence of the person – the self – is afforded a degree of mobility, not only in space but also in time, normally denied in waking life. While the body of the sleeper is readily visible at some fixed location, the self may be roaming far afield (OO 41). A sorcerer, for example, may be observed lying asleep in his tent, but in his dream he meets you while you are out hunting in the forest. And sure enough, when you were hunting recently, you had an unnerving encounter with a bear. The bear was the sorcerer, who was 'bearwalking' (OO 36).[9]

Both Western and Ojibwa people might agree that, in a certain sense, dreaming liberates the mind from its bodily housing. But whereas in the Western conception this amounts to a taking leave of reality, for the Ojibwa it allows complete freedom of movement *within* the earthly and cosmic space of ordinary life. The dreaming mind, far from severing its already tenuous and provisional connection with the real world, is able to penetrate that world to the point where mind and world become indistinguishable. This difference of interpretation has its roots in fundamental ontological assumptions. Mainstream Western philosophy starts from the premise that the mind is distinct from the world; it is a facility that the person, presumed human, brings to the world in order to make sense of it. When it is not busy making sense of the world, during 'time off,' it dreams. For the Ojibwa, on the other hand, the mind subsists in the very involvement of the person in the world. Rather than approaching the world from a position outside it, the person in Ojibwa eyes can exist only as a being *in* the world, caught up in an ongoing set of relationships with components of the lived-in environment. And the meanings that are found in the world, far from being superimposed upon it by the mind, are drawn from the contexts of this personal involvement. Thus the dreaming self in its nocturnal journeys, far from taking a break from the demands of coping with reality, sets out in search of meanings that will help to make sense of the experiences of waking life.

With these observations in mind, let me return to the problem of metamorphosis. How are we to respond to the objections of the sceptic to the effect that whatever people may say, humans cannot really turn into eagles or bears, or thunder into a kind of hawk, or vice versa? From an Ojibwa perspective, this objection is not so much false as beside the point. Metamorphosis may not occur in ordinary waking life, but it certainly occurs in dreams. And as Hallowell is at pains to stress, 'there is nothing psychologically abstruse about the incorporation of dreams into the category of self-related experiences' (CE 96). The awareness of the self is as phenomenally real when one is dreaming as when one is awake, and these dream experiences are built into the constitution of the self by memory processes that are no different from those working on the experiences of waking life. Consider the case of the boy who, in the midst of a storm, witnessed the Thunder Bird in its hawk-like guise.

What if he was only dreaming? Even when awake, we too can some-times let our imaginations wander, and see things that are not 'really' there. But from the point of view of the experience of the self, it makes no difference whether the boy was awake, daydreaming, or actually asleep. He still saw the bird, was moved to wonder by its presence, and remembered the encounter for the rest of his life. Experiences under-gone when asleep are just as much a part of autobiographical memory as are experiences when awake (OO 42).

If, then, we accept that, whether awake or asleep, the person's en-counters are those of a being-in-the-world, it follows, as Hallowell puts it, 'that metamorphosis can be *personally* experienced' (CE 180). Far from covering over a solid substrate of literal reality with layer upon layer of illusion, dreams penetrate beneath the surface of the world, to render it transparent, so that one can see into it with a clarity and vision that is not possible in ordinary life. In dreams, for the Ojibwa, the world is opened up to the dreamer, it is revealed. This is why they attach such a tremendous importance to dreaming as a source of knowledge, for the knowledge revealed through dreams is also a source of power. Of course, this knowledge is of a different kind from what people in the West call science. As I pointed out in the introduction, the very project of natural science is premised on the detachment of the human subject from the world that is the object of his or her enquiry. The Ojibwa, starting off from the opposite premise – that the subject can exist only as a being *in* the world – have arrived at something quite different: not a natural science but a 'poetics of dwelling' (Ingold 1998, 179). And it is within the context of such a poetics that Ojibwa ideas about metamor-phosis, the personhood of the sun, the winds and thunder, the liveli-ness of stones, and so on, should be understood.

The Sounds of Speech

I shall return, in the conclusion to this chapter, to the relation between poetics and science. Before doing so, I should like to elaborate further on the contrast between Western and Ojibwa models of the person with particular reference to the one criterion that, more than any other, is adduced to justify claims to the unique status of humanity: namely, the capacity for speech. For the Ojibwa, according to Hallowell, the essen-tial powers of personhood include, besides speech, sentience, volition, and memory. Those of us brought up in the Western tradition of thought would have no particular problem with this idea. We do have a problem, however, when it comes to the attribution of these powers to non-human animals, and even more of a problem in attributing them to things that we would regard as inanimate. To give a lead into this problem, let me recount one more anecdote from Hallowell's Ojibwa study. An old man and his wife are sitting in their tent, and a storm is raging outside. There is thunder and lightning. The thunder comes in a series of claps. The old man listens intently. Then he turns to his wife and asks, quite casually and in a matter-of-fact tone of voice, 'Did you hear what was said?' 'No,' she replies, 'I didn't catch it' (OO 34). What are we to make of this?

Certainly, so long as we remain with a Western view of the nature of sentience, volition, memory, and speech, the story seems incredible. The language of agency that we are accustomed to use posits a being, the agent, who is endowed with will and purpose, and whose existence and identity are given independently of any action that he or she chooses to initiate. Thus, I may or may not choose to speak, or I may decide to say one thing rather than another, but as a being with intentions and purposes – that is, as a person – I am not the same as my speech. Likewise, I may choose to clap my hands, but as a physical event in the world, the clap exists apart from myself – the person who claps. Notice the similarity between this notion of agency, as an inherent attribute of persons as distinct from their overt behaviour, and the notion of animacy built into the Western conception of 'living things,' which, as we have already seen, construes life as a substantive property of objects as distinct from their movement in the world.

Does the thunder, then, clap like I do? Though we might say 'the thunder claps,' we know perfectly well that we are speaking figuratively, as though there were some being in the heavens with intentions and purposes rather like our own, and who claps like a human person, except on a more awesome scale. In reality, we are sure there is no such cosmic being. And to get around the problem of how something can occur without an agent to produce it, we may use an alternative form of words, such as 'there was a clap of thunder.' The point is that thunder does not exist separately from its clap, in the way that I am supposed to exist separately from mine. Rather, the clap *is* thunder; it is the acoustic form of thunder's phenomenal presence in the world. Through the clap, the thunder audibly exists for those who hear it. Let me put this contrast in another way, while keeping for the moment to the terms of the Western model of personal agency. When I speak, or for that matter when I clap, it is because I have an idea. My concern is to communicate that idea, and I do so by means of coded signs or signals that travel in the medium of sound. By converting ideas in the mind into physical impulses in the world, information is transmitted. But the thunder is not transmitting a message. Of course, it affects us; we are moved by the sound, perhaps a little scared. But we do not look for a message in the sound or ask, as did the old man in Hallowell's story, 'Did you hear what was said?'

As this example shows, Western thought systematically distinguishes the sounds of speech, along with other sound-producing gestures whose purpose is to give outward expression to inner ideas or mental states, from the sounds of nature that are just there but have not been produced by anybody. My clap and the thunderclap fall on either side of this division. And the dichotomy between interior mental states and their outward physical or behavioural expression that underwrites this conception of the distinctiveness of speech also applies to the way we tend to think about other aspects of personhood such as sentience, volition, and memory. Thus, volition implies the intentionality of action, but Western thought sees intentionality as residing not in the action itself but in a thought or plan that the mind places before the action and which the latter is supposed to execute. Likewise, we are inclined to think of memory as a store of images in the mind, rather than of remembering as an activity situated in the world. And we talk about sentience in terms of inner states or 'feelings,' instead of focusing on the perceptual activity of feeling the world around us. In short, the self, as the locus of ideas, plans, memories and feelings, seems to exist as a substantive entity quite independently of where it is and what it does.

Behind all this is a model of the person that, as we have already seen, identifies the self with an interior intelligence, the conscious mind, enclosed by its physical container, the body. According to this model, the body picks up sensory signals from the world around it and passes them to the mind, which processes them to form images or representations. Through a logical manipulation of these representations, the mind formulates plans of action, which are then passed as instructions for the body to execute in the world. The mind itself may be envisaged as many-layered, with outer layers of consciousness covering over deeper, more subterranean levels of the unconscious. Locked up in there, directly known only to ourselves, are our thoughts, feelings, and memories, which can only be released, and made known to others, by way of their bodily enactment in speech and gesture.

The Western Model

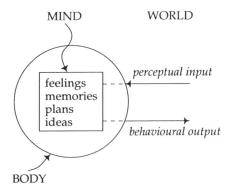

The Ojibwa Model

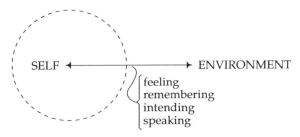

Figure 1.1   Western and Ojibwa models of the person

The Ojibwa model of the person, however, is quite different. As shown schematically in Figure 1.1, this model does not posit the self in advance of the person's entry into the world; rather, the self is constituted as a centre of agency and awareness in the process of its active engagement within an environment. Feeling, remembering, intending, and speaking are all aspects of that engagement, and through it the self continually comes into being.

In short, the Ojibwa self is relational. If we were to ask where it is, the answer would not be 'inside the head rather than out there in the world.' For the self exists, or rather becomes, in the unfolding of those very relations that are set up by virtue of a being's positioning *in* the world, reaching out into the environment – and connecting with other selves – along these relational pathways. Taking this view of the person, as Hallowell does, it is clear that no physical barrier can come between mind and world. 'Any inner-outer dichotomy,' he asserts, 'with the human skin as boundary, is psychologically irrelevant' (CE 88).[10] But this is precisely the dichotomy, as we have seen, by which speech and similar expressive gestures are conventionally distinguished from the sounds of nature. To take Hallowell at his word means having to adopt a quite different view of speech, not as the outward expression of inner thoughts, but as one of the ways in which the self manifests its presence in the world. Thus, when I speak or clap, I myself am not separate from the sound I produce, of my voice or the mutually percussive impact of my hands. These sounds are part of the way I am, they belong to my being as it issues forth into the environment. In other words, speech is not a mode of transmitting information or mental content; it is a way of *being alive*.

If we accept this view of speech, there is no longer anything so odd about supposing, as the Ojibwa do, that thunder can speak, and that other people can hear. The rumbling of thunder is the manifestation of its presence in the world, just as the sounds of human speaking, singing, clapping, or drumming are manifestations of ours. Indeed, the world is full of such sounds, each one the signature of a particular mode of life. As people move through their environment, they constantly listen to the speech of these manifold life forms, revealing each for what it is, and respond with speech of their own. Both non-human sounds, like thunder, and human speech have the power to move those who hear them, and both kinds of sound take their meaning from the contexts in which they are heard. There is no fundamental difference here. So when the old man asked his wife, as the thunder echoed through the sky, whether she heard what was said, he was not expecting an answer in the form of some proposition, as though the Thunder Bird had been trying to send them a message coded in sound, like a telegraph. When the boy, in our earlier example, ran to tell his parents about his vision of the Thunder Bird in its avian form, they may well have asked him, 'What did it look like?' This is the same kind of question the old man asked of his wife, though with regard to the Thunder Bird's acoustic rather than its visual presence.

Is there any significance, then, in the fact that the thunder was heard instead of seen? There is a long tradition, in the history of Western thought, of distinguishing between vision and hearing along the lines that the former is remote and objective, cutting the viewer off from things seen, whereas the latter is intimate and subjective, establishing a kind of interpenetration or resonance between the listener and the world. In vision, the world appears fixed and 'out there'; in hearing, as the musicologist Victor Zuckerkandl puts it, the world seems to flow 'from-out-there-toward-me-and-through-me' (Zuckerkandl 1956, 368; cited by Stoller 1989, 120). There are some hints, in Hallowell's account, that the Ojibwa might make a similar kind of distinction. Thus, he tells us that under no circumstances can the inner essence of the person, the soul, be a direct object of *visual* perception. 'What can be perceived visually is only that aspect of being that has some form or structure ... The only sensory mode under which it is possible to directly perceive the presence of souls ... is the auditory one' (CE 179–80). This could be explained on the grounds that in vision, we do not see light but things whose shapes and textures are revealed by the rays reflected from their outer surfaces, whereas what we hear is sound itself. And this sound, as we have seen, is of the essence of being rather than its outward expression.

However there are counter-indications, too, that the Ojibwa might not, or at least not always, make such a radical distinction between seeing and hearing. One is that ghosts, the outward form of spirits of the dead, can be heard as well as seen. They are known to whistle (CE 174). But more significantly, the notion that vision presents us with a world of fixed, objective things rests upon an assumption that is incompatible, in theory, with the relational model of the person presented above. This assumption, which is implicit in most studies of visual perception by Western psychologists, is that seeing things involves the formation of images in the mind on the basis of sensory data drawn from the play of light upon the retinal surfaces of the eyes. In an earlier section on the meaning of experience for the Ojibwa, I showed that for a being who is alive to its surroundings, experience does not mediate between things in the world and representations in the mind, but is intrinsic to the sensory coupling, in perception and action, of the awareness of the self to the movement of those features of the environment selected as foci of attention. This view of experience calls for a quite different theory of vision.

Such a theory would be premised on the perceiver as an active participant in an environment rather than a passive recipient of stimuli, one whose vision penetrates the world rather than holds up a mirror to it. In his famous essay 'Eye and Mind,' the philosopher Merleau-Ponty described the perceiver in just this sense, as a 'see-er.' Unlike the spectator who sets up before the mind a representation of an external reality, the see-er 'opens himself to the world.' In other words, he *watches what is going on*. Where the world of the spectator is fixed, that of the watcher is all movement. Imagine yourself following a flock of birds in flight. The movement of your eyes, your head, indeed your whole body, resonates with that of the birds across the sky. It is, to cite Merleau-Ponty once again, 'the natural consequence and the maturation of [your] vision' (Merleau-Ponty 1964, 162). Now, as a form of dynamic, sensory resonance, watching does not differ in principle from listening, and in ordinary life they are so closely intertwined as to be inseparable. I suspect that this is as true for the Ojibwa as for anyone else, and therefore that vision and hearing are not, in fact, sharply differentiated in their practice. Both are aspects of the total sensory involvement of the person in the world.

Before we leave the topic of hearing and speech, one more issue remains to be dealt with. It arises from Hallowell's remark, apropos of the old man's questioning of his wife about the thunder, that 'he was reacting to this sound in the same way as he would respond to a human being, whose words he did not understand' (OO 34). As we have seen, the world in which the Ojibwa dwell is polyglot, full of beings each with its own particular pattern of speech. It is tempting to compare these different patterns to the diverse languages of human communities, as though understanding the sounds of thunder, wind, the diverse forms of animal life, and so on were a problem of translation, of rendering meanings expressed in a multitude of foreign tongues in terms of one's own. Was the old man, then, asking his wife to translate for him? Were the words of the thunder spoken so quickly that, with his imperfect grasp of the language, he failed to understand what had been said? The metaphor of translation implies a certain view of language or speech, as a vehicle for the outward expression of inner ideas. To translate, then, is to 'carry across' an idea encoded in one expressive medium into the terms of another. I have argued, however, that in attributing the power of speech to thunder, the Ojibwa do not suppose that thunder is trying to transmit ideas to humans, but rather that its presence in the world, like that of other beings, whether human or other-than-human, can take an acoustic form. Responding to that presence with sensitivity and understanding is not therefore a matter of translation. It is more a matter of empathy. Total empathy is as hard to achieve as perfect translation; however, rather than shifting into another register of expression, it means taking on another way of being.

Full understanding, in short, is achieved *not through translation but through metamorphosis*. And this happens, above all, in dreams.

Naturalism and Animism

Are the Ojibwa animists? In recent anthropology the concept of animism has had a rather bad press, on account of its liberal use in the past to brand, as primitive superstition, systems of belief that allegedly attribute spirits or souls to things, living or non-living, which to any rational, thinking person are 'obviously' mere objects of nature. Philippe Descola, however, suggests a way of considering animism that is rather more respectful of indigenous understandings. Animism, he writes, is 'a kind of objectification of nature [that] endows natural beings not only with human dispositions, granting them the status of persons with human emotions and often the ability to talk, but also with social attributes – a hierarchy of positions, behaviours based on kinship, respect for certain norms of conduct' (Descola 1992, 114). Though Descola draws his ethnographic illustrations from Amazonian societies, this characterization of what he calls 'animic systems' would seem readily applicable to the Ojibwa case as depicted in Hallowell's account. Critically, in such a system, relations between persons – that is, *social* relations – can override the boundaries of humanity as a species. Thus, as Hallowell reports, 'the world of personal relations in which the Ojibwa live is a world in which vital social relations transcend those which are maintained with human beings' (OO 43). To this one might add that a person's social relations are carried on in the same space as, and are continuous with, relations with other constituents of their environment, that is, with non-persons. There is, then, no radical break between the domains of social and ecological relations.

   Following Descola's lead, it would be possible to draw a systematic comparison between the animism of peoples like the Ojibwa and the naturalism of Western thought and science. Whereas animism takes the relational character of the world as an ontological principle, against which the 'naturalness' of beings – the material forms in which they appear – stands out as unstable and problematic, naturalism takes it for granted that nature really exists, as an ontological domain of order and necessity where things are what they are, in themselves. Against this world of nature, it is the status and the forms of human culture that appear problematic (Descola 1996, 88; see also Viveiros de Castro 1998). Yet for Descola, animism and naturalism (along with totemism, which I shall not consider here) may be regarded as alternative 'schemata of praxis,' in other words, as 'mental models which organise the social objectivation of non-humans' (1996, 87). This appeal to the language of mental models, to the idea of accommodating beings that are really non-human into schemes of representation that construct them as social and therefore human, belongs squarely within a naturalist ontology, and it is from this that the terms of the comparison are derived. For what these terms do is preserve a space for 'really natural' nature, which is unaffected by the diverse constructions that the human mind might place upon it. Thus, the comparison between naturalism and animism, since it is done on naturalism's terms, is hardly a fair or balanced one (Ingold 1996, 120).

My purpose in this chapter has been to redress this imbalance. Instead of trying to comprehend Ojibwa understandings within a comparative framework that already presupposes the separation of mind and nature, I have been concerned with placing the mode of understanding of Western science within the context of the primary existential condition, revealed in Ojibwa thought and practice, of being alive to the world. Let me summarily take stock of these two approaches. The first posits a world 'out there' full of objects, animate and inanimate. The life process of animate objects, being the expression of their essential nature (nowadays understood as their genetic constitution) under given environmental conditions, is purely consequential, an 'effect.' Hence the invocation of an additional principle, of mind or consciousness, to account for the powers of intentionality and awareness that we normally attribute to persons. In animistic systems such as those of the Ojibwa, these powers are said to be projected onto non-human kinds. So long as we follow Descola in assuming that in reality, they are reserved for human beings, such projection is bound to be anthropomorphic. If, in other words, only humans *really* have intentions, then to represent non-humans such as bears *as though* they were persons with intentions is necessarily to represent them as human. That is why Descola builds a component of anthropomorphism into his very definition of animism, as a system that endows natural beings with human capacities. Only beings thus endowed, it seems, can have social relations.

Working from an Ojibwa notion of animacy, not as an empirical property of things but as an existential condition of being, my argument has followed an alternative path. This has been to envisage the world from the point of view of a being within it, as a total field of relations whose unfolding is tantamount to the process of life itself. Every being emerges, with its particular form, dispositions, and capacities, as a locus of growth – or, in Ojibwa terms, as a focus of power – within this field. Mind, then, is not added on to life but is immanent in the intentional engagement, in perception and action, of living beings with the constituents of their environments. Thus, the world is not an external domain of objects that I look *at*, or do things *to*, but is rather going on, or undergoing continuous generation, with me and around me. As such primary engagement is a condition of being, it must also be a condition of knowledge, whether or not the knowledge in question is deemed to be 'scientific.' All properly scientific knowledge rests on observation, but there can be no observation without participation – without the observer's coupling the movement of his or her attention to surrounding currents of activity. Thus, the approach I have followed here is not an *alternative* to science, as animism is to naturalism; it rather seeks to restore the practices of science to the contexts of human life in the world. For it is from such contexts that all knowledge grows.

This approach has two further implications that I would like briefly to explore. The first takes us back to the question of anthropomorphism, the second concerns what I shall call the 'genealogical model.' Natural science, as von Bertalanffy has put it (1955, 258–9), approaches the world through a 'progressive de-anthropomorphization,' that is, through the attempt to expunge from its notion of reality all that can be put down to human experience. Thus purified, nature is revealed to a detached human reason as a domain of things in themselves. Ojibwa ontology, too, could be said to entail a process of de-anthropomorphization, but this operates in a quite different direction. Instead of severing the link between reality and human experience, Ojibwa ontology recognizes the reality of the experience of other-than-human beings. All experience depends on taking up a position in the world, tied to a particular form of life, but for the Ojibwa the human is but one form out of many. This, of course, undermines the core assumption that Descola brings to his characterization of animistic systems as inherently anthropomorphic, namely, that experience depends on powers of awareness and intentionality that mark their possessors as uniquely human.

The genealogical model is a way of thinking about the relations between animate beings that rests on the assumption that every such being is specified, in its essential nature, prior to commencing its life in the world. According to the model, the elements of the specification are received as a kind of endowment, passed on independently of the being's interaction with its environment. And it is in the passing on or 'inheritance' of this endowment, from generation to generation, that relations are constituted. This model is central to the way modern biology conceives of species and their phylogenetic connections; it is also at the heart of the conventional anthropological understanding of kinship. Thus, a simple line on a kinship diagram indicates that some component of the essence of a person is received, by transmission, at the point of conception, ahead of that person's growth in an environment. From this model, it is easy to derive the following propositions: first, membership of the human – or any other – species is fixed by birth; secondly, the animals most closely related to humans are those, namely the great apes, with which they have the closest genealogical connections; and thirdly, human kinship relations cannot cut across the species barrier.

From the Ojibwa perspective, none of these propositions is valid. We have seen that beings can change from one species form to another, that the animals closest to humans are those such as bears and eagles that are fellow participants in the same life-world, and that one specific category of kin – namely 'grandfathers' – admits persons of both human and other-than-human kinds. At a more fundamental level, however, Ojibwa ontology is incompatible with the genealogical model. If the forms of beings are not expressed but generated within the life process, then these forms cannot be passed on as part of any context-independent specification. One cannot, in other words, lay down the form that a being will take independently of the circumstances of its life in the world. Kinship, in particular, is not about handing down components of a person specification, but about the ways in which other persons in my environment, through their presence, their activities, and the nurturance they provide, contribute to the process of my own growth and well-being. And since these others may be non-human as well as human, there is nothing in the least strange about the extension of kinship relations across the species boundary. To receive blessings from my other-than-human grandfathers, it is not necessary to suppose that I am descended from them in the genealogical sense.

Conclusion

Ever since Darwin, Western science has cleaved strongly to the view that humans differ from other animals in degree rather than kind. Yet it is a view that has raised more problems than it has solved. For if we ask on what scale these differences of degree are to be measured, it turns out to be one that places human beings unequivocally at the top. It is the scale of the rise of reason, and its gradual triumph over the shackles of instinct. Where Darwin differed from many (though by no means all) of his predecessors was in both attributing powers of reasoning to sub-human animals and recognizing the powerful sway of instinct even on the behaviour of human beings. As he argued in *The Descent of Man* (1871, chap. 3 and 4), the beginnings of reason can be found far down in the scale of nature, but only with the emergence of humanity did it begin to gain the upper hand. In short, for Darwin and his many followers, the evolution of species in nature was also an evolution that progressively liberated the mind from the promptings of innate dispo-sition. Moreover, in bringing the rise of science and civilization within the compass of the same evolutionary process that had made humans out of apes, and apes out of creatures lower in the scale, Darwin was forced to attribute the ascendancy of reason in the West to innate endowment, a conclusion that is utterly unacceptable today. Modern science has responded, by and large, by dissociating the historical process of civilization from the evolution of the species, thereby com-promising the thesis of continuity. Humans are made to appear differ-ent in degree, not kind, from their evolutionary antecedents by attributing the movement of history to a process that differs in kind, not degree, from the process of evolution!

I have been searching, in this chapter, for a way to understand the continuity of the relations between human beings and all the other inhabitants of the earth that does not fall foul of the difficulties of the argument by degree – an argument that is unashamedly anthropocen-tric in taking human powers of intellect as the measure of all things, that can only comprehend the evolution of species in nature by suppos-ing an evolution of reason that takes them out of it, and that, if applied consistently, is incompatible with any ethical commitment to shared human potential. I have tried to show that the ontology of a non-Western people, the Ojibwa, points the way towards a solution. I do not mean to suggest for one moment that the Ojibwa orientation to life in the world is without paradoxes of its own. Nor would I wish to argue that it offers a viable substitute for science.

Earlier, I suggested that what the Ojibwa have arrived at is not an alternative science of nature but a poetics of dwelling. In the past, there has been a tendency to write off such poetics as the outpourings of a primitive mentality that has been superseded by the rise of the modern scientific world view. My conclusion, to the contrary, is that scientific activity is always, and necessarily, grounded in a poetics of dwelling. Rather than sweeping it under the carpet, as an embarrassment, I believe this is something worth celebrating, and that doing so will also help us do better science.

NOTES

1 The designation is problematic because the existential condition of dwelling in an environment (or what phenomenological philosophy calls 'being-in-the-world'), and the kind of practical knowledge this engenders, is common to people everywhere, whether or not they happen to be citizens of so-called Western countries.

2 Hallowell's work was carried out in the 1930s among the people of the Berens River band, numbering about nine hundred. These people were known as the Saulteaux (derived from *Saulteurs*, a name given them by French traders). In much of his earlier work, Hallowell himself referred to them by this name (Hallowell 1955). Many other authors refer to the people inclusively as Ojibway. An alternative designation, officially adopted by the Bureau of American Ethnology, was Chippewa (Hallowell 1955, 115). However, Wub-e-ke-niew (1995, xviii), who refers to his people of Red Lake as Ahnishinahbæó'jibway, claims that 'Chippewa' was an entirely artificial category that the U.S. Government created by lumping them together with French Métis people in the region involved in the fur trade. For the sake of simplicity and consistency with Hallowell's later usage, I will retain the term Ojibwa.

3 All the ethnographic material in this chapter, unless stated to the contrary, is drawn either from this article, or from the earlier collection of Hallowell's essays, *Culture and Experience* (1955). Page references will be provided only for direct quotations from these sources, or where I cite very specific points. 'Ojibwa Ontology, Behavior and World View' will be abbreviated throughout as OO, and *Culture and Experience* as CE.

4 From my (so far) very limited and superficial reading of the ethnography on native Amazonian societies, I have been startled by the recurrence of just the same themes here too. The parallels are extraordinary, and warrant further investigation (see, especially, Descola 1992, 1996, and Viveiros de Castro 1998).

5 This is a wonderful example of what Viveiros de Castro calls 'perspectiv-

ism,' namely the conception 'according to which the world is inhabited by different sorts of subjects or persons, human or non-human, which apprehend the world from distinct points of view' (1996, 469). To be a person is to assume a particular subject-position, and every person, respectively in their own sphere, will perceive the world in the same way – in the way that persons generally do. But what they see will be different, depending on the position or form of life they have taken up. Thus, if beaver are food for human persons, then they are food for non-human persons also, such as for the Thunder Bird and the 'masters' of the hawks. But what are 'beaver' for the birds are batrachians and reptiles from the perspective of humans.

6 Significantly, while spirits of the dead and grandfathers have the same dual structure of inner essence and outward form, only the former can appear as ghosts, since the latter never die (CE, 179–80).

7 See Ingold (1998, 160–3) for further discussion of this strategy.

8 In his chapter on 'language,' Wub-e-ke-niew explains that in his native Ahnishinahbæó'jibway, 'rather than acting upon the world … one acts in concert with the other beings with whom one shares Grandmother Earth … A person harmoniously "meets the Lake," rather than "going to get water"' (Wub-e-ke-niew 1995, 218).

9 As this example shows, the very openness of the Ojibwa self to the world, especially in dreams, has its downside, for it renders the self peculiarly vulnerable to the potentially hostile intent of other persons. This accounts for people's chronic anxiety, vividly documented by Hallowell (CE 250–90), about falling victim to sorcery and other kinds of covert attack, for the mutual suspicion that lurks beneath the placid surface of interpersonal life, and for what, to the outsider, looks like an exaggerated concern to avoid causing offence to others (OO 40, 47).

10 Much later, and without reference to Hallowell, Gregory Bateson made exactly the same point. 'The mental world,' he declared, 'is not limited by the skin' (Bateson 1973, 429).

REFERENCES

Bateson, G. 1973. *Steps to an Ecology of Mind*. London: Granada.
Black, M.B. 1977. 'Ojibwa Power Belief System.' In R.D. Fogelson and R.N. Adams, eds., *The Anthropology of Power: Ethnographic Studies from Asia, Oceania, and the New World*, 141–51. New York: Academic Press.

Darwin, C. 1871. *The Descent of Man, and Selection in Relation to Sex*. London: John Murray.

Descola, P. 1992. 'Societies of Nature and the Nature of Society.' In A. Kuper, ed., *Conceptualizing Society*, 107–26. London: Routledge.

– 1996. 'Constructing Natures: Symbolic Ecology and Social Practice.' In P. Descola and G. Palsson, eds., *Nature and Society: Anthropological Perspectives*, 82–102. London: Routledge.

Hallowell, A.I. 1955. *Culture and Experience*. Philadelphia: University of Pennsylvania Press.

– 1960. 'Ojibwa Ontology, Behavior and World View.' In S. Diamond, ed., *Culture in History: Essays in Honor of Paul Radin*, 19–52. New York: Columbia University Press.

Ingold, T. 1993. 'The Temporality of the Landscape.' *World Archaeology* 25 (2): 152–174.

– 1996. 'Hunting and Gathering as Ways of Perceiving the Environment.' In R. Ellen and K. Fukui, eds., *Redefining Nature: Ecology, Culture and Domestication*, 117–55. Oxford: Berg.

– 1998. 'Culture, Nature, Environment: Steps to an Ecology of Life.' In B. Cartledge, ed., *Mind, Brain and the Environment*, 158–80. Oxford: Oxford University Press.

Merleau-Ponty, M. 1964. 'Eye and Mind.' In J.M. Edie, ed., *The Primacy of Perception and Other Essays on Phenomenological Psychology, the Philosophy of Art, History and Politics*, 159–90. Evanston, IL: Northwestern University Press.

Scott, C. 1989. 'Knowledge Construction among Cree Hunters: Metaphors and Literal Understanding.' *Journal de la Société des Américanistes* 75: 193–208.

Stoller, P. 1989. *The Taste of Ethnographic Things: the Senses in Anthropology*. Philadelphia: University of Pennsylvania Press.

Viveiros de Castro, E. 1998. 'Cosmological Deixis and Amerindian Perspectivism: A View from Amazonia.' JRAI (*Journal of the Royal Anthropological Institute*) (N.S.) 4 (3): 469–88.

von Bertalanffy, L. 1955. 'An Essay on the Relativity of Categories.' *Philosophy of Science* 22: 243–63.

Wub-e-ke-niew. 1995. *We Have the Right to Exist*. New York City: Black Thistle Press.

Zuckerkandl, V. 1956. *Sound and Symbol: Music and the External World*. Trans. W.R. Trask. Bollingen Series, 44. Princeton: Princeton University Press.

Chapter Two

Ontology, Ancestral Order, and Agencies among the Kukatja of the Australian Western Desert

SYLVIE POIRIER

The question of ontologies is fundamental in ethnographic encounters and anthropology for two reasons: first, because it refers to Being and what members of a culture have to say about it; and second, because it is linked to knowledge and action. All ontologies are value-laden (Overing 1985, 7), and one major obstacle to understanding ontologies other than one's own lies in how to recognize their local value as truth. This difficulty becomes particularly obvious when we are dealing not so much with different world views as with different ways of being-in-the-world. Accordingly, acquaintance with the ontologies and episte-mologies of other cultures requires a degree of humility on the part of the ethnographer (7). Through a process of objectification and by taking seriously what others say about their social worlds, ethnographers may arrive at a certain understanding of other ontologies. However, they remain constantly aware that they do not necessarily experience and perceive the world the way the cultural Other perceives it (Geertz 1983, 56). The process of objectification that emerges from these encounters or discoveries is an explicitly creative one (Hastrup 1995).

In his recent work, Sahlins reminds us that 'objectivity is culturally constituted, it is always a distinctive ontology' (1995, 169). Referring to Lévi-Strauss, and to the *pensée sauvage* as a form of empirical thought, he writes that if human sensory capacities are in effect universal, it remains that 'a sensory perception is not yet an empirical judgment, since the latter depends on criteria of objectivity which are never the only ones possible' (162–3). In a way, this assertion intersects with the claim by phenomenologists for whom meaning is part of the perceptual act and is culturally (and contextually) constructed. He adds, 'One cannot simply posit another people's judgments of "reality" a priori, by

laden ontologies, they do, however, differ from one another, and give rise to different understandings and praxis. Yet, 'the one truth does not go against the truth of the other' (Overing 1985, 5), as both add to the diversity and richness of human knowledge and action in the world. The conception of the wind as a link to the ancestral order, as a form of protection and nourishment to breath and the spirit, conveys a sense of 'permeability' between the body-self and the surrounding countryside. The body participates in action as a mediator between ancestral, human, and environmental elements, thus transcending the Cartesian absolute of a division between mind and body. Furthermore, the possibility that the whistling of the wind can be heard as a message from either an ancestral or a non-human agency is also a true experience to the degree that such an assertion indeed makes sense to the Kukatja. And, because it makes sense, it may call forth either a contextual interpretation, which in itself represents an action (Ricoeur 1986), or a process of objectification, which is a creative act. Within the local structuration of personal experience and collective forms of expression, humans, ancestors, and, in this case, the wind are all engaged as distinct yet consubstantial agencies in a reciprocal, intimate, and communicative relationship.

If we reduce these cultural cosmologies and ontologies to simple 'beliefs' that are destined to shatter upon meeting up with Western rationality, then we are merely sidestepping the difficult task involved in understanding other ways of being-in-the-world. In theoretical and empirical terms, cosmologies/ontologies must be viewed as instances of cultural rationality in their own right, and indeed as 'knowledge' (Lewis 1994).

In this chapter, I will explore a number of different facets of the ontology of the Kukatja, focusing on how they perceive, experience, and interact with a powerful, personified, and sentient 'landscape,' as networks of named places.[2] While much has been written on Australian Aboriginals' conception of a mythical landscape, recent work has brought out the role of landscape in mediating between present experience and ancestral past, between the contingent and the mythical, between human and ancestral actions (Morphy 1995b; Rumsey 1994; Povinelli 1993, 1995). In line with these authors, and with respect to Kukatja ontologies and politics of (ritual) knowledge, I will discuss the immanent and consubstantial dimensions of the ancestral order and its ongoing presence, together in connection with human actions and realizations. An acrylic painting by an elder (now deceased) will provide the ground for a discussion of the ontological difference between 'itineraries' and 'maps' (de Certeau 1984) as two poles of experience.

Since the 1950s, along with members of the neighbouring language groups (Waltmatjari, Wangkatjunga, Mandiltjarra, Ngarti, Pintupi, Warlpiri), most Kukatja have lived in the communities of Wirrimanu (formerly the Balgo mission) and Yagga Yagga, on the northwestern fringe of the Gibson Desert.[3] Their 'ancestral connections,' to borrow an expression from Morphy (1991), extend further to the south, around the Mungkayi area (the Stansmore Range).[4]

'An Ontology of Dwelling'

Drawing on ethnographic works about various hunting and gathering societies, Ingold contrasts their ontologies with an ontology predominant in the West. He underscores a well-known feature of Western thought, namely, the 'absolute division between the contrary conditions of humanity and animality ... subjects and objects, persons and things, morality and physicality, reason and instinct, and above all, society and nature' (1996, 130). This conceptual division between culture and nature, on which we construct our view and experience of the world, is far from being universal, as various anthropological works have brought out. In that connection, I should like to cite Ingold at some length: 'hunter-gatherers do *not*, as a rule, approach their environment as an external world of nature that has to be "grasped" conceptually and appropriated symbolically within the terms of an imposed cultural design, as a precondition for effective action. They do not see themselves as mindful subjects having to contend with an alien world of physical objects; indeed the separation of mind and nature has no place in their thought and practice' (120). Likewise, he adds that the point of departure of Western ontology 'is that of a mind detached from the world and which has literally to formulate it – to build an intentional world in consciousness – prior to any attempt at engagement ... [whereas for hunter-gatherers] apprehending the world is not a matter of construction but of engagement, not of building but of dwelling, not of making a view *of* the world but of taking up a view *in* it' (121; author's emphasis).

In such an 'ontology of dwelling' – or a 'poetics of dwelling' (Ingold 2000) – in which there are no absolute divisions between cultural subjects and natural objects, humans and non-humans are equally endowed with sociality, and hence intentionality. Humans and non-humans both are engaged together in reciprocal relations of obligation and responsibility, exchange and sharing. Generalized reciprocity as a social practice, and sharing as an embodied cultural value, can also be applied to the way the Kukatja, like other contemporary hunters and gatherers, perceive and experience their relationship to their environment (Bird-David 1990, 1992, 1999). In Kukatja ontology, human beings are an integral part of a socio-cosmic environment that is forever unfolding through webs of agencies, in other words, networks of social relationships that also include non-human beings, ancestors, and named places that are endowed with personhood and have in common their sociality. Human actions and realizations, including hunting activities, ritual performances, or dreams, are intrinsic to this process of unfolding.

Places, Itineraries, and Networks

In the Kukatja system of knowledge and cultural objectivity, the world is the creation of ancestral actors who have travelled over the surface of the earth, underground, and in the heavens. In the course of hunting, fighting, dancing, singing, copulating, or urinating, they formed and named the rocks, hills, trees, riverbeds, stars, etc. Wherever they passed – preferably around rock holes – they sowed the reproductive essences (*kurruwari*) that the people feel responsible for nurturing and tending. The actions of ancestral beings, and also their belongings (boomerangs, spears, digging sticks, sacred boards, or other), footprints, and body parts, thus underwent a process of metamorphosis. These are embodied within the landscape (Munn 1970) – indeed, they *are* the landscape. Slight hollows in the ground are the footprints of *Karlaya* (Emu); a hill, the tail of *Marlu* (Kangaroo); a tree, the spear of one of the *Wati Kutjarra* (Two Initiated Men); white pebbles, the fat of *Wanyarra* (Rainbow Serpent). From the Aboriginal point of view, these topographical, plant and mineral features still embody the essence and the spirit of the ancestral beings and deceased relatives, who have merged with the ancestral order. One point I wish to stress here, and to which I will return below, is that the ancestors go on living and travelling forever (often underground).

Working among the Belyuen of Northern Australia, Povinelli writes that, from the Aboriginal perspective, 'all matter is the congealed labor of mythic action' (1993, 137). While we tend to see hunters and gatherers as people who do not build, transform, or act upon the landscape, their ontology seems, as Ingold has remarked, to assert the precise opposite, wherein 'form arises and is held in place within action: it is movement congealed' (1996: 146).

As they travel, either on their own, in couples, or in groups, the ancestral beings named the places that they visited in the course of their journeys. These places are called *ngurra*. The word *ngurra* is translated as one's 'country,' and applies as much to these permanent ancestral sites as to the more temporary human camps (Myers 1986, 54–7), inasmuch as both leave traces on the ground and inscribe the landscape. Narratives provide Aboriginals with a form for objectifying these ancestral journeys; the itineraries of the ancestral beings are (re)created over a stretch of land in what constitutes a series of *ngurra*. The whole desert area, and far beyond, is thus crisscrossed with ancestral tracks, which not only link the underground, the heavens, and the surface of the earth, but which also bind together humans, ancestors, and named places as kin within complex and dynamic networks of relationships. These *ngurra* and ancestral itineraries are the wellsprings of social webs of rights and responsibilities, exchanges and alliances. Elsewhere, I have called these named sites 'the gardens of the nomad' (Poirier 1996). Metaphorically speaking, they are indeed gardens, which are shaped by ancestral actions. Like any other garden, they must be tended, cared for, and, when necessary, transformed; this is, in fact, the object of human actions and realizations.

One quality that is intrinsic to the political and ritual expressions of these mythical itineraries and is worth mentioning here is 'openness' – the possibility that new meanings or new episodes in relation to ancestral journeys, in relation to itineraries, can be revealed. I have devoted much comment elsewhere to how these itineraries, as ideological structures of permanence, are in keeping with events, contingencies, or revelations, and are 'open' to (re)interpretation and negotiation (Poirier 1992, 1996), at least in the Western Desert. Humans are not mere spectators who roam the countryside narrating and singing the great deeds of ancestral heroes, nor are they in essence 'confronted with a *fait accompli*, a fixed topographical structure, within which [they] must operate' (Munn 1970, 147). These ancestral journeys are partly the expressions of a local type of historicity and consciousness that has been inscribed in named places. Aboriginal people are active participants in the construction, reproduction, and (re)interpretation of these mythical tracks. It is partly at this level that individual (and collective) knowledge and achievement come into play.

Personal Identity as a Composite and Dynamic Configuration

At this point, it is necessary to describe, at least briefly, the composite character of personal identity; in other words, the personal configuration of 'ancestral connections.' Kukatja personal identity is indeed composite and dynamic, drawing on various affiliations to named sites located along ancestral itineraries. It is also in part constructed and achieved through ritual activities and the acquisition of sacred knowledge, as well as through individual experiences. In Western Desert societies, various criteria can be drawn on to confirm one's ancestral connections in terms of an affiliation to a 'country' (*ngurra*) and a responsibility towards it. For the Pintupi, a society closely related to the Kukatja, Myers (1986) identifies ten such criteria that clearly illustrate the complexity underlying personal identity and its unfolding over a lifetime. A person has rights to and responsibilities towards different 'countries,' thus entitling him or her to the associated mythico-ritual knowledge. Aside from the rights to countries inherited from the four grandparents, the most highly valued ancestral connection is certainly to the place of conception, which is located where the spirit-child (*kurruwari*) penetrated the mother's womb and metamorphosed into a human form. A person is thus the incarnation of the ancestral being (and essence) associated with such a site; they are consubstantial. Men and women often refer to themselves in the first person by using the name of the ancestral being of whom they are the expression; their relationship is one of intimacy.

In Aboriginal societies, the concept of knowledge is land-based, as Rose has aptly summed up: 'Within one's country, access to knowledge (subject to the "usual" circumscriptions of age, gender and intelligence) is a right. Beyond the parameters of what can legitimately be defined as one's country, access to knowledge is a privilege' (1994, 3). The criteria of exclusion from/inclusion within sacred knowledge are relative rather than absolute, and are contextually re-evaluated and negotiated according to events and individual abilities, requests, and acquaintance with mythical knowledge (see Poirier 2001).

With respect to local systems of knowledge and structuration of experience, it must be stressed that while personal familiarity with mythico-ritual knowledge, along with its enactment and embodiment, enhances spiritual power, it also allows for greater communication and intimacy with the ancestral agencies. In Aboriginal ideology, such personal achievement is highly valued. This again is another form of local engagement with (or involvement in) a powerful, sentient landscape. Such ancestral powers must indeed by treated with great care. That which is secret-sacred (*tarruku*) – named places, songs, designs, or cultual objects – is governed by a set of rules that only knowledgeable men and women ('Lawmen' and 'Lawwomen,' or 'businessmen' and businesswomen' in pidgin) can manipulate and potentially negotiate (Dussart 2000).

At death, the spirit (*kurrunpa*) of the individual returns to the named site where he or she was conceived, thereupon merging once again with its ancestral (and spiritual) essence and identifying with the ancestors that dwell there.

Ancestral Immanence and Consubstantiality

The ancestral order – that is, *Tjukurrpa* in Kukatja and other Western Desert languages – is without doubt an all-encompassing, multivocal reality. Habitually translated as 'Dreaming,' *Tjukurrpa* denotes the original essence that permeates all that is: the ancestral beings, their actions, the sites they named, and the itineraries they inscribed. It also refers to the Law (which the Kukatja also term 'business'), which not only informs the complex network of exchanges and alliances but also mediates personal entitlement to a country and its associated mythico-ritual knowledge. From an Aboriginal perspective, the *Tjukurrpa* is true (*mularrpa*).

These various dimensions of the ancestral order have been well documented in Australian Aboriginal ethnography. What I wish to explore here is a number of its more everyday manifestations. As a part of the interpretative process, I will consider three interrelated dimensions of the *Tjukurrpa*, namely, its immanence, its consubstantiality, and the ongoing interactions between the ancestors and humans. In the ideology and value system of the Kukatja, that which is ancestral is hierarchically superior, but it is also essentially immanent, in contrast with the Judaeo-Christian cosmology in which the Creator is transcendent. On the basis of such immanence, the value of communication, reciprocity, and intimacy between the ancestors and humans must be taken seriously – that is, as true – if we are to understand the local structuration of experience.

As the original essence, the *Tjukurrpa* represents an ongoing presence, which is continuously being re-embodied and actualized. This is made evident in the reproductive cycles, where it 'is continually coming out of the ground and being re-embodied as a living entity, as well as continually returning to the ground in death' (Munn 1973, 199). Ancestral, human, and non-human agencies are not only intrinsically linked in their becoming, they are also consubstantial. Everything that is, be it rock, wind, plant, human, or animal, shares the same ancestral essence. Ingold's words seem relevant here when he talks of 'the creative unfolding of an entire field of relations within which beings emerge and take the particular forms they do, each in relation to the others' (2000, 19).

Local narratives of conception provide evidence not only of consubstantiality but also of the permeability of forms and the high value attaching to metamorphosis. For every one of her children, a mother necessarily has a conception story that testifies to where and how the child came into being, which thus confirms the child's intrinsic link to ancestral sites and agencies. This narrative is constructed on the basis of events that occurred during pregnancy. To some degree, it is a necessary condition to the unfolding of one's identity. Out of *Tjukurrpa*, the spirit-child (*kurruwari*) will, as an agency, momentarily metamorphose into an animal, a plant, an object (ritual or other), or one of the 'natural' elements (i.e., cloud, rain, or wind). At this moment, the agent of conception (*tjarriny*) will be identified with the child-to-be. When, thereafter, it comes into contact with the future mother through a dream, ingestion, or other means, it will metamorphose into a human fetus. As with the wind when it is transformed into breath and spirit upon penetrating the human body, the spirit-child will be transformed upon entering the mother's body. Owing to the principle of consubstantiality involving ancestral, human, and non-human agencies, such metamorphosis conveys its own cultural objectivity.

Metamorphosis is key to understanding the permeability and consubstantiality of forms – in other words, the passage from one state of being to another. The entire landscape came into being through the initial metamorphosis of ancestral actions, body parts, and objects. Humans in turn come into being following the metamorphosis of the spirit-child. At death, one's spirit (*kurrunpa*) will merge again with the ancestral essence of his or her place of conception. Furthermore, in narratives of their life experiences, elder men and women may refer to instances where they had to metamorphose into an animal form in order, for example, to elude a potential danger. Such narratives exemplify a kind of complicity with the ancestors and their power.

The spirit-child can also make its presence known to the mother or a relative by way of a dream. Through dreams, the spirit-child makes known its intention to penetrate within the mother and undergo metamorphosis. At this point, it should be stressed that in the Kukatja system of thought and knowledge, dream experiences mediate between the ancestral and human realms. Dreaming is without doubt the favoured space-time of exchange and communication with the ancestral beings and deceased relatives (Poirier 1994, 1996, 2003). It is through dream experiences that Kukatja men and women meet with ancestors at specific places falling within their country. All dream narratives are necessarily spatially located, and the dreamer will always specify the *ngurra* (country or places) where the action occurred. Dreaming also has an influence on the reproductive well-being of one's country, in terms both spiritual and material. One day, commenting on the abundance of wild food in her country near Mungkayi, Napangarti added, 'This is good country, we are good dreamers.' As a part of human action, dreaming is yet another form of Kukatja involvement in the landscape, as well as a form of communication with the ancestral order.

On the basis of their embodiment within the landscape and their ongoing presence, ancestors can be encountered in daily activities either in the bush while hunting and gathering, or in and around the community. To the extent that ancestral beings are 'everywhen' (Stanner 1979, 24), narratives of such encounters are not only meaningful, they also occur fairly often, judging from their frequency during my stays among the Kukatja. Although they are very rarely seen, except in dreams, the ancestral beings are nevertheless able to make their presence known by a variety of means, or to manifest themselves in a range of different forms. For example, they can send messages through the wind, or assume the form of clouds, or slap someone on the shoulder. A person may also just 'feel' their presence. Such manifestations will be given meaning and interpreted contextually, in accordance with recent events (accident, pregnancy, or death) and the site where they occurred.

It is also during ritual gatherings and performances that the ancestral beings are liable to make their presence known through a sign of some kind. In their discussions of this type of presence in a ritual context, the women seem to hold the view that the ancestors, male or female, come to ensure that the ritual is being properly staged. By their presence, they play more of a protective and supervisory role (e.g., protecting the women's ceremonial grounds from unwanted eyes) than a role designed to impart power to the ritual per se, although this possibility is certainly not to be dismissed. Some Kukatja are of the opinion that the ancestors may come for enjoyment's sake. As one woman put it, 'They enjoy the singing and the dancing.' Such encounters or ancestral manifestations are perceived by individuals with varying degrees of apprehension and self-assurance, according to their age, current situation, and the extent of their personal knowledge and acquaintance with ancestral power.

A Personified, Sentient 'Landscape'

The concept of the person is fundamental to understanding Aboriginal ontology – and any ontology, for that matter. To contrast Aboriginal and Western notions of the person, one might say that in the former, networks of social relations are viewed as being intrinsically embodied within the person,[5] whereas in the latter they are conceived as being external to the individual, who is constituted as an autonomous moral entity. Earlier, I pointed out how ancestral connections are integral to one's composite identity. At this point, I would like to take up another aspect of the local notion of person, one that also includes named sites.

In the Western Desert, the human individual is an integral part of networks of social relationships and ancestral connections – i.e., networks of territorial and ritual affiliation and responsibility that also involve named places as persons. In turn, in their insertion along ancestral itineraries, named places are not a template (or a culturalized, political space) patterning the workings of kinship and ritual networks; they are themselves constitutive of such networks. The Kukatja refer to named places as 'kin' (*walytja*). They are persons in a literal, not a metaphorical, sense. The identity, and also the becoming, of the place-person and the human person are indissociable. Accordingly, the Kukatja view and experience their relationship to the named sites with which they are affiliated in a way that is intimate, reciprocal, and communicative.

An example. The spirit of the deceased father of a Kukatja/Walmatjarri rainmaker now lives in Kutal, one of the many abodes and expressions of *Wanayarra*, the Rainbow Snake. The deceased father and the Snake are both referred to as the 'old man.' The current rainmaker will also be referred to by the same name after his death. Kutal is not only the abode of *Wanayarra*, it *is Wanayarra*. Kutal is the public name of this place-person. It can be uttered freely, whereas *Wanayarra* is used with a great deal of circumspection. The rainmaker would often call his deceased father Kutal. As a merging of identities, Kutal is at once the site, the ancestral being, and deceased relatives.

Like persons and their human kin, named places have feelings. Their 'shared identity' is also a 'shared sensibility.' The cultural emotions existing between human kin, such as compassion, grief, and loneliness, which Myers has so vividly portrayed as the representation and expression of shared identity or kinship with another (Myers 1979, 1986, 1988), also apply to named places as kin. For Aboriginal people, sites are sentient; they feel a pang of longing for the human persons with whom they are affiliated, in the same way that people might feel homesick. In turn, Aboriginals 'feel sorry' for their 'country' (ngurra), often saying pityingly, 'yawi' (i.e., poor fellow). The spirit of the place-person may send messages to its human kin, most often by way of dreams, if the affiliated human persons are far away or have failed to look after the place properly. When Aboriginals longs for a place that they are unable to visit, or when they feel that a site (as the dwelling place of ancestral spirits) feels lonely because it has not been visited for a long time, they will address the place in song. The song is sung to soothe their pain, communicate their feeling to the place, and excuse themselves for being negligent and absent.

In her work among the Belyuen of northern Australia, Povinelli (1993, 1995) has brought out how places are indeed quite sensitive to by-products of human activities, such as speech and sweat. When Belyuen women visit sites to which they are affiliated while out on the land hunting small game or gathering, or simply visiting relatives (that is, embodied named sites), they feel that the site is receptive to their presence. They are confident that the site will respond positively by ensuring the reproduction of ancestral essences and, with this, economic resources. Povinelli writes, 'Human labor does, however, congeal in the countryside in a positive way in the long run. People who live and labor in an area permeate the region with their words and sweat. When they die, they are embodied at the site; their spirit/self resides there' (1993, 152). The landscape is thus the congealed product of mythic and human actions, and of their interrelated unfolding.

Nowadays, when it has become difficult for some people in Wirrimanu and Yagga Yagga to visit their sites of affiliation, dream experiences represent an important means by which they can journey to such places, to meet and carry on a dialogue with the ancestral beings and deceased parents, and to remind themselves that someone cares. For the Kukatja, this value of exchange and communication, reciprocity and intimacy, between the human person and the place-person is a fundamental, integral component of the local structuration of experience. From their point of view, this value stands as truth (*mularrpa*).

Interpreting the Landscape

The interpretation of indexical and iconic signs in the landscape is another form of Kukatja engagement, of their active participation in the unfolding of their environment, and of the continual 'business' of actualizing the *Tjukurrpa*. Birds, lizards, kangaroos, ants, the wind, and even rocks are sentient beings and agencies that are capable of communicating something to humans. Kukatja men and women are constantly on the lookout for signs that could reveal new knowledge of some kind or another, whether of an ecological, political, or poetic variety, thus demonstrating how all these aspects are closely intertwined in Kukatja expressions and experiences.

Needless to say, as hunters and gatherers, the Kukatja are acute observers of their physical environment. They are masters of the art of reading tracks (*tjina*). Indeed, everyone can recognize the footprints of a great number of community members. The same applies to animal tracks, of either large game such as kangaroos, emus, or wild turkeys, or small game such as various snakes and lizards. Even the fine lines formed on sandy soil by yams (*karnti*) or other tubers do not escape their sharp eyesight. Such knowledge is acquired at a very young age. I myself tried to achieve competence in the art of track reading, but in vain. Despite all my efforts, and the enormous patience of my Kukatja teachers, I still have difficulty distinguishing the track of a snake from that left by a lizard. When I actually manage to make such a distinction, I am unable to tell in what direction the animal was heading, how long ago it passed through, whether it was male or female, or how much fatty tissue it had.

By acquiring such knowledge, hunters and gatherers do not seek to control their natural environment; rather, they aim to refine and consolidate their relationship to this milieu as well as their knowledge of the sentient entities that dwell within it. For hunters and gatherers like the Kukatja, the understanding and interpretation of such indexical signs is not so much an act of decoding as a dialogue between sentient beings sharing the same socio-cosmic environment. The following example provides a good illustration of this aspect of dialogue. A group of women had gone gathering *lukarrara*, a type of sedge grass. The plant's fine black and white seeds are usually gathered around ant holes in the earth, then ground and made into damper, a type of unleavened bread that is cooked in hot ashes. The women arrived at a place where *lukarrara* is usually quite abundant. To their disappointment, they found only small quantities of the grass around the various ant holes. They then asked a young nursing mother to drop some of her breast milk on the sand. The young woman did not understand why she should do so, and so an elderly woman explained that the ants would smell the milk and become aware of their presence. Knowing that humans like the sweetness of *lukarrara*, the ants would reciprocate by gathering plenty of seeds – but also in exchange for the breast milk.

The following encounter provides an additional example of a particularly intense and aesthetically evocative performance. I was out hunting and gathering with a group of men and women. The woman I was accompanying had been following the track of a lizard for some time. Owing to the hardness of the soil, the track would be imperceptible for a short distance and would then re-emerge a short way further on. At one point, I gave up hunting out of sheer exhaustion, but continued to watch my friend from a distance. I admired her agility and perceptiveness. Her digging stick at the ready, she was now closing in on her prey. She knew quite well that the large lizard would have to hide underground if it were to try to escape. That was the moment she would be able to get hold of it. Aware that she was drawing closer with every passing minute, she now quickened her pace. Suddenly, however, she stopped in her tracks, and did not move for several seconds. Then she started to weave back and forth like a snake. At that point, I understood that the tracks of two different animals – a poisonous snake and a lizard – had crossed one another in the desert soil. I knew the woman hunter well enough to recall that she was deeply afraid of snakes. As I went to join her, she remained silent, merely pointing out the snake track to me. Her entire body-self participated in this new presence; she had become the snake. Her spontaneous performance was both moving and laden with meaning. Through her dance, she had been warning me at some distance of a potential danger. However, she did not refer to the snake by name, which would have amounted to calling it and bringing it closer. The performance also enabled her to exorcize her fears. Any other woman would have continued tracking the lizard, but my friend chose instead to stop hunting.

Of course, animal tracks, as a kind of indexical sign, are not the only signs one is likely to come across while moving within a named, personified, and sentient landscape. Aboriginal people are also constantly engaged in detecting signs that might have been left by the ancestors in a more or less distant past, but which have gone unnoticed until that time. Some signs may contain relevant information or offer new knowledge. As Povinelli (1995) has pointed out, while rock is sensitive to the presence of humans, so too are humans sensitive to the message of rocks. To make this point clear, I will give another example.

Once, as on so many other occasions, I was out walking in the bush with a group of men, women, and children, looking for small game and gathering various things. Tjampitjin, a male adult, came across a flat rock measuring about thirty square centimetres that had a number of peculiar designs on it. It was what Westerners would call 'natural' designs, or the 'work of Nature.' For Tjampitjin and his companions, though, it was an ancestral action that had been inscribed (or congealed) in the rock – that is, a potential message to be interpreted and understood. In terms of ontology, he and the rock were equally engaged in the narrative unfolding of a socio-cosmic environment. In terms of epistemology, the rock was considered likely to reveal new knowledge pertaining to ancestral actions and itineraries.

The country we were in at the time had been named and formed by the *Wati Kutjarra* (the Two Initiated Men), ancestral actors who had travelled widely throughout the Western Desert. In his work of interpretation, Tjampitjin understood that they had inscribed the rock. By the same token, the rock was revealing a message, telling a story. In the language of the rock, as it was interpreted and understood, Tjampitjin saw surrounding hills and rocky outcrops, in addition to the presence of *puliki* (bullocks) and two salt lakes, which actually lay further to the southeast. The story thus told by and through the rock was another proof of the passage of the *Wati Kutjarra* through this specific site, at a time, moreover, when *puliki* had come to the area – that is, in the period following the arrival of the *Kartiya* (White man). The message of the rock confirmed the *puliki*'s active involvement in the landscape as one agency among others. In a way, the surrounding landscape had not changed for me, but for my Kukatja friends it was a kind of new unfolding that revealed once more the presence of the *Wati Kutjarra*, as well as their relatively recent encounter with the *puliki*. In another time and place, and in another context, the story could have been different. Certainly, the text that had been revealed through the rock was open to different interpretations.

Tjampitjin used his knowledge of this particular country to decipher the patterns of the rock. In itself, this interpretation was an act of participation in, and communication with, the surrounding landscape. And in this instance, the interpretative act did not lead to the re-configuration of ancestral itineraries as might well have been the case. However, it does illustrate another kind of everyday Aboriginal in-volvement in a sentient, evocative environment, one in which the land-scape is not given once and for all, but is forever revealing itself to those who are open to it and actively engaged with it. As an act of interpreta-tion, Tjampitjin's gloss on the rock's 'text' was also an act of creation (Ricoeur 1986); through the work of interpretation, what was unknown becomes known. To a certain extent, the local narrative according to which the *Wati Kutjarra* inscribed the rock is not the end point of the process, but is, rather, the starting point, or pretext, upon which hu-mans will thereafter interpret contextually, in order to gain 'knowl-edge.' On the basis of Peirce's typology, such signs have an indexical and iconic value to them. The *Wati Kutjarra* left these marks during their passage through the area; therein lies the indexical value. Consid-ered as the 'true' likeness of the surrounding country, these signs never-theless offer iconicity of a sort that is fundamentally polysemic and contextual.

To say that the Kukatja, or hunters and gatherers in general, are more ecologically minded, closer to nature, and so on, is a misguided asser-tion, one which subjects a specific cultural reality to the terms of our own interpretation and which fails to present this reality in terms of its own cultural objectivity and values. In the Kukatja world, ecological and mythico-ritual varieties of knowledge, indexical and iconic signs, human and ancestral actions are all the interrelated expressions of an unfolding (and manifold) reality. As a powerful, sentient entity, the landscape is forever revealing itself to the hunter and to the Lawmen and Lawwomen, occasionally at the cost of great hardship and perse-verance. Such revelations – in other words, the 'everywhen,' and the contextual actualizations of the *Tjukurrpa* (the Law) – are made possible by means of the sensitive engagement, the praxis and achievements of social and ritual actors. The landscape, including the heavens and the below-ground, provides the basis of epistemology and most of the texts of the semiosphere, in which all sentient beings and agencies interact and communicate with one another, and thereby become acquainted with one another.

Singing and Painting the Country

In addition to storytelling and mythical narratives relating to a country, knowledge also comes in the form of songs, designs, and dances, which correspond to every named site along an ancestral track. The core of ritual performances, these series can be more or less elaborate depending on the political and spiritual relevance of the site. As enactment and performance, these aesthetic forms are another expression of an Aboriginal ontology of dwelling.

Ritual activities and performances are highly valued modes of knowledge and experience. It is by participating in rituals and acquiring knowledge that one's composite identity is collectively recognized. However, as a ritual corpus, these aesthetic forms are not immutable. They are capable of undergoing transformation, with new sequences occasionally being created and others falling into disuse, depending on events, contingencies, actions and revelations. It is through dreams that the ancestors may reveal new songs, designs, or dances to humans. This initial revelation will be subject to further elaboration, and will have to be collectively recognized (Poirier 1996; Dussart 2000, 139–76).

From the perspective of the Kukatja, the acts of singing, painting, and dancing are acts of communication with, and participation in, the ancestral order. When the Kukatja represent a particular country (and the Law associated with it) in painting, song, or dance, they are unequivocally demonstrating their connections and rights to the particular country thus represented – it is a political act. It is also a performative and communicative act. In painting, singing, and dancing, the Kukatja directly address the sensibility of the place-person as the embodiment of the ancestral beings and the deceased. These forms thus constitute a dialogue, a way of expressing their shared identity and sensibility. They enhance the Kukatja's empathy for their country as a dwelling place for the ancestors. Empowerment is a recurrent theme in local discourses on ritual activities. One of the multiple purposes of rituals is, as one Kukatja man put it, 'to make people and the country stronger [*marrka*].' As in the previous example of the wind, which permeates the human body, becoming breath and empowering the spirit, the ancestral power will, when momentarily embodied in ritual body paintings, for example, penetrate a person's being, making him or her stronger (*marrka*). Dancing is also highly valued. As bare feet slip rhythmically over the sandy soil, the ground becomes 'inscribed.' Conversely, it is said that the dance steps can be heard underground by the ancestral beings.

Once more, as in the preceding example of the wind, the body-self becomes a mediator between ancestral, human and environmental agencies. The dancing body is a 'moving' agent (Farnell 1995).

In non-ritual contexts, such as hunting and gathering activities, the Kukatja also engage in singing. The songs invoke the ancestor (public song lines) who has inscribed the land they are walking over. The kangaroo, the lizard, the yam, or the bush tomato can also be subjects of song. Songs are sung to give strength to the child or the anthropologist who occasionally become tired from walking in the heat. The Kukatja also sing out to their prey, thus engaging in a dialogue.

Songs and designs, along with storytelling and mythical narratives, are forms that objectify ancestral and human action as congealed in the landscape. In addition, the act of putting one's country into narrative, singing, and painting is an act of communication and participation: they are political and aesthetic forms of involvement. When Aboriginals paint or sing, they are enacting their intrinsic relation to the site and living out the ancestral actions and events being portrayed. In so doing, they are participating in the well-being of the country and related kin, and strengthening their connections to both. While a definite sense of responsibility attaches to this act, and a set of rules, according to the local politics of (ritual) knowledge, has to be respected, there is, however, room for individual creativity.

I would also like to take up another, relatively recent form of objectification and creative expression – Western Desert acrylic painting. This medium was introduced into the Wirrimanu area in the early 1980s, and it has by now become quite well-known throughout the world.[6]

Spatial Stories

> What the map cuts up, the story cuts across.
>
> Certeau, *The Practice of Everyday Life*

With the advent of canvas and acrylic paint in the Wirrimanu area, Kukatja art, like that of neighbouring groups such as the Warlpiri and the Pintupi, became a medium of artistic expression, and a commodity as well. Western Desert painting, like Australian Aboriginal art in general, does not admit of easy classification with respect to the contemporary art scene (Myers 1992, Morphy 1995a). The adoption of acrylic painting as a medium has surely signified a major challenge for Aboriginal people, who were accustomed to working on the ground in sand paintings or on the human body using 'natural' pigments (Anderson and Dussart 1988). It has also had implications for the reinterpretation of local criteria governing access to knowledge, and raised issues of what can be painted and exhibited by whom and when. All the same, the case of acrylic painting and the international art market illustrates how Western Desert Aborigines have brought a clear sense of cultural resistance and innovation to their appropriation of modernity. I would like to focus in particular on one such acrylic painting, which speaks directly to the issue of the ontological obstacles in intercultural relations. The painting provides me with a basis for a series of reflections on the distinctions that de Certeau drew between the 'map' and the 'itinerary,' which represent the twin poles of experience (Certeau 1984, 115–31).

The author of the painting, a member of the Tjupurrula subsection, died in May 1994.[7] I became acquainted with him in the early 1980s. Like most people from the area, Tjupurrula was of mixed descent, in his case Kukatja-Pintupi. When he came to the Balgo mission in the early 1950s, he was a young adult, in his early thirties or thereabouts. In his lifetime, he became an accomplished Lawman who was feared and respected over a wide area. He was also a *marparn* (medicine man) and a warrior, who never hesitated to apply traditional Law when he felt that this was necessary to the well-being of his people and the country. He could be fierce, but also gentle at times. His body bore many marks: initiation marks, mostly lines that crossed his chest; scars resulting from the many fights he had during his lifetime; and spear marks he had inflicted on himself following the death of relatives. His life history could be read from these various body marks. More than any other elder, Tjupurrula would openly defy *Kartiya* (and missionary) authority. His line of conduct was dictated solely by ancestral Law, *Tjukurrpa*.

His life itinerary and personal configuration of ancestral connections was also intimately bound up with mythic action and narrative, as depicted in the painting. As with all Aboriginal painting, this example tells a land-related story, which I shall summarize here. This story is part of a major initiatory cycle and itineraries that overlap onto many countries, thus falling under the responsibility of different groups. The painting refers to an important episode that occurred at Maruwa (the concentric circles in the centre), one of the many Aboriginal names for the Lake Mackay area. It was here that the *Kanaputa* (the Digging Stick Women) met the *Tingarri* (Initiated Men), novices and men. The *Tingarri*

Figure 2.1 Donkeyman Lee Tjupurrula, *Kanaputa/Tingarri*, 1989, acrylic on canvas, 180 × 120 cm. The painting depicts a *Tjukurrpa* event that occurred at Lake Mackay, involving the *Kanaputa* (Digging Stick Women) and the *Tingarri* (Initiated Men). Private collection.

and the novices had established their camp on top of a hill, out of sight (the long wavy line around Maruwa), in preparation for initiation ceremonies. The *Kanaputa*, at the time young, nubile women (the three concentric circles to the right represent the women, and the parallel lines, their digging sticks), were unaware of the presence of the novices until a sign informed them of this. They then invited the young novices, their future husbands, to join them in lovemaking. When the Initiated Men realized this, they became so angry that they lit a huge bush fire, which killed all the novices. The *Kanaputa* were also targeted but managed to escape by diving into a nearby lake and then travelling underground; they also succeeded in making off with the sacred objects (*tarruku*). From there, as the story goes, the *Kanaputa* kept on travelling in various directions, singing and dancing along the way. From the Aboriginal point of view, the painting – that is, the story and the experiencing of the story thus painted and narrated – extends far beyond the frame itself.

A most interesting feature of Tjupurrula's painting is the fact that he used the contours of Australia to represent the contours of the *Kanaputa*'s ceremonial ground. When Glowczewski remarked to him that people might think that his painting represented Australia surrounded by the sea, he replied, 'What I have said is true. Maybe both are true [*mularrpa*]' (Glowczewski 1991, 11). Undoubtedly, from his point of view, the 'congealed labour' of the ancestors, as well as their actions and itineraries, is embodied in the Australian landscape alongside *Kartiya* landmarks, boundaries, and involvement in the land. In his painting, he is challenging the co-existence of two ontological (and epistemological) ways of relating to the country.

In order to make my point clearer, I think it useful to refer to the work of de Certeau, when he draws a distinction between the 'map' and the 'itinerary' as representing two poles of experience. The main ontological difference between the two is that the former is descriptive, 'a plane projection totalizing observations,' whereas the latter is performative, 'a discursive series of operations' (1984, 119). The map describes a space, whereas the itinerary narrates movements in space.[8]

Westerners often tend to present Aboriginal acrylic paintings as maps that are at the same time mythical and topographical. By doing so, we are trying to translate their ontology of dwelling into our own ontology of building. Tjupurrula's painting is a good example of how these painted spatial stories are not maps, at least not in the Western meaning of the word. For Aboriginal people, they are itineraries – that is, actions and movements within a named, personified land. Maps are fixed, whereas itineraries are open-ended, forever unfolding. I might add that the difference between the map and the itinerary, as two poles of experience, is another way of expressing what the Aborigines call the Two Laws, that of the *Kartiya* and their own.

The inspiration for Western Desert acrylic paintings is located in the expressions and experiences of spatial trajectories. As stories, they are multivocal, open to revelation, reinterpretation, and negotiation. The stories are dialogic and open-ended, as is clearly illustrated in the way Tjurpurrula extends this spatially located episode far beyond the original area where the ancestral action actually occurred – namely, Lake Mackay. I pointed out above how, from the Aboriginal perspective, painting is always a political act, as it confirms one's identity with respect to a 'country.' By extending the *Tingarri* and *Kanaputa* founding performance and narrative to the whole of Australia, Tjupurrula is to a certain extent making a 'nationalist' statement. Deriving from the ongoing presence of the ancestral order, Aboriginal identity is itself inscribed and embodied within the Australian landscape.

Concluding Comments

I have attempted in this chapter to explore the Kukatja understanding of human knowledge of, and human action in, the world. Whether a dialogue with ants, an encounter with an ancestor, a revelatory dream, the deciphering of a stone, a hunting trip, a ritual performance or a painting – all provide examples of the multifaceted, processual engagement of Aboriginal people with a powerful, sentient environment. The field of human action, including breathing, dreaming, dancing, speaking, singing, hunting, and so forth, unfolds within a world of permeable and negotiable boundaries between various agencies.

In their interaction with their environment, the Aboriginal people sense and value something that I, as a Westerner, was unable to perceive – that is, the ancestral but ongoing presence and spiritual power embodied within the landscape, and with this, their intrinsic link to that landscape. Ancestrality, as it has been presented here, is not a referent (or a given) in Western ontology and thought systems, hence it does not fall within our perceptual acts. One way to make the ancestral order decipherable in terms of Western thinking would be to translate it as a form of knowledge.

NOTES

My research with the Kukatja was made possible through grants from the Social Sciences and Humanities Research Council of Canada and the Australian Institute of Aboriginal and Torres Strait Islanders Studies. I am most grateful for their support. I would also like to thank Eric Schwimmer and John Clammer for their very valuable comments on previous versions of this paper.

1 I do not wish to suggest that wind is always experienced in this way at all times by the Kukatja. I wish only to present and interpret an example that provides insight into Kukatja cultural expressions and structuration of experience.
2 Recent cross-cultural studies have conceptualized the 'landscape' as a cultural process (Hirsch 1995), thus as something different from a solely representational, objectified, and hence static reality. Hirsch defines this process as being located between place and space, foreground actuality and background potentiality, image and representation. See also Feld and Basso (1996) on the anthropology of place.
3 These groups are not bounded entities in terms of either demography or geography. Indeed, those who have come to be called Kukatja are usually of mixed descent – i.e., either Kukatja/Pintupi, or Kukatja/Ngarti, or Kukatja/Walmatjari, etc. This provides illustration of the value attaching to the scope and negotiability of their ancestral connections.
4 Fieldwork was conducted in the Wirrimanu (Balgo) area from August 1980 to January 1982, from March 1987 to March 1988, and for a few weeks in 1994 and 1998.
5 While the theme of the 'fractal' or 'dividual' person has been widely documented in New Guinean ethnography, it has not received much attention in Australian Aboriginal ethnography, which nevertheless offers an interesting basis for comparison.
6 See Watson (1996) for a thorough analysis of women's acrylic paintings in the Wirrimanu (Balgo) area.
7 The painting, which dates to 1989, appeared in an exhibit organized by the French anthropologist Barbara Glowczewski, in Grasse, France, in 1991. A photograph of the painting appears in the exhibit catalogue (Glowczewski 1991, 47). Out of respect for the local prohibition on using the name of a deceased person, the artist's name will go unmentioned. I shall refer to him by using the subsection name.
8 The ontological distinction between the 'map' and the 'itinerary' shares

some similarities with the distinction made by Deleuze and Guattari (1980) between the 'tree,' as an image dominant in Western thought, and the 'rhizome,' as a metaphor more representative of the nomadic thought and way of being-in-the-world.

REFERENCES

Anderson, C., and F. Dussart. 1988. 'Dreamings in Acrylic: Western Desert Art.' In P. Sutton, ed., *Dreamings: The Art of Aboriginal Australia*, 89–142. New York: George Braziller Publishers.
Bird-David, N. 1990. 'The Giving Environment: Another Perspective on the Economic System of Gatherer-Hunters.' *Current Anthropology* 31: 189–96.
– 1992. 'Beyond the Hunting and Gathering Mode of Subsistence: Culture-Sensitive Observations on the Nayaka and Other Modern Hunter-Gatherers.' *Man* 27: 19–44.
– 1999. 'Animism' Revisited: Personhood, Environment, and Relational Epistemology.' *Current Anthropology*, 40 (Supplement): S67–91.
Certeau, M. de.1984. *The Practice of Everyday Life*. Berkeley: University of California Press.
Deleuze, G., and F. Guattari. 1980. *Mille Plateaux*. Paris: Éditions de Minuit.
Dussart, F. 2000. *The Politics of Ritual in an Aboriginal Settlement*. Washington: Smithsonian Institution Press.
Farnell, B. 1995. *Do You See What I Mean? Plain Indians Sign Talk and the Embodiment of Action*. Austin: University of Texas Press.
Feld, S., and K.H. Basso. 1996. *Senses of Place*. Santa Fe: School of American Research Press.
Geertz, C. 1983. *Local Knowledge*. New York: Basic Books.
Glowczewski, B. 1991. *Yapa. Peintres Aborigènes de Balgo et de Lajamanu*. Paris: Baudoin Lebon.
Hastrup, K. 1995. *A Passage to Anthropology*. London: Routledge.
Hirsch, E. 1995. 'Landscape: Between Place and Space.' In E. Hirsch and M. O'Hanlon, eds., *The Anthropology of Landscape: Perspectives on Place and Space*, 1–30. Oxford: Clarendon Press.
Hirsch, E. and M. O'Hanlon, eds. 1995. *The Anthropology of Landscape: Perspectives on Place and Space*. Oxford: Clarendon Press.
Ingold, T. 1996. 'Hunting and Gathering as Ways of Perceiving the Environment.' In R. Ellen and K. Fukui, eds., *Redefining Nature: Ecology, Culture and Domestication*, 117–55. Oxford: Berg.
– 2000. *The Perception of the Environment*. London: Routledge.

Lewis, G. 1994. 'Magic, Religion and the Rationality of Belief.' In T. Ingold, ed., *Companion Encyclopedia of Anthropology*, 563–91. London: Routledge.

Morphy, H. 1991. *Ancestral Connections: Art and an Aboriginal System of Knowledge*. Chicago: University of Chicago Press.

– 1995a. 'Aboriginal Art in a Global Context.' In D. Miller, ed., *Worlds Apart: Modernity Through the Prism of the Local*, 211–39. London: Routledge.

– 1995b. 'Landscape and the Reproduction of the Ancestral Past.' In E. Hirsch and M. O'Hanlon, eds., *The Anthropology of Landscape: Perspectives on Place and Space*, 184–209. Oxford: Clarendon Press.

Munn, N.D. 1970. 'The Transformation of Subjects into Objects in Walbiri and Pitjantjatjara Myth.' In R.M. Berndt, ed., *Australian Aboriginal Anthropology*, 141–63. Nedlands: University of Western Australia Press.

– 1973. 'The Spatial Presentation of Cosmic Order in Walbiri Iconography.' In J.A. Forge, ed., *Primitive Art and Society*, 193–220. London: Oxford University Press.

Myers, F. 1979. 'Emotions and the Self: A Theory of Personhood and Political Order among Pintupi Aborigines.' *Ethos* 7: 343–70.

– 1986. *Pintupi Country, Pintupi Self: Sentiment, Place and Politics among Western Desert Aborigines*. Washington, D.C.: Smithsonian Institution Press.

– 1988. 'The Logic and Meaning of Anger among Pintupi Aborigines.' *Man* 23: 589–610.

– 1992. 'Representing Culture: The Production of Discourse(s) for Aboriginal Acrylic Paintings.' In G.E. Marcus, ed., *Rereading Cultural Anthropology*, 319–55. Durham: Duke Universtiy.

Overing, J. 1985. 'Introduction.' In J. Overing, ed., *Reason and Morality*, 1–29. London: Tavistock Publications.

Peile, A.R. 1985. 'Le concept du vent, du souffle et de l'âme chez les Aborigènes dans le désert de l'Australie.' *Bulletin ethnomédical* 33: 75–83.

– 1997. *Body and Soul: An Aboriginal View*. Carlisle, Western Australia: Hesperian Press.

Poirier, S. 1992. 'Nomadic Rituals. Networks of Ritual Exchanges Among Women of the Australian Western Desert.' *Man* 27 (4): 757–6.

– 1994. 'La mise en œuvre sociale du rêve. Un exemple australien.' *Anthropologie et sociétés* 18(2): 105–19.

– 1996. *Les jardins du nomade. Cosmologie, territoire et personne dans le désert occidental australien*. Münster: Lit, with the support of the CNRS (Paris).

– 2001. 'Les politiques du savoir rituel. Réflexions sur les relations de genre chez les Kukatja (désert occidental australien).' In C. Alès and C. Barraud, eds., *Sexe relatif ou sexe absolu?*, 111–33. Paris: Éditions de la Maison des sciences de l'homme.

- 2003. '"This is good country. We are good dreamers." Dreams and Dreaming in the Australian Western Desert.' In R. Lohmann, ed., *Dream Travelers: Sleep Experiences and Culture in the Western Pacific,* 107–25. New York: Palgrave Macmillan.

Povinelli, E.A. 1993. *Labor's Lot: The Power, History and Culture of Aboriginal Action.* Chicago: University of Chicago Press.

- 1995. 'Do Rocks Listen? The Cultural Politics of Apprehending Australian Aboriginal Labor.' *American Anthropologist* 97 (3): 506–18.

Ricoeur, P. 1986. *Du texte à l'action. Essais d'herméneutique II.* Paris: Seuil.

Rose, D.B. 1994. 'Whose Confidentiality? Whose Intellectual Property?' In M. Edmunds, ed., *Claims to Knowledge, Claims to Country,* 1–11. Canberra: AIATSIS.

Rumsey, A. 1994. 'The Dreaming, Human Agency and Inscriptive Practice.' *Oceania* 65: 116–30.

Sahlins, M. 1995. *How 'Natives' Think. About Captain Cook, for Example.* Chicago: University of Chicago Press.

Stanner, W.E.H. 1979. *White Man Got No Dreaming: Essays 1938–1973.* Canberra: Australian National University Press.

Watson, C. 1996. '*Kuruwarri, the Generative Force: Balgo Women's Contemporary Paintings and Their Relationship with Traditional Media.*' MA thesis, Australian National University, Canberra.

Chapter Three

The Politics of Animism

JOHN CLAMMER

'Animism' is a term that has almost entirely dropped out of anthropological discourse in the West. It has not, however, disappeared from the intellectual vocabulary of the East and is still evoked there in a number of guises. Discourses *about* animism abound in South-East Asia, for example, where forms of Indigenous religion and their expression through media such as shamanism suggest that the term still has some utility. It is in Japan, however, and possibly only in Japan, that the concept of animism is still widely used as a way of explaining the distinctiveness of the national culture and as a vehicle for constructing a model of Japanese society, which, unlike classical Western sociological theories, explicitly locates nature as part of the constitution of that society. It is perhaps no coincidence, too, that many strands of deep ecology and so-called New Age thinking in the West have begun to offer a vision of society and of humanity's place in the universe that is remarkably parallel to ideas that have wide intellectual currency in Japan.

This all suggests a number of potentially fruitful directions in which the exploration of the idea of animism might be taken. First, it may be that, while the term itself has disappeared from usage in mainstream anthropology, it is in fact still useful, and a sympathetic reading of the history of the concept might show that it is valuable in organizing our understanding of both Indigenous knowledge systems and new social movements that invoke nature as their central principle. Second, the fact that intellectual discourse in one of the world's major cultures uses the idea of animism to express and encapsulate a complex of questions relating to identity, society-nature relationships, and images of the self is not only interesting and worthy of exploration in itself, but should alert us to the possibility that there are indeed alternative modes of social analysis, starting from different premises about what is significant and leading to different conclusions about the actual dynamics of social organization. The increasing significance of ecological, feminist, and New Age thinking in effecting intellectual currents suggests that such ideas, long current in Japan, are, despite their no doubt very different sources, becoming more and more widely diffused.

Third, and rarely commented on, is the political significance of animism. Anthropological discussions of animism have left this dimension untouched. It is a major thesis of this paper, however, that animism has profound political implications: it contains a model of human–nature relationships beyond the sociological categories of the state; it is extremely difficult to codify or to convert into any easily administrable theological system; and when it is linked with expressions such as shamanism it can become subversive, a form of power residing in implicit knowledge, a counter-discourse (Taussig 1987), and indeed a way of undermining the categories of conventional science. These qualities can be stated in the abstract. Here, however, I will attempt to illustrate them through the inner history of one of the major struggles in early modern Japanese history – the attempt by the state to impose a systematized and bureaucratized framework ('state Shintô') on the amorphous, localized, and diversified forms of Japanese folk religion ('shrine Shintô') in the late nineteenth century.

This case study illustrates very well the political dynamics of animism (Shintô being interpreted here as a complex and specific form of animism) and the problems of containing it within a model of organized and hierarchical religious categories. Given Shintô's close association with what is often glossed as Japanese 'nationalism' but is in reality somewhat closer to the idea of patrimony, an analysis of Shintô as the major Indigenous religious tradition in Japan also permits an approach to the triad of identity/land/descent, which is not only basic to Japanese self-understanding but will also be found to underly many of the disputes between Indigenous Peoples internationally and the state over land ownership and the exploitation of resources on or under that land. The logic of the Japanese case and the particular ontology that the Japanese have created speaks surprisingly, but directly, to the concerns of Indigenous Peoples in many other parts of the world. The continuing liveliness of debates about animism in contemporary Japan also points to a somewhat unusual form of argument that provides an alternative political language which might be of considerable interest to ecologists, individuals, and groups involved in struggles for identity, land, and the right to be recognized as part of nature rather than as some kind of entity opposed to it.

Recovering the History of Animism

The history of the concept of animism is usually traced to the definition first proffered by E.B. Tylor in *Primitive Culture* (1871): 'The deep lying doctrine of Spiritual Beings, which embodies the very essence of Spiritualistic as opposed to Materialistic philosophy' (Tylor 1871, 7). In Tylor's understanding of animism, however, the central concern was not merely with the definition of the term, but rather with its use in an evolutionary theory of the origins of religion. Animism in this framework was seen by Tylor as the earliest form of religion. The nineteenth-century concern with origins was pushed even further back in R.R. Marett's subsequent theory of 'preanimism' or 'animatism' – a phase preceding the formulation of ideas of spiritual beings consisting of belief in, or recognition of, a primal force, a homogeneous and undifferentiated power not yet individualized into specific spiritual entities – a concept or rather intuition of what A. van Gennep in *Les Rites de Passage* (1909) called 'dynamism.' In Tylor's original theory there are two mixed elements: a characterization of animism as a system of spirit beliefs, of nature inhabited by a myriad of beings in which the boundaries between the spiritual and the material are effectively dissolved, and the evolutionary preoccupation with origins.

Interestingly, even as scholars of Shintô have carefully avoided the animistic dimension of their subject, so critics of the original anthropological formulation of animism have largely ignored its potential significance (and revolutionary implications for ideas of the self, matter, human-nature relationships) in favour of concentrating on the shortcomings of the evolutionary model proposed by both Tylor and Marett.

In the entry on animism in the usually authoritative *Encyclopedia of Religion* (Eliade 1987), the whole idea is considered to be of interest only because of its role in the intellectual history of religious studies. Further, animism is considered to be wholly contaminated by its association with an anthropology arising from colonialism, and is regarded as a form of pre-scientific, positivist reductionism, to be classified as one of a class of competing late-nineteenth-century theories of primal forms of religion (e.g., Spencer's ancestor worship, Frazer's magic, Schmidt's primal monotheism, and Durkheim's totemism). The author of the entry, one Kees Bolle, considers that 'The theories of animism and animatism are difficult to take seriously in our own time, given the psychological sophistication that has come to be taken for granted in intellectual circles since Freud ... At present, prehistorians and anthropologists would agree that Tylor's theory has little bearing on anything they would consider a religious phenomenon' (Bolle 1987, 297–8).

This depressingly narrow-minded reading of animism, which sees the whole phenomenon only in terms of a now discredited nineteenth-century anthropological theory, not only entirely overlooks the vitality of the concept in contemporary anthropological, Japanological, and neo-ecological discourse, but does substantial violence to Tylor's conception of what was involved in animism. If we can bracket the question of origins, it is important to remember that Tylor was concerned with two additional things. The first was the establishment or delimitation of the concept of reality as non-material, or nature as spiritualized. While Tylor was indeed exercised by the task of arguing that this approach was the source of religion, he was also committed to arguing that, while 'primitive,' this dimension was real to those who held it, and that this dimension, while supplanted in great measure by the advance of the dominant literate world religions, was never entirely suppressed, as any scholar of contemporary Buddhism or Islam will willingly attest.

The second was the linking of this phenomenon of an animated or panentheistic cosmos not to the hypothetical question of its putative original status, but to a range of other phenomena that provide the idea of animism with a context, even a rational one. There are two primary phenomena here: dreams and death. And neither are explained more satisfactorily now than they were in the nineteenth century, despite the 'psychological sophistication' so lauded by Bolle. Dreams, which have exercised the imaginative and professional capacities of many twentieth-century anthropologists and psychologists, not to say mystics and New Agers, do indeed seem to many people, and not only 'primitives,' to provide a door to realms beyond mundane experience. Since dreams appear to be no less real than the waking world, they intimate a world beyond the confines of normal time-space constrictions, in turn suggesting a vision of the universe somewhat beyond ordinary materialism. Death, which to many suggests the continuity rather than the cessation of being, in almost all cases involves spirit beliefs of one kind or another. When combined with the almost universal belief – a belief also common in many parts of the industrialized

West – in nature spirits or beings (fairies, gnomes, spirits, and so on), Tylor not unreasonably supposed that animism, far from being an irrational or sub-scientific view, actually has quite a good theoretical and experiential basis.

The association of animism with what we now consider passé intellectualist theories of the origins of religion (which, by the way, actually remains an entirely legitimate and perhaps vital field of intellectual inquiry) has deterred most subsequent generations of anthropologists from making much use of the term (although it does surface almost inevitably, even if in a disguised form, in studies of more currently respectable themes such as shamanism). From the complex and tortuous history of the term in late-nineteenth- and early-twentieth-century anthropology, however, certain valuable ideas do emerge that still have major theoretical implications.

First, the question of animism raises the issue of its relationship to its close cousin, totemism – the classification of social groups in terms of animals, or natural objects or phenomena. Interestingly, while the notion of animism has fallen out of general anthropological usage, rather more (although not a lot of) attention has been paid to totemism, including an important book in the development of anthropological structuralism by none other than Lévi-Strauss (1962).

Second, animism, embodying as it does an experiential, active, and everyday relationship to creatures and things in nature, does not diminish 'religion' to its point of ('primitive') origin, but to the contrary expands it by including nature, dissolving the boundary between the animate and inanimate, spiritualizing the mundane, and locating the core of religion in praxis rather than belief and in social-experiential forms rather than in theology.

Third, because of the variety of forms of relationship between humans and animal and plant species (including their relationship to totemic animals), animism is closely linked to taboo and sacrifice – also major themes in the intellectual history of anthropology. Through taboo animism is linked to yet a wider range of issues – some, such as the notion of 'mana,' being of central anthropological significance, and others, such as the links between animism and vitalism, of rather wider philosophical interest. These themes, in turn, are related in a very organic way to the position of ancestors – of ancestors as totemic animals, as the focus of a spiritist form of religious observance, or as a constituting factor in corporate kin groups and forming the epistemological basis for the continuity of such groups (lineages in particular).

As some scholars of totemism have also suggested, animistic beliefs are also functional to the preservation of the ecology, as reverence precludes the destruction of natural species.

And fourth, animism in some of its forms involves a theory of souls, in which natural phenomena have autonomous souls or the souls of 'dead' humans now inhabit animals or other natural phenomena. Such a belief further ties animism to the ideas of ancestralism and of existence after death, and in some cases to practices of taboo.

Two points need to be made here. First, the theory of animism, far from being a defunct nineteenth-century aberration, is of profound interest in itself and proves to have close ties with many other dominating themes in what might be termed the 'classical' tradition of anthropology. Second, acquaintance with Shintô suggests that many of these same themes may very fruitfully be brought to bear on a reading of a 'religion' that is centrally concerned with the world of spirits (both animal, natural, and deified humans [kami]), with ancestralism and the constitution of micro-social groups (corporate households or ie), and with a macro-social group (Japan itself) and ideas of taboo, refracted through concepts of pollution and purity.

Shintô: The Alternative Politics of Nature

Where and how does this rethinking of animism connect with the Japanese experience? Here I will argue that there are two ways that this connection can be made: through a rereading or reinterpretation of Shintô from this perspective, and from an understanding of the political implications of immanent religion.

Shintô is probably one of the least understood of the world's major religions. Scholarly attention to it has been weak, probably because of its character, which is diffuse and hard to systematize, and its associations with pre-war and wartime fascism and ultra-nationalism. Shintô nonetheless constitutes the basic substratum of Japanese religion, it is actively important and utilized in relation to life-cycle rituals in contemporary Japan, it has modified and even transformed the other major religious traditions in Japan (especially Buddhism), and it has been the major inspiration for many of the so-called New Religions that have proliferated in Japan since the late nineteenth century. It is, in other words, very much a living religion, but studies of it, especially those available in languages other than Japanese, have tended to concentrate on its architecture, its rituals, or its connections with ultra-nationalism.

Few have attempted to interpret its inner cosmology. Here I will attempt briefly to do that, and in so doing argue that Shintô does indeed have close links with politics, but with a radical form of alternative politics that has little to do with the forms of state nationalism with which it has so often been associated. That it is connected with forms of cultural nationalism there is no doubt, but I will argue here that these forms actually directly subvert state nationalism. The continuing vitality of animistic discourse in Japanese intellectual, and especially anthropological, discussion suggests a widespread diffusion of animistic thinking through a wide range of Japanese institutions.

The place to start this analysis is through an account of the struggles between 'shrine,' or localized folk, Shintô, and 'state,' or government-directed and bureaucratized, Shintô. At issue here is not only a history of a periphery/centre conflict, but also of attempts to define what Shintô is and to represent that definition as the only correct or possible one – the struggle for definitions is actually that of attempting to achieve or resist ideological hegemony, and as such it is inevitably deeply political.

'Shintô' in its most general meaning refers to a complex of beliefs and, more importantly, practices encapsulating an understanding of human-cosmos relationships. Historically, it has never been a single thing, but rather a loosely connected set of localized behaviours, Japanese in its specific configurations, but with many parallels to nature-based religions elsewhere and sharing with them some of their typical manifestations, such as shamanism. There was consequently no concern with 'defining' the term 'Shintô' – no intellectual, religious, or political reason – until the late nineteenth century, following the Meiji restoration of 1868 and the subsequent national project of modernization without westernization, when governmental attempts to systematize and control religion and direct it to nationalistic ends led directly to the contestation of the meaning of the 'way of the gods' (*Shin-tô*). It is only then that Shintô begins to be seen as a 'religion'; prior to the late nineteenth century it can be better seen as an ecology – an expression of human-nature relationships in the context of an animistic universe.

While the origin of the term "Shintô" itself is unclear, by the late nineteenth century two broad categories of contested meanings had emerged: nationalistic meanings stressing ancestor worship, the religious systematization of patriarchy, and the recognition of the emperor as a living *kami*, or deity; and meanings arising from the ethnography of actual practices stressing Shintô as 'hylozoism or pan-psychism, a point of view wherein *kami* is taken to signify the "psyche" which exhibits itself in all the forms and forces of nature' (Holton 1965, 32). The former definition is, to use M.N. Srinivas's term, a 'Sanskritized' version deriving its legitimacy from its connection to an ancient literate tradition, the belief being that the origins and essential nature of Shintô (including the pantheon of distinctively Japanese deities, the position of the emperor, and the ancestral links between the Japanese people and the mythology of divine origins of the country and the race), appear in the founding charters of Japan embedded in the literary classics, the *Kojiki*, the *Nihongi* and the *Norito*. The latter definition has less claim to formal legitimacy, being rooted in what much contemporary literature persists in calling 'nature worship' (a complete misnomer as I will later argue) and ancestralism lacking any systematic 'theology,' and without any administrative or organized intellectual apparatus for negotiating as a body either with the state or with the imported and powerful Buddhist and Confucian traditions. Indeed, the structure of shrine Shintô (so called because of its localization in specific centres of practice) reflects its cosmology: diffused, immanent, processual.

These characteristics partly explain why so little attention has been given to the content and practice of shrine Shintô; it is simply harder to study than the organized and bureaucratically managed state Shintô and sect (*Shûha*) Shintô. Indeed, shrine Shintô has assimilated so many features of the other two that, except for its concentration on the celebration of local festivals (*matsuri*), it has largely come to resemble them. But there seems to be an ideological factor, too. State propaganda against local expressions of Shintô, together with the powerful association between pre-war ultranationalism and Shintô, has established an almost complete scholarly hegemony of views on what constitutes the field of Shintô studies. The effect has been to a great extent exactly what the state intended after the Meiji restoration, when it disestablished Buddhism and set about the active revival of an officially approved version of Shintô – the denaturing of folk religion and its neutralization as a political force. Despite this the fundamental nature of 'basic' Shintô has not been entirely eradicated, and it is to the implications of this that we will now turn.

Between 1899 and 1900 the Japanese government promulgated a number of measures designed to bring Shintô under direct bureaucratic control, and in doing so to declare that these reforms were separate from any concern with 'religion': to eliminate the religious character of the official shrines and instead to link Shintô to an ideologically constructed version of Japanese history in which loyalty and patriotism became the essence of morality (Holton 1965, 31–2). The principal *kami*, or deified humans, became those of the imperial line, beginning with the sun goddess Amaterasuomikami, now redesignated as the divine ancestress of the imperial family. Politics, ethics, education, religion, and a sense of distinct ethnicity and global purpose were all united under the notion of *Yamato Damashii* – the 'great way,' or perhaps the Japanese 'spirit' or 'soul,' identified in the reforms with state Shintô. Folk religion thus became converted into a national-ethical system with the emperor at its centre, and it took on universalist and expansionist overtones as a new generation of bureaucrat-theologians began to expound the theory of Shintô as the basis of all religions, or rather, to separate this idea from that of Tylor, as the best expression of all religions – as an inclusive system embracing and subsuming all the other major religions. Paradoxically, in asserting this 'basic' quality it became necessary for these theologians to, in very Tylorian fashion, equate Shintô with 'primitive' religion elsewhere (e.g., Kakeki 1912) in claiming the unity of religion, law, politics, and ethics in these systems of belief and practice. Parallel to what Carol Gluck (1985) has called the 'denaturing' of politics in Meiji Japan went the denaturing of religion.

While in Gluck's terminology 'denaturing' is meant metaphorically, in the case of the suppression of shrine Shintô we might use the term quite literally. To illustrate this we need to briefly sketch some of the key cosmological elements in shrine Shintô. Shintô has been described by some as homocentric rather than theocentric (Holton 1965, 114), but this is only partly true. *Kami* can be forces of nature, and they can also be humans, and while Shintô clearly has a notion of deities in the plural, there is no one Supreme Being. All religions are, in practice, more or less human-centred in that the people who follow them seek protection, health, and benefits, and this is equally true of Shintô. But a major difference between Shintô and most other major systems of belief is that the boundaries between the human, the natural, and the divine are extremely permeable.

The father of *Kokugaku*, or 'national learning' (the Shintô-inspired nativism of eighteenth-century Japan), Motoori Norinaga, in his attempt to define the essential characteristics of Japaneseness, emphasized the 'primitive' supernaturalism of Shintô, in which *kami* are not only heavenly deities and equally *mitama* or the tutelary spirits of shrines, but also humans, animals, birds, plants, mountains, rocks, oceans, lakes, and, in particular, spectacular manifestations of nature such as waterfalls. Emperors may be *tôtsu kami*, or 'distant kami,' but even they are, or were, human, and every locality, village, or even family contains their own 'close kami,' in the case of ancestors. Thunder is *naru kami*, or 'sounding *kami*,' foxes are *kami*, and indeed a whole cult of the fox as tutelary deity of shrines (*Inari* shrines) exists in Japan. Unusual phenomena may also be *kami* – the *kodama*, or echo, being a good example, although the term *kodama* itself actually means 'tree spirit.'

Kami then are not just deified humans; 'nature spirits,' or *kami* of nature, may also reflect or refer to each other. The result is a dense network of spiritual influences at work in nature giving rise to a cosmology much closer to the occult vision of such modern seers as Rudolf Steiner (e.g., Steiner 1995) than it is to anything conceivable in Western materialism or positivistic science. The notion of *kami* then has parallels with notions found in other cosmological systems – *mana* in Polynesia, the *Manitou* of the Algonquins, or the *kalou* of the Fijians (on the latter see Clammer 1976). Early-twentieth-century studies of shrine Shintô confirm this plethora of *kami*, including the mythical founding parents of the Japanese race *Izanagi* and *Izanami*; the moon god; the harvest god; *Ukemochi no kami*, the great food goddess, and the *kami* of the five elements, of the sea, trees, mountains, grasses, rivers, wells, kitchens, privies; the *kami* of trades, protectors of the comings and goings of ships; phallic *kami*; *kami* who bring intelligence and happiness, those who bring illness and misfortune, spirits of foxes and badgers and the spirits of enemies living and dead.

Some of these *kami* are still active, as evidenced in the phallic cults or festivals that centre on a number of well-known shrines in contemporary Japan. But rather than seeing this kind of religious praxis as antithetical to faiths that have a personal deity at their centre, we should see shrine Shintô as a radical personalization of the universe: the heavens and in particular the earth are subject to a personification that clearly links Shintô to North American and Siberian religions, from which it may have indeed received early influences (Irimoto and Yamada 1993). The earth-as-mother motif, widely distributed in world ethnology, appears in shrine Shintô not in abstract form, but concretely, as food-giver. This has led at least one Japanese anthropologist to argue that rice, long the central staple of the diet, constitutes what is in effect the central *kami* of Japanese cosmology, and from this derives the basis of the Japanese image of the self (Ohnuki-Tierney 1993). While this view is simplistic in that it ignores other features of what is actually a very complex and dynamic religious world view, and it takes only one aspect of the images of the Japanese self for the whole (cf. Rosenberger 1992), it does correctly point to the central role of nature and of the products of nature in the constitution of the Japanese sense of self (Clammer 1995).

In interpreting or re-interpreting shrine Shintô, I would argue that this permeable sense of human-nature boundaries, the view of nature as sanctuary and source of true being, and the effects of these on sense of self are actually the keys to understanding. The distortion of elements in Shintô for nationalistic political purposes (such as the co-option of the sun *kami*, now the symbol on the national flag) should not blind us to the radical epistemological implications of this form of cosmology. For Shintô's central concern with purity and the avoidance of pollution represents not an empty ritualism, but a set of techniques to break through into that world parallel to and interpenetrating with the quotidian, to pass through the permeable boundary, and to ensure that the positive forces that exist on the other side of the boundary in turn pass through into the human realm. Shrine Shintô should thus be seen not, as in functionalist explanations, an attempt to control nature, but rather to achieve something closer to Lévy-Bruhl's now widely discredited notion of 'participation' (Lévy-Bruhl 1933).

It is against this background of folk Shintô (*Minzoku Shintô*) that two major issues can be raised. The first issue is politics. Why was the Meiji government so concerned with bringing shrine Shintô under its heavy-handed bureaucratic control? If Shintô is merely 'nature worship' it should be harmless enough to the organs of government in a modernizing state. The desire, and indeed the practice, at the turn of the century of ruthlessly suppressing what had clearly been the native religion for hundreds of years suggests a deeper level of dynamics than merely the desire to bring ever wider zones of society under bureaucratic control. The second issue is understanding the continuing vitality of animistic thinking not amongst the 'folk,' but amongst Japanese intellectuals. What does this probably unique trend mean, and why does it exist? These two issues will prove both in practice and conceptualization to be closely linked, and it is to them that we will now turn.

Popular or folk Shintô (*Minzoku Shintô*) possesses several characteristics that make it difficult to manage or bureaucratize: it is highly polytheistic, and it is also inherently pantheistic. It appears that originally there were no shrines, but that shrines grew up at sites, often of great natural beauty, where *kami* were supposed to reside and/or where agricultural, healing, or purification rites were carried out. Today there are shrines, although the number is much smaller than it was at the end of the Edo (Tokugawa) period, after which the new Meiji government set about their systematic destruction and amalgamation. Religious sites need not be shrines at all, but are today often rocks or, in particular, trees, marked by a straw belt (*shimenawa*) tied around them to mark them as *kami* or the residences of *kami*. The rites of popular Shintô – purification, honouring home and field deities, the divination of dreams – do not require formal sites for their performance. In some cases whole vast natural features may become such sites, as in the case of mountain worship such as practised by the Fusôkyô and Jikkôkyô sects, which worship Mount Fuji, or the Ontakekyô, which worship Mount Ontake, in Nagano prefecture. Purification sects that undertake water purification for the cultivation of mind and body centre on waterfalls.

The diffusion and localism of popular Shintô makes it impossible to organize bureaucratically, a challenge to the Meiji and all subsequent governments with their strong centralizing, bureaucratizing, and state-building sentiments, and equally impossible to organize into a coherent conceptual system that can be classified, systematized and theologically controlled. The ethics of popular Shintô, centring on the idea of *makoto no kokoro* (sincerity, or 'heart of truth') are essentially individualistic. The conversion of state Shintô into a system embodying nationalism, loyalty, and Emperor veneration was something of an ideological triumph (or disaster, given its long-term historical consequences) for the Meiji and subsequent governments. The pilgrimage tradition in which large numbers of peasants left their homes and travelled in huge groups to the major Shintô centres, and especially to the Grand Shrine at Ise, as much for travel and for pleasure as from any religious motives, meanwhile neglecting their fields and causing crowd-control problems for the government along the pilgrimage routes, posed yet further security problems for a state bent on the very Foucaultian project of classification, control, and order. The diffused and localized nature of popular Shintô make it a potential source of resistance, implicitly, if not explicitly, to the centralizing tendencies of the state.

Parallel to the political unification of Japan and the literal colonization of the periphery (Tohoku and Hokkaido in particular) went an attempt at ideological unification and colonization. And just as in very different geographical and historical contexts shamanism and the control of everyday implicit knowledge emerged as the foci of resistance to colonialism (e.g., Taussig 1987) and in which cults of healing, purification, and ancestralism became the vehicles for subverting ideological hegemony, so too in Japan the cosmology of popular Shintô stands over against the state-directed ethics and politics of official Shintô. The sense of land, of a physical and inalienable patrimony, is interesting too in this context. State Shintô had as one of its major objectives the identification of land not with particular localities, but with Japan as a whole. Popular Shintô, on the other hand, is intensely local; *kami* are very specific to a particular place. While this does indeed foster identification with land or territory in a very restricted sense, it does not create a sense of 'land' in any abstract way. Ancestral association with particular places is strong, but under the conditions of premodern feudalism this identification was not with land as *property*, but with land as *resource* and with land as *numinous entity* – as the site and source of the spiritual and regenerating forces of nature. This is an important distinction. Peasant movements in Japan, and indeed later industrial movements, were not so much struggles for *rights* as for *benevolence*: the recognition of a 'great chain of being' in which peasants or workers, while remaining as such, had expectations not only of relief from overburdening taxation and the like, but also for their spiritual rights to be observed by those with power (Smith 1989, 89).

Animism then has many implications, all of which are in a broad sense political: it represents an alternative ontology, it constitutes an 'ecology' as much as a 'religion,' and it has implications for the nature and sources of social conflict, especially when they involve an animistic paradigm coming into contact with a rationalizing one. Misunderstandings of Native claims to land rights is perhaps one of the best illustrations of this, but it is by no means the *only* one, a point worth making as conflict between modern state governments and Indigenous Peoples often seems to be phrased purely in terms of land disputes. Conflict over land rather than the source difficulty should really be seen as reflecting a deeper ontological disagreement. The historical conflict between popular and state Shintô and its long-term fallout illustrates the range of these ontological issues very clearly and likewise demonstrates that competing ontologies are not only cultural, but also political.

And in some important ways the implicit politics of popular Shintô were, and are, more realistic than those of the state, which assumed that by organizing religion it could control modes of coherence – that by shaping religious institutions it could control thought. In fact, this can never be done, as Geoffery Benjamin has aptly expressed it in his suggestion 'That religion constitutes a phenomenologically distinct area of human action that we enter into largely as a result of the way in which consciousness is organized in our species. That religious traditions (the "religions" of the world) are institutionally shaped so as to *prevent* the articulated expression of the key coherence-imposing relationships on which the embedding "culture" (by which is meant cultural regimes) and "societies" (i.e. politics) are based' (Benjamin 1987, 3). Popular Shintô, by refusing or being unable to systematically articulate its theology and practice, actually allows a dynamic and constantly reconceptualized set of relationships or interpenetrations to take place between people and cosmos that the bureaucratic variety cannot achieve. The relative lack of *language* (e.g., prayers, chants, scriptures) to articulate popular Shintô means precisely that the entrapment in language, the difficulties of communicating, and, to paraphrase Jan Van Baal's words, the resulting 'essential loneliness of the human subject' is bypassed.

This does not entirely banish existential anxiety about the mental representations used to organize life, but it does mean that this anxiety, where it occurs, is of a radically different kind and is resolved through radically different channels. After a brief discussion of the continuing role of animism in contemporary Japanese intellectual life, I will return to this fundamental issue: the relationship of the politics of the self to the politics of the state.

It is probably true to say that in no other major industrialized country is there still, or has there ever been, widespread discussion of animism as part of ordinary intellectual discourse. However, this is the case in Japan, and has been at least since the beginning of the last century. In a discussion of this phenomenon Tsurumi Kazuko relates this vitality of the idea of animism to three important thinkers of the early modern period: Yanagita Kunio, the folklorist and ethnographer; Minakata Kumagusu, who combined a career in microbiology with a reputation as a folklorist and is considered a forerunner of the environmental movement in Japan; and Imanishi Kinji, an ecological biologist who later turned to anthropology (Tsurumi 1992). Tsurumi sees these pioneers as both rediscovering the animistic views of nature held by ordinary rural Japanese, and as creating on the basis of this a view of science as something that should be symbiotic with nature, and indeed she joins the debate herself by explicitly suggesting that 'It is my contention that animistic views of nature hold significant potential to contribute to the search for such a relatively non-violent science and technology' (3). In pursuing this thesis Tsurumi argues that 'Just as Christianity destroyed 'pagan animism' in Europe (following the analysis of Lynn White, Jr), so it was the emperor ideology in the name of state Shintôism, that attempted to destroy animistic belief in nature in Japan at the incipient stage of modernization' (4). The work of Yanagita in describing in detail the ethnography of regional cultures in Japan in the early years of the twentieth century did much to resist this trend, and the recent rediscovery and popularity of Yanagita in Japan and amongst anthropologists of Japan (e.g., Kawada 1992) suggests the resurfacing of a whole tradition of ideas current in early modern Japan, contemporary with and parallel to those of E.B. Tylor and others in Europe. The movements that grew out of this tradition included both critiques of modernization, the concept of ecology, and an early version of the environmental movement in Japan, and some distinctive rejections of Darwinian theories of natural selection and their replacement by alternative views not at all well known outside of Japan (Imanishi 1970).

These ideas are still alive and well. One contemporary example is the work of the anthropologist Iwata Keiji, much of whose writing (e.g., Iwata 1989, 1991) has been devoted to exploring the idea of animism, examining its manifestations in a range of societies, especially in South-East Asia, and in considering its application to the understanding of Japanese culture. In his work Iwata argues that animism is not an early or underdeveloped form of religion. He sees it rather as a cosmic sense, or sense of the cosmos, the analysis of which helps us to reconstruct the relationship between human beings and nature. Accordingly, when we are born we have a natural animistic vision (a view, interestingly, supported by a number of recent articles in the *Journal of Genetic Psychology* and in *Developmental Psychology* and elsewhere, e.g., Kennedy 1987); this is diminished by the process of adult socialization, but returns in old age when the categories created by socialization tend to fade and a 'natural religion,' which Iwata associates with the character of Zen, reasserts itself (Iwata 1991, 262).

Iwata's theory is of particular interest to anthropologists since he relates it to a range of other cultural phenomena. One of these is the close association between animism and shamanism, which he sees as the technique for detecting the voice of the *kami*. Another is his theory of naming: he theorizes that naming comes not from an arbitrary linguistic relationship between object and name, but is rather the technique of 'how to recognize things' – inside the name there is a 'spirit.' His theory of intercultural relations is interesting in this respect, too. He argues that when groups confront one another in any form of communication each group is forced to face the *kami* of the *other* group. Even this, though at a fundamental level and in a very Buddhist way, Iwata sees as being a provisional characterization, since his view is ultimately a vitalist one: that animism is not just the theory that animals and plants have a spirit, but is the view that there is actually one spirit that embodies itself in form, but which itself exists infinitely beyond shape (Iwata 1991, 181).

This finally leads Iwata to the view that the universe is pervaded by the numinous and that intellectual discussion of animism ultimately misses the point – to be understood animism must actually be *encountered*. Animism constitutes what he calls 'The Third Mirror' – a meeting with oneself through the stripping off of one's cultural clothes (Iwata 1991, 182). This finally results in a critique of deep ecology as a movement that is still too materialistic because of its unwillingness or inability to penetrate to deep enough levels, and a theory of the formation of Japanese society in which he contrasts Western societies constructed on the ultimate basis of history with the culture of Japan as having emerged organically from an animistic view of the cosmos (Iwata 1989, 250).

It should be apparent from the foregoing that there are several things going on in Japanese discourses of animism. At one level there is the project of rediscovering and propagating a cosmology, a vitalistic model of the universe with deep roots in folk Shintô modified by certain strands of Buddhism, especially the very Japanese theory of the ultimate or potential Buddhahood of all things – not only people, but also animals, plants, and so-called inanimate objects (LaFleur 1974). (This also helps one to understand why, at the same time as the Meiji government set about suppressing shrine Shintô it also set about suppressing Buddhism, not only because a large number of Shintô shrines were administered by Buddhist priests, so close had the symbiosis between the two religions become, but because Buddhism had so fully accommodated itself to the demand for a theory of nature. Even today many Buddhist temples contain small Shintô shrines within their precincts.) This cosmology has numerous implications, including such ideas as Japanese theories of the body being one with the mind and as reflecting *ki*, or universal energy, in their composition and activity (Yuasa 1987, 1993).

At the second level there is a sociology: not just a negative sociology in the sense of a critique of modernity, but one that is also positive – a vision of how society should be organized to reflect the vitalistic forces that underly it. Yanagita Kunio's own work reflects this, even if not in a fully developed way. His ethnographic studies of folklore and local religions led him to a variety of conclusions about the way in which Japanese society should develop. These include a critique of modernity in the sense of the spiritual effects of individualization; belief in the necessity of a non-aggressive economy and agriculture; the theory that the *ie*, or extended family, was the basis of social solidarity in Japan and that land tenure should be linked to the *ie*, rather than to individual ownership; that ethical principles are embodied in folk Shintô, which balances individualism and localism with society and kinship like nothing else, and as such is a way of harmonizing horizontal ties and hierarchy. Yanagita was indeed critical of Buddhism precisely because he saw it as being too individualistic and correspondingly weak in its ethical and social dimensions.

These considerations point to the third level, that of politics. Here again Yanagita is a good example. His sociology led him directly to politics: he believed that if his theory of Japanese society was correct, it pointed to the view that state Shintô is superficial because it is merely political – it does not speak to the actual spiritual lives of the Japanese; and that it is possible, indeed desirable, to have nationalism without the state – nationalism being understood as a form of solidarity based on shared values, which in his view are the values of folk Shintô. Shintô in this sense is the basis of Japanese nationhood, but in ways undreamed of by the architects of state Shintô. Folk Shintô is politically subversive because it points to a mode of thinking, organization, and rootedness in the universe beyond politics. This having been said, we can now turn to developing a more synthetic account of the deep politics of animism, something that necessarily lies beyond the concept of politics as normally received.

Self/Other and Nature/Nation

Shintô (at least folk and shrine Shintô), as is well known, lacks a systematic theology, although a certain class of scholars has worked hard to provide state Shintô with one. The reason for this lies somewhat beyond the dubious explanation that folk religions, being informal and local, have no institutional mechanism for systematizing themselves. This is that they are essentially not pre-reflective (i.e., primitive), but are organized in such a way that reflective verbalization (language) is much less necessary to their practice than it is in centralized religions, especially the 'religions of the book.' Ritual, music, and dance constitute the important expressive performances rather than rhetoric. Tacit knowledge in such contexts is not so much hidden (*pace* Benjamin 1987, 6), but as with Taussig's shamans, becomes articulated (in appropriate contexts) and hence the source of power. Benjamin does indeed seem to suggest that this is true of animism: 'The result is that, unless our consciousness has been severely subverted in some way by other modes, we will prefer always to treat the world as relatively undifferentiated and as possessing subjectivity. In its basic manifestation this preference constitutes classical animism' (6–7). Belief in such a context is rarely articulated or even articulable, except in some condensed and apologetic form after the event. This is not simply to assert the rather obvious fact that animism is practical (or experiential, in Iwata's terms) rather than theoretical or theological, put to point to something deeper in the structure of animism itself as a mode of relating to the world.

What this also implies is that the relationship between self and other has to be reformulated in that the animistic world view calls into question the essentialist assumptions of many Western views of the self or the individual (Morris 1991). The self is transformable and mutable. This is true both at the level of the Japanese (and Chinese) preoccupation with self-cultivation (understood not as narcissism but as a moral activity) and at the cosmological level (the human self of today becomes the *kami* of tomorrow). In the vitalistic world view all selves are in a sense manifestations of the 'Great Self' (a view also found in some varieties of Japanese Buddhism).

The 'other' in this context has to be radically redefined. It is not nature as in many Western traditions, nor is it necessarily people, especially those not bound to the same set of kinship or quasi-kin relations, particularly as the sphere of kinship is linked to the sphere of cosmology. Just as the human realm and that of animals interpenetrate, so do cosmos and kinship, the particular link between them being the ancestors – those who have become *kami* and in return influence mundane human life. The 'other,' rather, becomes the person outside of this circle of participation. While in Shintô (given its vitalistic world view) there should logically be no outsiders, in practice the nexus between racial identity, place, or territory and the specifically Japanese expressions of animistic religion has given rise to the image of the Japanese as homogeneous and as exclusive – a charmed circle that none may enter except by birth. As one well-known expounder of modern Shintô puts it, 'Shintô is racial religion' (Ono 1990, 111). This specific dynamic of exclusion, in some ways structurally similar to that operating in the caste system (Dumont 1980), has its origins not in racialism, but (also like caste) in a cosmology, a fact that helps exceedingly in interpretating Japanese culture, its constant insider/outsider dialectic (Akasaka 1987), and the role that this has played in Japanese history.

Significantly, recent studies of Japanese identity have used metaphors from nature, including those of rice and the monkey, as mediators between the human and animal because of nature's closeness to people biologically and socially, which also allows it to become a medium of critique and challenge to the assumptions of Japanese culture and society (Ohnuki-Tierney 1987, 1993). Coherence then exists in the Shintô mode of orientation to the world through a two-part process: through and somewhat parallel to, but, given its animistic assumptions also different from, the Buddhist viewpoint, involving the self intimately with the 'other' within the system but drawing a clear boundary between those socially classified as outside the system, weak boundaries within, but strong boundaries without. The result is a strong emphasis on communality, hence the major significance of the 'group' in Japanese society.

All this has major implications for a number of cultural areas beyond the very fundamental question of the identity of the self. One of these is that nature becomes part of the constitution of society, not its 'other' (Clammer 1995, 59–81). Another is directly political. As Benjamin notes in his seminal but little-known paper, 'Because the different modes of orientation generate different modes of interpersonal attention and different interactional styles, in any one polity (i.e. a social network institutionalized or thought of as a power dominated domain) those who wish to achieve and maintain power for themselves will strive to establish just one of the orientational modes as the overt over-arching mode in the culture of the people they wish to dominate. This they will do by actively (although not necessarily thinkingly) relating those patterns of action and communication that generate the different orientational modes in the dominated individuals 'ontology' (Benjamin 1987, 13). This exactly encapsulates the process of the suppression of shrine Shintô by the modernizing Meiji state.

Interestingly, rather than just encapsulating folk Shintô and separating it from the 'legitimate' concerns of the state, the Meiji government clearly saw folk Shintô as a threat. If left alone as an autonomous area of life it would not in practice remain apart from the interests of the government, but would interfere with them: it would in fact subvert the centralizing state building and attempts to achieve 'modernity' (with all its attendant transformations of the self) embarked upon by the holders of political power. To prevent this 'escape' from modernity, folk Shintô had to be suppressed – its implications are too powerful for the modernizing ('transcendental cultural regimes' in Benjamin's terminology) and centralizing Japanese state, involved as all states must be in the constant construction of itself and the persuasion of those to whom the idea of the state is not at all a natural one, that it is the only legitimate framework of reality and politics. Animism is not easily digestible by the modern state, not least because the view of the self that it propagates is incompatible with the systematized classification and surveillance characteristic of modern polities.

Animism, Ontology, and Multiculturalism

Animism, of which I have suggested Shintô is a sophisticated example, creates a world view in which humans are a product of nature and nature is in a sense is a product of humans, both through the literal intervention of humans in nature through activities such as agriculture and through the activities of *kami* as former humans. This perspective, which transcends the sterile categories of the social constructivists, is not just a Durkheimian attempt to see culture deifying itself through nature. As such it is necessary to reject the organizing idea expressed by the early Taussig in his study of Colombian plantation workers and Bolivian tin miners. Much of it organized around ideas about nature: 'Appealing to nature, to the paradoxical extreme wherein certain lifeless things are seen to be animated, is merely one historical specific manifestation of that probably universal tendency whereby any culture externalizes its social categories onto nature, and then turns to nature to validate its social norm as natural' (Taussig 1980, 33). The picture I have been suggesting goes far beyond this, and hence the displacement of the point of conflict between modernity and animism to nature from society. Animism is not the *worship* of nature, and the function of ritual in Shintô is not so much to get things done (there is very little petitionary prayer) as to affirm, exemplify, and continually keep open the channels to a metaphysical and ontological reality.

The somewhat abused concept of animism actually reflects a deep ecological consciousness, one that sees the environment not merely as an object, but as something inseparable from the species-being of humanity. A rethinking of the relevance of animism also has substantial theoretical implications for anthropology and allows old topics –

totemism, shamanism, ancestralism, 'participation' – to be approached in fresh ways. In the specific context of Japan, it allows both a fresh reading of the nature of Shintô and of the role of Shintô in modern Japanese history. The powerful re-emergence of animistic ideas in 'New Age' thinking should also be taken very seriously, for whereas the New Age tends to be treated as beneath notice by many sociologists, I would see it as a genuine and far-reaching social movement struggling with the issues of the reform of consciousness in a world increasingly in economic, political, ecological, and epistemological crisis. In turn, it has connections with the ecological movement proper, with the revival of interest in Asian systems of thought, with the rediscovery of American Indian spirituality, with mainstream religion through media such as the 'creation spirituality' movement (Fox 1991), and with a widely read popular literature on what was once called the 'occult' but which now deals openly with theories of such things as the animate life of objects and their power (e.g., Watson 1991). As such, animism connects with a whole field of issues that have emerged or been rediscovered in the contemporary cultural scene – concern with selfhood, the body, death, animal liberation, dreams, alternative medicine, organic farming, macrobiotics, and meditation, to name a few of the prominent ones.

Of course, not all 'animisms' are the same, and as with all other phenomena that have a social expression, a comparative approach is necessary. The animism of the Iban, the animism of Shintô, and the animism of New Agers who wish to argue for the retention of the 'wild' in an industrializing world are not necessarily identical, but they are likely to share many common features at the level of basic ontological and epistemological assumptions. Also important is the fact that this world view also constitutes or implies a politics. The study of the history of Shintô in modern Japan illustrates this very clearly, and no doubt parallel cases could be invoked, such as that of Indigenous people in East Malaysia struggling against logging and deforestation, in which what appears to be, in the conventional sense, simply a political or ecological movement, is actually an ontological struggle. Habitat reflects cosmology, and what is occurring in such instances is the struggle between modes of being, a view reflected in insightful fictional form by Daniel Quinn in his novel Ishmael (1992). The politics of nature is actually ontology. It is for this reason that struggles over land rights between governments and Indigenous Peoples, or struggles for cultural recognition (such as with the Ainu in contemporary Japan), often seem so irresolvable. Usually the two parties are talking at entirely different levels; their epistemologies are radically different. When these cases come to court the problem becomes even more acute, since the language and categories of the formal legal process can rarely contain such possibilities, being largely predicated upon a rationalistic world view in which a positivistic model of cause and effect is in use.

This casts some interesting light on the currently hotly debated issue of multiculturalism. For the most part, argument about multiculturalism has been phrased in terms of gender, race, or 'culture' itself, and the differences between groups posed in these terms. Here I am suggesting that in many cases this debate could fruitfully be recast in terms of ideas of nature and people-nature relationships. Conflicts between groups that appear to be 'cultural' in many cases actually turn out to be ontological.

The recent 'rediscovery' of Shintô in certain circles in Japan reflects this, especially as there are signs of a shift in the definition of Shintô itself. In a fairly recent book available in an English translation, Fujisawa has the following statement: 'Shintô means the Way (Tao in Chinese) of kami, designating the cosmic vitality generative of all beings, animate and inanimate. We understand by the Way a permanent centre of the universe to be apprehended with incessant mutations. Kami is taken to mean the productive power of Taiichi: the Great Ultimate or Great Void' (Fujisawa 1977, 27). In the same book, Fujisawa relates Shintô to the metaphysics of Zen and to Western depth psychology, and defines Shintô as 'metaphysical realism' (60) and as 'cosmic Vitalism' (65), and he argues specifically against the 'perversion of Shintô theory and beliefs into militaristic and ultra-nationalistic propaganda' (55). The other strand in the re-evaluation of Shintô is very explicitly its connection to nature and its presentation to the world, still suspicious of its old nationalistic leanings, in these terms (International Shintô Foundation 1995).

A rereading of the significance of Shintô coincides with and sheds light not only on the perennial question of self/other and insider/ outsider relationships, but coincides also with the expressions of animistic ideas in contemporary social movements (the New Age and creation spirituality movements being amongst the best examples, together with alternative healing and the fact that in any bookshop today one can find books on the 'Tao' of everything from management to Winnie the Pooh). Most significantly, however, it is in the deep ecology movement that a seriously rethought re-evaluation of animism has occurred, centring on the concept of hylozoism (a 'scientifically formulated animism'), which regards life as one of the properties of matter (Fox 1990, 40).

The implications are many. First, there needs to be a re-evaluation of nineteenth-century anthropology and recognition that it saw, even if through a glass darkly and in an environment where evolutionism and imperialism were major factors, depths and connections in human cultures beyond the ken of later generations of positivist anthropologists, for whom disputes about religion were simply not part of their context. The wider organization of society and the micro-organization of the professional life of intellectuals has much to do with what can be conceived, as Bauman has recently so cogently argued with respect to ideas of death (Bauman 1992). Secondly, it is time for a fresh reading of Shintô, both to better understand its place amongst the major religions of the world and to rescue its essence from the politicizing efforts of its reformers, so that it may speak again to issues of broad human interest – ecology being a principal one – and to the question of the relationships of self/other, self/nature, self/nation, and nation/nature. Thirdly, the reconsideration of the position of animism in human thought opens a dialogue between 'religion' and ecology and suggests models of the universe beyond those of conventional science. Practical issues such as multiculturalism and the struggles of Indigenous Peoples for land rights are aspects of this. Finally, and at root, shrine versus state Shintô illustrates very clearly how conflicts at the political or cultural levels are often in fact ontological ones. What blocks communication is the attempt of two groups of people to speak to one another from differing world views – a fact that often goes unrecognized or becomes virtually unrecognizable in many well-meaning attempts at dispute resolution or legal mediation. Animism suggests that there is no pure object-world. Nature remains enchanted. For the Japanese, nature is indeed part of social self-image; there is no gap between humans and the rest of creation, and when society, especially urban society, creates one, the recovery of humanness requires a return to nature, a lesson that might well be taken to heart as we progress towards a world that some are already calling 'post-materialist.'

Beyond the immediate scope of this essay, but certainly suggested by it, are convergences with some interesting strands of contemporary social theory and with some of the perennial preoccupations of Japanology. A major commentator on the emergence of 'postmodern' cultural and social forms is the French sociologist Michel Maffesoli, who has developed an argument about the 'end of individualism' posed in a form that resonates in a remarkable way with the position being expounded here. Maffesoli sees the collapse of the 'great collective values' and the current preoccupation with the self not as a retreat from the world, but as signalling a shift to 'a sort of tribalism which is based at the same time on the spirit of religion (*religare*) and on localism (proxemics, nature)' (1996, 40). The context of Maffesoli's study is the decline of individualism in the West. But in Japan an age of individualism has never begun, for reasons that are parallel to those identified by Maffesoli as indicating the shift to a new era in the West: 'There is no longer a separation between the cosmos and society, nor within the social whole. On the contrary we are witness to what might be deemed *the culturalization of nature and the naturalization of culture*' (66).

Japan, as many observers have noted, appears to Western eyes to be a highly eroticized culture, themes of sexuality pervading both popular culture and classical literature. The erotics of culture in Japan are closely related to Shintô through the link between sexuality and nature reflected in ideas of fertility, phallic cults, symbolism (e.g., of water), and through understandings of the body and of body/mind and body/cosmos (e.g., the theory of *ki* energy) and their mediation through notions of pollution and purity. The formal patriarchy of Japanese social structure is in practice modified by the occupancy of women of two vital sacred spaces: the area of shamanism and the area of the household, or *ie*. The view that the *ie* is simply a sociological family or household is now widely challenged, and it has been suggested that a better translation would be 'sacred familialism' (Heine 1995) in which women, as the agents of reproduction, link the sociological and the natural. The *ie*, in stressing continuity over time, integrates memory and nature through the cult of the ancestors. The *ie* in practice brings together decentric and horizontal lines of authority with centric and vertical ones. The *hiden*, or 'concealment,' lying at the heart of the *ie* expresses its character as a group organized around the preservation of an identity that externalizes itself in a sociological form while not being itself entirely a sociological entity, but rather the meeting point of nature and culture.

The postmodern concern with aestheticization finds its prototype in Japan but in an unexpected form, one which, far from separating art and nature, relates them in an intimate way, a synthesis rooted in Shintô. Here is the context in which immediate experience, *naka ima* (the 'eternal present'), is synthesized with the demands of actual everyday life and the need for continuity in the *ie*, the 'sacred family.' The liminality of persons in relation to the cosmos and the silences and spaces (*ma*) of Japanese aesthetics (Pilgrim 1995) are seen to be part of a single complex. Aesthetics and politics indeed turn out to be aspects of the whole in traditional Japanese thought, a fact which underlies the utopian expressions and aspirations of Japanese nativism past and present (Nosco 1990). They also help to explain some of the deep structures of Japanese thought and action, in particular the permanent tension between statism and its desire to co-opt nativist thought and direct it to its own nationalistic ends, and the resistance to this stemming from an Indigenous vision of humanity's place in the cosmos. This view still expresses itself in Japanese social movements (e.g., the anti-nuclear movement) and keeps alive a form of animism difficult to assimilate to the rationality and abstractions of modernism. The Japanese project this century might be seen as the struggle between those desiring to 'overcome modernity' (*kindai no chokoku*) through the enterprise of nationalistic state-building, and those who seek to overcome it through its subversion in a modernity whose roots in nature are left uncut.

REFERENCES

Akasaka N. 1987. *Ijin-ron Josetu*. Tokyo: Sunagoya Shobo.
Bauman, Z. 1992. *Mortality, Immortality and Other Life Strategies*. Cambridge: Polity.
Benjamin, G. 1987. *Notes on the Deep Sociology of Religion*. Working Paper No. 85, Department of Sociology: National University of Singapore.
Bolle, K.W. 1987. 'Animism and Animatism.' In M. Eliade, ed., *The Encyclopedia of Religion*, 296–302. New York: Macmillan.
Clammer, J. 1976. *Literacy and Social Change: A Case Study of Fiji*. Leiden: E.J. Brill.
– 1995. *Difference and Modernity: Social Theory and Contemporary Japanese Society*. London: Kegan Paul International.
Dumont, L. 1980. *Homo Hierachicus: The Caste System and Its Implications*. Chicago: Chicago University Press.
Eliade, M. 1987. *The Encyclopedia of Religion*. New York: Macmillan Publishing Co.
Fox, W. 1990. *Towards a Transpersonal Ecology: Developing New Foundations for Environmentalism*. Boston: Shambhala.

Fox, M. 1991. *Creation Spirituality: Liberating Gifts for the Peoples of the Earth*. San Francisco: Harper San Francisco.

Fujisawa C. 1977. *Zen and Shintô*. Westport, CT: Greenwood.

Gennep, A. van. 1909. *Les rites de passage*. Paris: Nourry.

Gluck, C. 1985. *Japan's Modern Myths: Ideology in the Late Meiji Period*. Princeton: Princeton University Press.

Heine, S. 1995. '*Ie*-Ism ("Sacred Familialism") and the Discourse of Postmodernism in Relation to Nativism/Nationalism/Nihonism.' In C. Wei-Hsun Fu and S. Heine., eds., *Japan in Traditional and Postmodern Perspectives*, 25–53. Albany: State University of New York Press.

Holton, D.C. 1965 [1922]. *The Political Philosophy of Modern Shintô: A Study of the State Religion of Japan*. Tokyo: Yushodo.

International Shintô Foundation. 1995. *Shintô to Nihon Bunka* (Shintô and Japanese culture). Tokyo: International Shintô Foundation.

Imanishi K. 1970. *Watashi no Shinkaron* (My theory of evolution). Tokyo: Shisakusha.

Irimoto T. and Yamada T. 1993. *Circumpolar Religion and Ecology: An Anthropology of the North*. Tokyo: Tokyo University Press.

Iwata K. 1989. *Kami to Kami* (God and gods). Tokyo: Kôdansha Gakujutsu Bunko.

– 1991. *Soumokuchûgyo no Jinruigaku* (Anthropology of animism). Tokyo: Kôdansha Gakujutsu Bunko.

Kakeki K. 1912. *Koshinto Taigi* (The essentials of old Shintô). Tokyo: Kobundo.

Kawada, M. 1993. *The Origins of Ethnography in Japan: Yanagita Kunio and his Times*. London: Kegan Paul International.

Kennedy, D. 1987. 'Fools, Young Children, Animism and the Scientific World Picture.' *Philosophy Today* 33: 374–81.

LaFleur, W.R. 1974. 'Saigyô and the Buddhist Value of Nature.' *History of Religions* 13: 93–118, 227–48.

Lévi-Strauss, C. 1962. *Le Totémisme aujourd'hui*. Paris: Presses Universitaires de France.

Lévy-Bruhl, L. 1933. *Le Surnaturel et la nature dans la mentalité primitive*. Paris: Alcan.

Maffesoli, M. 1996. *The Time of the Tribes: The Decline of Individualism in Mass Society*. London: Sage.

Marett, R.R. 1914. *The Threshold of Religion*. 2nd ed. N.P.

Morris, B. 1991. *Western Conceptions of the Individual*. Oxford: Berg.

Nosco, P. 1990. *Remembering Paradise: Nativism and Nostalgia in Eighteenth Century Japan*. Cambridge: Council on East Asian Studies.

Ohnuki-Tierney, E. 1987. *The Monkey as Mirror: Symbolic Transformations in Japanese History and Ritual.* Princeton: Princeton University Press.

– 1993. *Rice as Self: Japanese Identities through Time.* Princeton: Princeton University Press.

Ono S. 1990. *Shintô: The Kami Way.* Tokyo: Charles E. Tuttle.

Pilgrim, R.B. 1995. 'Intervals (*Ma*) in Space and Time: Foundations for a Religio-Aesthetic Paradigm in Japan.' In C. Wei-Hsun Fu and S. Heine, eds., *Japan in Traditional and Postmodern Perspectives,* 55–80. Albany: State University of New York Press.

Quinn, D. 1992. *Ishmael.* New York: Bantam/Turner.

Rosenberger N. 1992. *Japanese Sense of Self.* Cambridge: Cambridge University Press.

Smith, T.C. 1989. *Native Sources of Japanese Industrialization, 1750–1920.* Berkeley: University of California Press.

Steiner, R. 1995. *Nature Spirits.* London: Rudolf Steiner Press.

Taussig, M. 1980. *The Devil and Commodity Fetishism in South America.* Chapel Hill: University of North Carolina Press.

– 1987. *Shamanism, Colonialism and the Wild Man: A Study in Terror and Healing.* Chicago: University of Chicago Press.

Tsurumi K. 1992. *Animism and Science.* Tokyo: Sophia University Institute of International Relations. Research Paper A-58.

Tylor, E.B. 1871. *Primitive Culture.* 2 volumes. London: John Murray.

Watson, L. 1991. *The Nature of Things: The Secret Life of Inanimate Objects.* London: Sceptre.

Yuasa, Y. 1987. *The Body: Towards an Eastern Mind-Body Theory.* Albany: State University of New York Press.

– 1993. *The Body, Self-Cultivation and Ki-Energy.* Albany: State University of New York Press.

PART II

Beyond Positional Identities

In systems where several mutually unintelligible ontologies coexist, conflicts have been seen to arise that 'have to do with the day-to-day and on-the-ground relations of power, deference and entitlement, social affiliation and distance — with the social-interactional, social-relational structures of the lived world' (Holland et al. 1998, 127). Such conflicts can be analysed using constructivist theories like Bourdieu's. However, ontological questions arise when conflicts originate in 'narrativised or figurative identities' that 'have to do with the stories, acts and characters that make the world a cultural world' (127), based on a set of highly diverse philosophical categories. Cases have been quoted where a person's relational (or positional) identity is in direct conflict with his figurative identity (138–40), but there are also cases where the narrativized identities of a minority culture are so unintelligible to the majority that they have no place in the social-interactional (i.e., positional) structures of the society in question. This happens where a majority system based on a science of nature encounters a minority system that relies on a 'poetics of dwelling.'

In David Parkin's analysis of Zanzibar, the latent power inherent in an ancient, no longer sovereign system was mobilized to create chaos in a supposedly modern, rational political mainstream by the re-enactment of an old narrative about hidden demonic forces, symbolizing true facts of historical suffering. The method demonstrated by Parkin treats historical narratives as rational explanations, each in the framework of its own ontology.

Sylvie Vincent's analysis of Innu data is likewise based on the coexistence, in Canada, of historical narratives that are based on incompatible ontologies. While the Zanzibari analysis explains apparently anomalous behaviour patterns, Vincent explains the radical incompatibility of Canadian historical narratives by the argument that historiographies mirror the ontological vision of each authoring culture's national self. History told by a minority nation, if incompatible with mainstream history, is not just political propaganda but a true account of a distinct ontological perspective. Moreover, both Parkin and Vincent show how the reconstruction of historical figured worlds may play a positive role in strengthening minorities' positional identity.

REFERENCES

Holland, D., W. Lachicotte, D. Skinner, and C. Cain. 1998. *Identity and Agency in Cultural Worlds*. Cambridge: Harvard University Press.

Chapter Four

In the Nature of the Human Landscape: Provenances in the Making of Zanzibari Politics

DAVID PARKIN

It has long been argued in anthropology that earlier attempts to separate nature from society/culture and show how far they reflect each other are a Western analytical imposition, for in other non-Western ontologies and epistemologies the so-called natural and socio-cultural seem to be much more part of each other and less distinguishable as separate categories. Hobart (1978) describes how on the island of Bali, Brahmanic hierarchy is likened to the flow of water from the island's centrally placed mountain to the sea, and therefore as the flow of purity from high to low. The people have no need to rephrase this, as might a political anthropologist, as a device to legitimate Brahmanic hierarchy by making it seem a part of nature. For them, the purity of down-flowing water and of Brahmanic status and action in relation to lower castes are aspects of the same understanding of the principle of purity. Marriott (1976) further suggests that co-resident Brahmins are bound together by particles that are simultaneously moral (socio-cultural) and physiological (natural). Indigenous theories of human nature are thus often embedded in what Westerners translate as the social, cultural, and eco-cosmological. Thus, a shaman or political big man may *ipso facto* embody 'natural' qualities deriving from the flora, fauna, and features of landscape.

The following case from coastal East Africa describes how people differentiate each other as belonging to overlapping groups premised on certain intrinsic characteristics by invoking animal and geographical images of a violent past extending into the present. It suggests that, while landscape is a geographical metaphor, it also provides a remarkably powerful historical reminder of how peoples have behaved in the past and may conceivably behave in the future. It is a map that essentializes human difference across time.

An Ethnographic Case

'Popobawa' (meaning 'bat wing') is a term that emphasizes that aspect of a bat which looms large and casts a shadow on the ground. The term was used to refer to a spirit that has a habit of sweeping across large areas of the Zanzibar islands of Unguja [also known as Zanzibar] and Pemba at times of political crisis.[1] It appeared in 1965 in Pemba, a year after the revolutionary massacres and purges in this island state. It recurred in March 1995, lasting from just before until just after Ramadan in Pemba but continuing in Unguja, and was coloured by the run-up to the state's first multiparty national elections. For instance, people in Pemba considered that it had left their island to attack the political opposition based in Unguja. In the case of Pemba, it developed into a reported seven hundred manifestations. During both periods, the starting point appears to have been in southern Pemba. It is difficult to say why it recurred in 1995 and not, say, during a severe famine in 1971–2. However, it is relevant to note that, at the time of the first registrations of political parties in anticipation of the 1995 multiparty elections, there arose a witch-finding movement led by a man named Tokelo from the Tanzanian coastal town of Tanga. Since Tokelo came to be generally regarded by the people of Pemba as a fake, some argued that the subsequent Popobawa movement was his revenge for not having been paid for his services there. There are many local theories explaining Popobawa, but a common feature is its association with political change, or an anticipation of change, set in the context of division and rivalry between Pemba and Unguja.

In the 1960s Popobawa was reported to have sodomized men and women on Pemba, but in 1995 such incidents were reported only in Unguja. On both islands Popobawa knocked people down, including children, and beat them. It climbed over roofs and entered houses, exhibiting great force, and attacked people, causing them to flee from their homes. Many preferred to sleep outside and at a distance from human habitation. At night numerous terrified people would sleep by the side of unlit tarmacked roads, close to passing vehicles, at considerable risk to their lives.

Sitings of Popobawa stopped on Pemba after a few weeks when a couple of men, one an MP, were 'discovered' to have brought Popobawa to the island. People then realized that this had been a political attempt on the part of the ruling party, which Pemba opposed, to divert Pemba's voters from concentrating on their own party's political campaign. This seems to have been the final of a number of explanations of the phenomenon.

Evidently, to have a vicious spirit terrorizing people of its own volition is absolutely unacceptable. That it should be controlled by human rivals is only politically unacceptable and ceases then to be so terrifying. Using old terminology, we might say here that the inexplicably non-human becomes rationalized as the humanly calculating. The fantasy of *mysterium tremendum* becomes political sleight of hand.

Before Popobawa stopped, however, there is no doubting the sheer panic and fear that gripped people, and their willingness to risk life, limb, and property rather than face the monster.

Emergent Themes

Associated with Popobawa are the themes of, on the one hand, power and control, and on the other, human oppression and degradation. These latter themes refer to such matters as perverse sexuality, environmental uncleanliness and an ability to slip like a shadow through (dirty) cracks, ugliness and bestiality, foul odours and offences against bodily aesthetics (much underwritten by assumptions of improper Islamic behaviour relating to sex), and washing and worshipping in a state of spiritual uncleanliness.

Ordinarily, Zanzibari spirits possess individual humans or are their familiars, and although they may cause suffering, they are not lethal, but can be appeased or driven out. Many move in and out of fashion, with names that denote various places, events, eras, sultans, and ethnic groups. Together they constitute a pantheistic narrative of migration, ethnicity, power, and human suffering.

The occurrence of a special spirit like Popobawa unleashes suffering randomly, and Popobawa was not at first thought controllable. People saw themselves as reduced to the status of objects to be violated and beaten indiscriminately. In other contexts I have heard people refer to themselves as having been treated as mere objects, 'As if we were slaves and mere nothings,' an allusion to Zanzibar's past as a major slave entrepôt and its historical slave-based plantation economy.

What are such extensive spirit movements about? If spirits are sometimes mnemonics recalling the past, does Popobawa recreate the fears and terror of the oppression and brutality suffered by the people of Zanzibar during and since slavery, a subject normally too delicate to be mentioned? If we regard the Popobawa movement as part of the political election in Zanzibar and not just an accidental prelude to it, then it can indeed be regarded as part of a continuing trajectory of communal violence that continues into the present.

During the 1995 political election campaign, a surfeit of past events was worked into rhetorical promises of a better future, bringing together old fears and new possibilities. Would there be another massacre, not just of political parties against each other but of 'racial' groups or *kabila*? This fear was presented not as a formulaic political argument, but as what we translate as imagined suffering and terror, a kind of emotional pre-emptive strike, clearing the spiritual ground before the argument of political campaign began. It is as if people knew that issues of power are not settled by rational debate but by past and present resentments of privation and oppression.

The Critique from Violence and Suffering

In dealing with such issues of power, my own focus has for some time been less on the oppressors and more on the victims, who are not, however, seen as always passively suffering but as sometimes able to turn their suffering against their oppressors, playing on the ambivalence of, for instance, violence as contaminating the perpetrator as well as the victim. I am not alone in this approach, for a number of anthropologists have recently also reconvened grimmer versions of Victor Turner's notion of a 'community of suffering' (1957). This notion now extends far beyond the twenty-eight souls making up his Ndembu village. The idea may still be described as occurring in specific localities, but these are seen as reflecting and counter-reflecting each other in an irreducible global chain of overlapping features.

Consider the books. Although one or two Marxist and Marxisant studies in the 1970s linked ideas of suffering directly to adverse economic conditions and exploitation (Parkin 1994 [1972]), it was not until the mid-1980s that we had a kind of updated version of the problem of inexplicable, horrific, unacceptable, and endless human evil, analysed, as one might Zande withcraft, as explanatory systems (O'Flaherty 1976; Parkin 1985), but stressing more the existential dilemmas occasioned by the impossibility of perfect human choice.

This somewhat metaphysical treatment of evil has recently been overlaid by more immediate concerns ranging from the Holocaust to Bosnia and Rwanda. However, in ways that combine analysis with disaster, with the peripheries becoming the centres, there was already an emerging plethora of studies with similar themes: Wendy James on disaster, warfare, and famine in the Sudan (1994), David Lan on warfare and spirit possession in Zimbabwe (1985), Paul Richards on war, conflict, and deforestation in Sierra Leone and Liberia (1992), Richard Werbner on Tears of the Dead, also in Zimbabwe (1991), Nancy Scheper-Hughes on 'death without weeping' in Brazil (1992), and Murray Last on healing the wounds of war in Africa (forthcoming).

As part of this re-emphasis on suffering bodies and disaster zones and landscapes, we have had analyses of political or state violence or violence generally (Riches 1986; Kapferer 1988; Bloch 1986). The focus extends to mental as well as bodily torture and punishment. These are vividly combined in Judith Zur's work on Guatemalan widows, whose menfolk were victims of the Guatemalan war (1997).

In some respects these empirical and often passionately expressed concerns have taken the place of political analysis in anthropology, even to the extent of abridging, and so no longer acknowledging, the Foucauldian concern with power as ever-immanent and no longer to be seen as the property of formal office and personalized control (Spencer 1997). Indeed, these concerns now brush shoulders with questions of anarchy that were current half a century ago. The popular media image may not perhaps be that of 'ordered anarchy' but is more that of global forces of persuasion, consumerism, and predation running out of control against the anthropological insistence that, desperately dispersed and reduced though they may be by war, famine, disease or migration, peoples still constitute themselves in the image of a rule-governed extended local grouping or diaspora.

This dispersive nature of locality, that is, the disaster zone within which people still try to preserve a sense of territorial autochthony, has brought with it a theoretical concern with landscape (Bender 1993; Hirsch and O'Hanlon 1995; Tilley 1994; McDonald 1997) and body as sites on which collective and personal memories are etched or scarred, and from which narratives may be extracted, all interpretively contestable of course. Being more than simply passive bearers of memorial inscriptions, landscapes and bodies may be used to carry their memories into engagement with the world. Putting memories to claims of belonging is, after all, the social evidence of being.

Forcing Free Elections

Anthropology has tried to expunge the essentialized 'isms' of being and theory from its own vocabulary (e.g., from tribalism to postmodernism), but they have reappeared as other peoples' essentialisms and so as our subject matter, as, for instance, nationalism, Islamicism, and other forms of so-called fundamentalism, to which may be added such perennials as capitalism and consumerism. They are, of course, as much 'ours' as 'theirs' for we ourselves live them daily, and they are certainly part of the continuing contemporary challenge to our methods.

For example, given their undeniable importance and effect on peoples' lives, how, as anthropologists, do we understand the International Monetary Fund's demands throughout Africa and elsewhere for multi-party democracy and fully enfranchised political elections, both of which are premised on essentialized assumptions of universal applica-bility and consequence, and now embraced as such by millions of ordinary people throughout the world? Studying elections seems bor-ing by comparison with, say, annual rites of renewal or periodic pil-grimages traditionally observed in all their ritual splendour. But placed in the context of the real or imagined violence and suffering that these elections sometimes invoke, and of the stories of past and potential triumphs, horror, and shame inscribed in the human bodies and physi-cal landscapes among which they occur, elections seem more like rapid myths in the making and cry out for the conceptual unpacking that anthropologists are good at.

There were extensive preparations in the run-up to the first national multiparty elections in Zanzibar in 1995. *Pace* some journalists, the issues were not simply those of interests being specified and repre-sented by competing political parties, such as the promise by the new party of more jobs and better living conditions, or the promise by the party in power of a continuation of the stability and steady progress that it claims to have achieved since independence over thirty years ago. Drawing on the metaphorical use of landscape in recent anthropol-ogy, I see these election promises of prosperity and progress as the rapidly moving, immediate foreground issues that you are likely to find anywhere in African states experimenting with parliamentary de-mocracy. This is the 'sameness' that seems to typify so many studies of so-called global cultural homogenization and consumerism, and of which we may justifiably complain.

The background, however, is made up of matters that are seemingly at a distance from anything we might call politics and are very much part of the distinctive history of the region. They are the implicit assumptions – the things taken for granted and judged 'natural' if sometimes disliked, and which have no set language in which to be expressed. Yet these background factors can be squeezed, so to speak, into mundane, global platitudinous concerns that are immediately recognizable in the usual rhetoric of modern competitive politics. Squeezing the esoteric into the mundane produces a kind of doubletalk. You say one thing but you are referring to any number of other things, some of which are understood as such depending on the interpreter.

Hirsch (1995) and other contributors in Hirsch and O'Hanlon (1995) make the interesting suggestion that background images and foreground representations are mutually implicating: staid everyday phenomena are lifted out of the ordinary, while fantazised images are tied to reality. But compressing the limitless potentiality of background history into the foregrounded actuality of the everyday, may, I think, do more than this. The compression of limitless historical reimagination, or of 'dreamtime,' into the more limited representational possibilities of everyday speech and actions results in a kind of image overload or conceptual excess, a 'fantasization' of built-up historical bricolage. Impossible promises proliferate and jostle with mythicized claims of being and becoming that defy normally held constraints of time and space, as happened in Zanzibar in the run-up to the elections.

I am using the above landscape metaphor rather than the usual surface and depth dichotomy because I think the latter's structuralist duality shuffles us off into directions I do not want to take, such as that of the mind as an uninvited guest. I would prefer the distinctive and long-lasting ideas of a particular region, in this case Swahili-speaking Zanzibar, to be my guest. But what are the background and foreground concerns among the Zanzibari population?

The republic of Zanzibar consists of two main islands: Unguja, identified in tourist brochures and some maps as 'Zanzibar,' and Pemba, which has very little tourism. The inhabitants of each island regard Unguja, with a population of about half a million, as benefiting swiftly from tourist-related development, and Pemba, population three hundred thousand people, as an impoverished source of labour for Unguja or the Tanzanian mainland. Both islands are almost entirely Muslim, mainly Sunni, with a few adherents of Shia. There is also a small, but influential, community of Ibadi. The Ibadi are important because they tend to come, or at least claim to come, from Oman, the Gulf State of which Zanzibar was politically once a part and which has recently started playing a renewed and important role in the life and politics of Zanzibar.

Until about 1989, the year the Berlin wall fell and Zanzibar finally broke with the East German government and Communism, Unguja was as impoverished as Pemba is today. Today, even a casual visit to the islands impresses on the visitor the emerging and significant differences between them; although material inequality exists among Unguja's population, there is more money in circulation and much more display of consumer goods.

Two political parties competed in the 1995 Zanzibar elections: the governing party, the Chama Cha Mapinduzi (CCM), which has ruled Zanzibar's two islands almost since independence (with a change of name from English to Swahili, from TANU to CCM); and a newer party, the Civic United Front (CUF). The CCM retained its control by winning twenty-six parliamentary seats against CUF's twenty-four. Its leader, Salim Amour, also retained Zanzibar's presidency, gaining 50.2 per cent of the vote as against the 48.8 per cent achieved by Hamed, the CUF leader. The narrowness of these wins reinforced the accusations of vote rigging and illegal voting registration that were being made before the elections (international observers were not generally much in evidence). Despite the figures, it is clear from observation that almost everyone on Pemba supported the new party, while a probable slight majority on Unguja supported the party in power, whose president was anyway duly re-elected.

Members of ethnic minorities, particularly so-called Arabs and Indians, and those with property, as well as many ordinary people, expressed considerable fear that the elections would erupt in fighting and massacres on the scale of Zanzibar's notorious unrest of 1964 – the year the Sultan's mainly Arab government was toppled and an African socialist revolutionary government installed, the precursor of the present but much mellowed ruling party, the CCM. At that time the newly formed republic of Zanzibar joined what was then mainland Tanganyika to form the political union of Tanzania. In 1995 some members of the ethnic minorities, fearful of the effects of the elections and possessing means and contacts, dispatched their families and key valuables to Kenya, sometimes accompanying them, and boarded up their properties. In the event, there were electioneering skirmishes but very few deaths and injuries.

It is here that I can begin to talk about the background concerns, those of the *longue durée* of Zanzibar,[2] seemingly resistant to the foreground of immediate and rapidly passing events, and always likely, as I shall show, to spill over and submerge them. For instance, alongside the usual promises and counter-promises of more jobs and progress, supporters of the CUF on Pemba often wanted Zanzibar to be independent of the political union with the Tanzanian mainland, sometimes to the extent of urging a return to Omani Arab rule. Zanzibar, in fact, enjoys almost total autonomy within the union, and most CUF supporters felt that calling for the return of the Sultan was unrealistic and little more than a deliberate play with fantasy. But the wish for total independence from the mainland was widespread, for voters *did* want more trade and job possibilities with the Gulf States, emphasizing the past era of prosperity under Sultanate Arab rule, especially for the now impoverished Pemba, which under the Sultan had supplied most of the world's cloves.

This sense of a renewed past prosperity is reinforced by the fact that, on Unguja, Gulf Airways has increased its flights to Oman (Muscat) to three a week, having only started a service from the island three or four years before. An Unguja resident can buy cheap, duty-free goods in Muscat and fly them directly to Unguja and thence to other parts of Africa and the Indian Ocean islands, while a Pemba resident has the extra, lengthy, and complicated boat journey from Unguja to Pemba. Despite these differences, the renewed links with Oman and the Gulf are spoken of by both islanders as a return to a better, potentially more prosperous, and self-governing past. These concerns override the more immediately visible differences between the two islands, since they are here placed in opposition to the African mainland.

Bodily Origins and Futures

This hope for an Omani-Zanzibari economic and cultural renaissance is shared by both the so-called Omani Arabs, who include many Ibadi Muslims, and by many so-called Shirazi, who, despite appearances, regard themselves as originating more from outside Africa, including Shiraz in Persia, than from the African mainland, and who are mainly Sunni Muslims. People of acknowledged African mainland origin and those Shirazi (and other groups on Zanzibar) who have established interests over the years with the ruling party not surprisingly vote for the latter. It is they who invoke past Arab-controlled slavery as grounds for condemning any return to Omani hegemony. And, thinking back to the Popobawa movement, we here enter into more obviously background features to do with the invocation of the body, particularly the female body, as the source of images usually suppressed and undisclosed.

For instance, the privately observed but publicly undiscussed, shameful issue of slave descent plays a part in such memories of the past. It was on the body and its colour that such memories were inscribed and that threaten to become public questions but which should 'decently' remain unsaid. People ask, if slaves were described as black or 'African,' does this mean that prosperity under the former Omani Sultan was in fact mainly enjoyed by those described as 'white'? And who, therefore, can nowadays claim to be descended from whom in this melée?

The undiscussable shame attached to slave descent is in fact covered or glossed by what I can only call an aspect of the politics of appearance, particularly women's appearance, for it has become an often openly acknowledged ambition on the part of parents of all groups to marry their daughters 'up' into families of Arab or Arab-Swahili or Indian-Swahili descent with a view to producing grandchildren who will be regarded as and called 'white.' While discussing who is or is not of slave origin is highly offensive and strictly for private gossip and malice, there is no shame in wanting 'white' grandchildren using the respectable route of marriage. It is another, though reverse, way of talking about the same thing. Unlike slave descent, whose history cannot be altered, redefining your future progeny is a marriage strategy that is in principle open to all. The leaders of the previous socialist regime were ideologically opposed to this strategy, but evidently, in their own practices, saw it is an aestheticization of the forbidden discussion of who is or is not of even partial slave origin, a way of making public what was otherwise private.

Racial marrying up has in fact been given a new lease of life as a topic of discussion since the demise of the revolutionary government, whose first president, Karume, silenced it. Karume had forbidden the use of racial and ethnic labels, including those hinting at differences of slave and free origins, and had urged that racially mixed marriages be forced upon couples in order to produce progeny whose racial origins would be rendered too mixed to be relevant. (In the 1930s and 1940s, long before he became president of Zanzibar, Karume set up a football team called African Sports with a view to making it so excellent and admired that people would cease to denigrate the term 'African' as being associated with slave descent and would return dignity to black people [Fair 1997]. Later, as president, he was to ban the use of the ethnic-racial term 'Afro-Shirazi' to denote the ruling party and call it instead the 'revolutionary party,' Chama Cha Mapinduzi [CCM].)

Though spoken of only very discreetly, there is a strong memory of these forced marriages in the second half of the 1960s and early 1970s, in fact between 'African' men and women of 'Arab/Indian and Persian' descent, and of the measures taken by families desperate to get their daughters out of Zanzibar before they could occur. These recently expressed memories seem to act as a spur to the present revival of the old preference, in which girls are voluntarily 'married up' the racial hierarchy rather than being forcibly 'married down.' While forcible marriage 'downwards' was seen as a form of bodily violence, voluntary marrying up is regarded as a last stage in publicly approved female ornamentation that begins when the girl child is very young.

The renewed, openly expressed preference for marrying up occurs at two levels. First, there has been a remarkable acceleration of marriage between Zanzibar Omani women and Omani men (often of Zanzibari family origin) living in Muscat, who, aware of the much lower bridewealth compared with oil-rich Oman and of the reputations of Zanzibari women as dutiful, hard-working, and materially undemanding, seek them out through family, friendship, or trading links in Zanzibar. Zanzibaris of claimed Omani origin include young Ibadi Muslims in their teens and twenties who are in the forefront of Islamicism. As 'Arabs' attached to learned Muslim sheikhs only in their thirties, their lifestyles are often imitated by other young Zanzibaris, who are mainly Sunni Muslims, and many of whom call themselves Shirazi. Secondly, there is the phenomenon of Shirazi parents, the so-called Zanzibari Africans (as distinct from mainland Africans), who try to marry their daughters to Zanzibari men who have some claim to Arab or Indian ancestry. Such marriage strategies, despite their repudiation by Karume a generation ago, are in the ascent again in the post-socialist climate of capitalist fee-economic-zone entrepreneurship for they are believed to give better access to job, education, and trade opportunities as well as satisfying an aesthetic preference.

It is difficult also not to see in this new climate of entrepreneurship a modern, rather than a traditional, commoditization of marriageable women as they are duly packaged to appeal, though this is not how they see it, expressing instead a wish to marry up, and seeing self-packaging as a reasonable means to this end. The concern with how they look has its counterpart in the search for better health care, the point being that you cannot place daughters in 'good' marriages and have desirable progeny unless they are healthy as well as aesthetically pleasing. But alongside the election wish for better Omani links runs the complaint, especially in Pemba, that there are not enough bio-medicines available and that children suffer malnutrition and die frequently from malaria and other afflictions. Sick children become unhealthy brides, and so family histories are always under scrutiny for health, morality, and fruitfulness. The production of good brides requires good health care. But this is a fragile equation, because the history of medicine has its violent side, as does that of forcible mixed marriage, and may periodically erupt, so subverting long-term plans.

For instance, shortly after his accession to the presidency of Zanzibar in 1964, Karume is said to have ordered traditional healers to be rounded up and their wares confiscated. We do not know whether he ordered that they be beaten and killed. He did wish to eliminate such superstitions, as he regarded them, in the new socialist world he was creating, although it is also alleged that he genuinely feared the powers of these healers, who, as potential sorcerers, might kill or usurp him. In any event, the so-called guards or youth cadres who were sent out to detain and reprimand healers did commit acts of violence against them, including death, and more so in Unguja than Pemba, it seems. The result is that, to this very day, traditional healers do not practise openly, unlike in Mombasa, Kenya, where Islamic doctors have well-advertised clinics. Indeed, most healers and Islamic scholars who could do so fled Unguja for Kenya, with those less affected on Pemba taking the precaution of practising less visibly.

Alongside the dearth of Islamic and traditional healers, moreover, there were during the revolutionary government period few bio-medicines available. Their provision is now encouraged but only as part of the new entrepreneurial push for development, so that new pharmacies have been set up and have so far reaped big profits. In other words, it is now only those with money who have access to what they perceive to be adequate health care, and it is they who are most likely to aim for high-status marriage arrangements by way of exquisitely presented brides. Those who cannot afford such health care use the skills of the traditional healers who survived the Karume purges, continuing the story of majority suffering. (The complaint on Pemba and Unguja that there are not enough medicines, therefore, refers not to these expensive remedies but to the absence or insufficiency of government clinic medicines and, in Unguja, of traditional healing knowledge, both of which have suffered at the hands of the revolutionary government dating from Karume's period.)

Constraining Excesses

All communities are to some extent imagined, in that the concept of community presupposes a greater consensus of views, visibility, and territorially located interaction than is feasible, and my own description contributes to this imagining. On the other hand, the community of election voters in Zanzibar displays preferences and exclusions that are born of easily attestible suffering. This suffering, following what I have been saying, comprises

- a history of slavery and harsh, racially organized feudalism;
- the vengeful massacre of 1964, mainly in Unguja, when the revolution occurred;
- the purges of traditional healers, again mainly in Unguja;
- the marked reduction in health care and nutrition;
- the forced marriages of non-African girls;
- the constraints placed on Islam by the secular Communist government; and
- the voluntary exile of many Muslim scholars.

These factors were remembered, so to speak, in the fearful run-up to the presidential multiparty elections of September 1995. Their explicit mention was accompanied by

- feverish expectations and preparations for marriage with Omanis;
- an idealization of times under Arab rule;
- a frank acknowledgment that to have 'white' grandchildren was a major factor in marriage choices;
- an exaggeration of the benefits to be had from revived traditional healing and from the burgeoning new biomedical clinic-hospitals and pharmacies; and
- extremely expressed fears of massacres.

Under the cover of election rhetoric promising progress and prosperity, background issues entered the foreground of everyday talk. What's more, they generated their opposite in the form of future possibilities that teetered on the edge of the feasible and the fantastic, being hopes for the future which were to reverse the present results of the usually unremembered past.

Thus, joined with the highlighted fears of a return to the bodily violence of the revolutionary years is the call, sometimes direct and sometimes indirect, and more in Pemba than Unguja, of a return to an earlier period of rule by Omani Arabs, or at least of the values that allegedly prevailed at that time. In showing how the foregrounding of background features may produce an excess of expectations or fantasy, let me focus on Zanzibar in two areas. First, there is the emphasis on women's physical and sartorial appearance as the route to third-generation social and ethnic mobility; and, secondly, there is concern with the better health care that would help make this and the continuity of generations possible. Let me here repeat my suggestion that foregrounding background features during rhetorical polyphony, and compressing the *longue dureé* into contemporary events, is like promising too much in too short a time, producing the inevitable excesses and ambiguities of fantasy.

Taking women's appearance first, in Unguja the colossal purchase and use by, and for, women and girls of clothes, finery (including gold and silver jewellery), and perfumes, and their public display as ornaments good to marry with, clashes, according to radical young Muslim men, with the presence of white women tourists, whose consumerist ways are seen as dangerous. These young men led a campaign in 1992–3 against tourism, complaining that pure and virtuous Muslim women were dangerously exposed to the possibility of imitating scantily dressed, long-haired white women tourists. The young Muslims nailed up posters contrasting these semi-naked devil whores with their own pious Arabo-Swahili women dressed from top to toe in *hijab* and *buibui*, further associating the former with drink, drugs, and prostitution, and the latter with prayer and modest demeanour.

Their fears have a context and are not without foundation. Young men are expected to have a regular job, including self-employment, and the means to buy a house, as well as provide marriage payments, before they marry. Unemployment is high and they may have to wait years. I met a number of young men heartbroken by losing loves whom they could not yet afford as wives. In addition, the Zanzibari musical concerts called *taarab* (a term denoting the original Egyptian and Indian Ocean rim provenances of this now much evolved form of music) have become especially lavish occasions on which women switch from pious Islamic garb and modest, eyes-down comportment to glittering dress and jewellery, swaggering sexily to present gifts of money to the singers in order to communicate with a lover, or possible lover, or to a woman rival for that lover. In the newly emerging 'hypergamy' or marrying up of women, such developments are said to make women more desirable for the men who can afford to keep them, such as Omanis or well-to-do Zanzibaris. But these same factors withhold women from young men, whose Islamic piety may be their only resource. It is perhaps small wonder that Islamicism is in effect driven by young men, whatever the titular position of older clerics.

As regards medicine, I have mentioned already that, in the relative absence of traditional healers and their knowledge, and encouraged by the new capitalism, private pharmacies have sprung up and doctors have become entrepreneurial. Doctors are obliged to spend some of their time in the government hospital, but they devote much of it to their own private clinics. Many pharmacies have clinics attached to them, with more and more providing wards with beds and sometimes better biomedical equipment than is provided by the government hospital. Although the service *is* sometimes superior to that found in the government hospital, it is not aimed at, say, cerebral as distinct from bodily malaria nor at deep surgery, for which local and foreign expatriate doctors at the government hospital are regarded as indispensable.

Moreover, the privatized pharmacies and clinics are expensive yet popular, and people are prepared to become indebted in the belief that they are being offered exceptional health care. Here, too, one sees the commoditization of putative means to good health, purveyed as would other imported consumer goods identified as Western, although they are more likely to be of East Asian manufacture. Some Zanzibaris returned from long overseas exile have even mooted the possibility of setting up a factory producing biomedicines and equipment, which they could do easily in the absence of strict regulations governing the quality of such locally produced drugs.

Similarly, the new, private pharmacies can sell medicines that are not allowed in Europe and America and which are, of course, dumped in the Third World by large pharmaceutical companies. These factors go hand in hand with Western capitalist consumerism, including the way their women dress in *taarab* concerts, that radical young Muslims reject, just as they reject what they see as the decadent excesses of tourism, including not only the immorality of Western dress and the behaviour of white tourist women, but also that of tourist men who seek sodomy and engage in other non-Islamic behaviour – a major theme, it will be remembered, of the Popobawa spirit pandemic. Indeed, it can be argued that it is these young radicals who alone attempt to demystify the excesses or fantasies of the emerging consumerist culture, whose alleged significance is heightened during election promises. Their disillusionment with such circumstances eventually creates the appeal of Islamicism or radical Islam, even if only to a youthful but forceful minority, and that it is in the shadow of its coming that the formal hierarchy of religious office becomes politically prominent.

In other words, this is when the clerics are obliged to speak for or against militant representations of Islam pitched against consumerist images. At such times they cannot sit on the fence; both mosque and the informal institution of the *baraza* oblige them to hold a view, with the result that we get a picture of politico-religious hierarchy that seems formalized, enduring, and the stuff of which an earlier anthropology was made. In fact, our methodology now sees such formal structures not as central to social being but as supplementary to its crises of choice in the face of suffering, with disorder the starting point of analysis, and putative order an epiphenomenon dependent as a concept on claims of disaster.

I am not just appealing to the Durkheimian proposition that it is only in a crisis that you see enduring principles. I am saying that, in the foregrounded crisis that an election evokes, abundant shameful and fearful narratives from the past are made public and discussed, including racially or ethnically based slavery, forced marriage and massacre.

However – and this is where the analytical rhetoric of the global ecumene seems to have relevance – once made public, these disclosures about the past can easily be pushed into the background by an excess of consumerist fantasies centred on tourists, popular Western culture and goods, and a new politics of appearance. While some forget the past in favour of current images of consumerist hedonism, others, including radical Muslims, turn against such current 'decadence.' There is tension between the two: some frequent video shops purveying kung fu and pornographic movies, while others disdain such influences and distribute Islamic literature outside mosques on Fridays.

In this proliferation of, and competitive jostling between, the consumerist society of the spectacle, as Debord (1990) calls it, and images of history, we tend to say that consumerist preferences will emerge dominant and eventually reduce traditional images. It may well be that excesses of tradition recede, for the moment, as quickly as the electoral fever and the Popobawa spirit movement that evokes them. But such excesses make the point that, despite the alleged global sameness of popular and tourist goods and styles, existential issues of life and sexuality, death and violence, remain locally distinctive, reworked but evoking an agreed origin, which is what we mean by identity or local cultural resistance.

Conclusion

It seems that a surfeit of worldly promises and expectations, such as obtains in modern elections, gets caught up in a proliferation of unexplained sufferings rooted in the past. By remaining unexplained, they continue as possibilities or templates for more suffering. If I may reify, it is as if culture has failed to attend to unfinished business, such as the cultural justifications for cruelty or violence that are never quite believed and linger as resentments to be passed on to succeeding generations.

Of course, cultural business always remains unfinished, since, like the distant reaches of a landscape, there is infinitely more to create and call discovery. Another way of saying this is to convert the essentialized idea of culture into that of contestable knowledge, which is what the Popobawa spirit movement did. It subverted the sense of immediacy of a modern IMF-sponsored election. Perhaps such movements, in parallel with a modern election, are firefly myths, giving us glimpses, but no more, of practices and beliefs that obsess us with their unspeakability and elusiveness.

These unspeakable practices and beliefs from the past are part of a people's own 'otherness.' But they are the negative rather than positively remembered aspects: they are the underside of romanticized tradition. I suggest that this is a half-hidden, momentarily evoked negative internal otherness in the new worldly conscious selves of so-called developing societies. It results perhaps from exposure to the many overlapping and cross-cutting comparisons of national, ethnic, and religious identity to which all peoples are now subject through increasingly powerful global media reports and propaganda. The growing and in some cases newly 'invented' ethnic self-consciousness of many societies has led to an essentialization of identity that first stressed positive aspects (the more favourable rewriting of 'our' history) but may now also include the beginnings of a 'rediscovery' of the less palatable aspects of a people's past. A third phase might be that of internal critique, metaphorical hints of which are implicit in Zanzibar's Popobawa movement.

NOTES

1 I am grateful to Martin Walsh for first drawing this movement to my attention and for insightful comments on this and other matters during my time on Pemba island.
2 The reference is to the French school of history. The term *longue durée* is explicated in Fernand Braudel, *Écrits sur l'histoire* (Paris: Flammarion, 1969), 41–83. It includes the history of unconscious forms of sociability and of phenomena whose temporal progression is very slow, seemingly absent.

REFERENCES

Bender, B. 1993. *Landscape: Politics and Perspectives*. Oxford: Berg.
Bloch, M. 1986. *From Blessing to Violence: History and Ideology in the Circumcision Ritual of the Merina of Madagascar*. Cambridge: Cambridge University Press.
Davis, J. 1992. 'The Anthropology of Suffering.' *Journal of Refugee Studies* 5 (2): 151–61.
Debord, G. 1990. *Comments on the Society of the Spectacle*. London: Verso.
Fair, L. 1997. 'Playing Politics with Football.' *Africa* 67 (2): 224–51.
Hirsch, E. 1995. 'Landscape: Between Place and Space.' In E. Hirsch and M. O'Hanlon, eds., *The Anthropology of Landscape: Perspectives on Place and Space*, 1–30. Oxford: Clarendon.
Hirsch, E., and M. O'Hanlon, eds. 1995. *The Anthropology of Landscape: Perspectives on Place and Space*. Oxford: Clarendon.
Hobart, M. 1978. 'The Path from the Soul: The Legitimacy of Nature in Balinese Conceptions of Space.' In G. Milner, ed., *Natural Symbols in South East Asia*. London: School of Oriental and African Studies.
James, W. 1994. 'Civil War and "Ethnic Visibility": The Uduk of the Sudan-Ethiopia Border.' In K. Fukui and J. Markakis, eds., *Ethnicity and Conflict in the Horn of Africa*, 140–64. London: James Currey; Athens: Ohio University Press.
Kapferer, B. 1988. *Legends of People, Myths of State: Violence, Intolerance and Political Culture in Sri Lanka and Australia*. Washington, DC: Smithsonian Institution.
Lan, D. 1985. *Guns and Rain*. London: James Currey.
Last, M. Forthcoming. *Healing the Wounds of War in Africa*. Edinburgh: Edinburgh University Press.

McDonald, A.W. 1997. *Mandala and Landscape: Emerging Perceptions in Buddhist Studies No. 6.* New Delhi: D.K. Printworld.

Marriott, M. 1976. 'Hindu Transactions: Diversity without Dualism.' In B. Kapferer, ed., *Transaction and Meaning*, 163–90. Philadelphia: Institute for the Study of Human Issues (ISHI).

O'Flaherty, W. 1976. *The Origins of Evil in Hindu Mythology.* Berkeley: University of California Press.

Parkin, D. 1994 [1972]. *Palms, Wine and Witnesses.* Prospect Heights, OH: Waveland.

– 1985. *The Anthropology of Evil.* Oxford: Blackwell.

Richards, P. 1992. 'Saving the Rain Forest: Contested Futures in Conservation.' In S. Wallman, ed., *Contemporary Futures: Perspectives from Social Anthropology*, 138–53. London: Routledge.

Riches, D. 1986. *The Anthropology of Violence.* Oxford: Blackwell.

Scheper-Hughes, N. 1992. *Death without Weeping: The Violence of Everyday Life in Brazil.* Berkeley: University of California Press.

Spencer, J. 1997. 'Precolonialism and the Political Imagination.' *JRAI (Journal of the Royal Anthropological Institute)*, 3 (1): 1–19.

Tilley, C. 1994. *A Phenomenology of Landscape: Places, Paths and Monuments.* Oxford: Berg.

Turner, V.W. 1957. *Schism and Continuity in an African Society.* Manchester: Manchester University Press.

Werbner, R. 1991. *Tears of the Dead: The Social Biography of an African Family.* International African Library. Edinburgh: Edinburgh University Press.

Zur, J. 1997. '"Violent Memories": Quiche War Widows in Highland Guatemala.' Boulder, CO: Westview Press.

Chapter Five

Apparent Compatibility, Real Incompatibility: Native and Western Versions of History – The Innu Example

SYLVIE VINCENT

The backdrop to the questions I would like to examine in this text is a report by a task force that was commissioned by the government of Quebec to examine the teaching of history (programs, teacher education, class hours, etc.). One of the report's recommendations was to offer 'Native groups an equitable place' in primary and secondary school history programs 'in terms of the role they have played in the history of Quebec, Canada and the Americas' (Groupe de travail sur l'enseignement de l'histoire 1996, 74). Given the current state of research, one might ask how this 'equitable place' and this 'role' are to be defined. One might also set out to show how responding to this recommendation constitutes a challenge all by itself.

In my opinion, however, there is room for yet another, more fundamental question. Is it possible not only to provide a place for Native history, to the extent that material, written, and iconographic sources and Western conceptions make it possible to narrate this history, but to also provide a place for Native versions of this history? Without dwelling on the fact that there are eleven First Nations in Quebec or the technical complexity of such a venture, the question remains whether it is theoretically conceivable to conciliate or achieve coexistence between different ways of discussing the same past within the same course or in the same textbook.

It is also important to recall that this question has ramifications extending beyond the teaching of history and is intimately bound up with the everyday lives of Natives and non-Natives alike. Both groups must coexist on land in which their identity is rooted but for which they have developed differing representations, i.e., of this land and the events that have taken place on it. Nowadays, as Native people claim their right to self-government and to their own culture, diverging interpretations of the past have become a source of misunderstanding and tension. Thus, during round-table negotiations between Natives and non-Natives over the sharing of land and resources, a lack of familiarity with the historical origins and conceptual framework of the other side's point of view means that the obstacles to an agreement are not only economic, social, or political in nature, but they are also, and above all, cultural.

As both groups have increasingly come into direct contact with one another, the differences between Native and non-Native ways of knowledge have become more apparent. Most often at issue is knowledge involving the environment, for example, during an impact assessment for development projects. However, knowledge of the past is also an area that members of the Western scientific community claim they wish to take into consideration, although they provide little indication about the status they plan on according this knowledge.

Thus, is it possible to provide a place for Native knowledge of a past that concerns both Natives and non-Natives, as well as the land on which the two groups have come into contact with one another and which they have lived in either alone or together? I have used the following three themes as a basis for my reflections: the choice of events that are narrated; the interpretation of these events; and the temporal and conceptual framework into which they are fitted. The basis for my remarks comes from information collected among the Innu of the Middle and Lower North Shore of the Gulf of St Lawrence (in the eastern part of Quebec) between 1971 and 1993, and in particular data collected in Natashquan from 1971 to 1975 and again from 1992 to 1993.[1]

The Innu (whom the French called the Montagnais, a name now seldom used) are a member of the great Algonquian linguistic family. The Innu inhabiting Quebec now form nine communities, but settlement in villages is a relatively recent phenomenon, particularly in the eastern portion of their territory, which began in the 1950s and officially ended only in the 1970s (Savard 1975). The North Shore Innu who provided me with their version of history were born and raised prior to sedentarization. They took part in travels inland in small family groups between the months of August and June and participated in summer gatherings along the shore. The stories they told me or on which they based their accounts were ones that their elders, and most often their grandparents, had told them.

Choosing the Events to Be Narrated

The events that are chosen for narration vary from one historian, or one historical actor, to another (Lévi-Strauss 1962, 340). This fact is sufficiently obvious that it does not merit further comment here. Even within one and the same society, historians accord greater or lesser importance to events, themes, and specific subjects depending on the era in which they conducted their research, their own ideologies, and the development of their methods (see Le Goff and Nora 1974). History textbooks written in the 1950s, for example, devoted little space to the economy but a great deal to wars, little to women or to society as a whole but a great deal to political leaders. From one culture to another, the divergence between perspectives becomes even more palpable. If it is apparent that each people develops a discourse on its past, the examination of these discourses also shows that each people attaches more importance to some themes than to others and recalls the events that are peculiar to it.

In their own narratives, the Innu tell how their ancestors were able to support themselves, the causes of death among their people, their travels back and forth over the Quebec-Labrador peninsula, and the deeds and actions of other peoples and non-human beings who were in contact with their territory. Among the other peoples were the Mi'kmaq, the Inuit, the Iroquois, and the Europeans. The latter are mentioned in connection with, for example, their arrival in the seventeenth century, the dealings of the missionaries, the establishment of trading posts and the approaches taken by the traders, the settlement of the Acadians on the North Shore in the nineteenth century, and so forth. Events that occurred far from Innu territory or did not directly affect them are not narrated. Thus, while the Innu are aware of a period when the French and English were at war with one another, they do not specifically refer to the Conquest, the rebellions of 1837–8, the Union of Upper and Lower Canada, or the British North America Act of 1867 – all subjects that figure prominently in the teaching of Quebec history.

We must, of course, take notice of this fact, in addition to the scope of the territory covered in each version of the past. At first glance, however, it does not appear to represent a major obstacle to the harmonization of these versions. For the North Shore, for example, it is possible to imagine a kind of history that would present an Innu version of certain events, a non-Innu version of other events, and occasionally two versions of the same event. Such a history would offer two versions, for instance, of the alliance between the Montagnais and the French during the seventeenth century, the activities of the Oblate Fathers during the nineteenth century, or the opening of the mine in Schefferville in the 1950s. A description of the cod-fishing economy, on the other hand, would be based primarily on the Euro-Québécois version, whereas a description of the Caribou hunts inland and an explanation of the hunting economy would rely on the Innu version.

The Interpretations of Events

A second, more serious obstacle to the compatibility of these two versions of history arises in connection with the diverging interpretations that are made of the same events. I will give only one example here, but one that is important for both parties, in that it constitutes a myth of the origins of relations between the Innu and the Québécois of European descent.

A synthesis of the narratives collected from seven persons living in Natashquan presents the North Shore Innu version of history according to four main periods.[2] 1. Prior to the arrival of the French, the region of Quebec City was an Innu gathering point. 2. When the French arrived, they saw that the Innu lands were attractive. They asked if they could settle, and offered the Innu a form of economic aid in return. 3. Relations between the Innu and the French deteriorated, and as the French population constantly increased, the situation of the Innu became intolerable. 4. Thus, the Innu departed the region of Quebec City for other sites located further to the east along the St Lawrence River.

Now let us examine what the historians have written on this subject. The standard history textbooks or general histories of Quebec and Canada have devoted little comment to a possible alliance between the French and the Innu, except to mention that by allying himself with the Native people he met first at Tadoussac and then at Quebec City, Champlain automatically involved himself in the wars with the Iroquois (see, for example, Vaugeois and Lacoursière 1976, 54). Among specialists of Native history, however, recent research has made it possible to link the portrait that emerges from the archives with that provided by oral tradition.

On a point-by-point basis, it would appear that, first, for Parent, the Quebec City region during the seventeenth century was undoubtedly a gathering place controlled by the Montagnais (Innu): 'The influence of the Montagnais extended ... to Montréal [by way of the Laurentian coalition]. However, they considered the area around Québec City as the beginning of their country. This fact is confirmed on a number of counts' (Parent 1985, 239). Among the corroborating elements, Parent cites the fact that in 1624 the Montagnais wished to exact tolls from the Hurons who came to Quebec City, and the attestation that in 1637 Governor Montmagny was unable to forbid the Abenaki, who carried on trade with the English, access to Quebec City, without symbolically requesting the Montagnais to bar the Abenaki (239, 241).

Secondly, the idea that there had been an agreement between the French and the Montagnais in the early years of the seventeenth century was recently examined by Girard and Gagné, two historians belonging to the Groupe de recherche sur l'histoire, Chicoutimi. They reviewed the opinions of several authors, from Benjamin Sulte in 1882 to Bruce Trigger in 1985 and Olive Patricia Dickason in 1993; they demonstrated that there was a real 'alliance' between, on the one hand, Gravé Du Pont (the representative of the king of France) and Champlain, and, on the other, the Montagnais, Etchemin, and Algonquins, as represented by Anadabijou, the Montagnais chief of Tadoussac (Girard and Gagné 1995). This agreement was reached at Tadoussac in 1603, and it continued to be implemented after the settlement of the French at Quebec City in 1608. The resulting political, military, and commercial alliance enabled the French to settle on Montagnais territory.

Thirdly, a deterioration in the relations between the Montagnais and the French also appears to be a recognized fact. Among the supporting evidence is the murder of a number of French subjects by the Montagnais; the commotion created at Quebec City when a Montagnais claimed that the Jesuit missionaries had attempted to poison him (1626); the fact that by guiding the Kirke brothers from Tadoussac to Quebec City in 1629, a Montagnais had helped the English take over Quebec City; the refusal of the French to supply the Montagnais with guns (Innu oral tradition also affirms that the French were afraid the Innu would take back Quebec City); and the fact that the Montagnais forbade the French access to their rivers (Parent 1985, 239, 241).

Fourthly, and finally, the departure of the Montagnais from the area of Sillery and Quebec City also seems to be borne out by the archives. Parent ascribes this exodus to commercial disputes between the Montagnais and the French as well as to the Montagnais's fear of the Iroquois and epidemics.

By scrutinizing the archives, one can make a serious case that there are major parallels between accounts by representatives of the oral tradition and those of the written tradition. This does not imply, however, that there are no obstacles to reconciling both versions of the past. Although the sources appear to refer to the same events, the interpretations of these sources, and hence the meaning that is ascribed to these events in terms of understanding the current situation, are nevertheless dissimilar. In the following examples, I will take up a number of these diverging interpretations.

Some historians believe that in 1603 the French received authorization to inhabit the valley of the St Lawrence, or indeed the entire country (howsoever vaguely defined). For example, Mgr Victor Tremblay has brought out what he perceives to be respect for the rights of the Montagnais: 'Under the terms of this agreement, the French were *fully entitled* to come and settle in the St. Lawrence valley. Whereas, elsewhere, the Spanish, the Portuguese and the English imposed themselves, establishing their settlements without overly preoccupying themselves with the rights of the native peoples, here the French proceeded *in accordance with the existing rule of law*, settling as guests and allies of the inhabitants of this country under the terms of this agreement' (Tremblay 1963, 28, quoted in Girard and Gagné 1995, 7; my italics). And in his *Histoire de la Nouvelle-France*, Marcel Trudel asserted that 'At a solemn gathering, the French received general authorization to inhabit the country. *Natives were not despoiled* [of their lands]' (Trudel 1963, 268, quoted in Girard and Gagné 1995, 7; my italics).

According to the Innu, however, and they are categorical about this, only the region of Quebec City was to be left to the French, who, despite this injunction, rapidly spread out from this area and further and further into Innu territory. We are confronted here with two versions of history, that of the Innu, who are of the opinion that with the exception of the region of Quebec City, the entire territory of Quebec still comes under the authority of Natives, and that of the other inhabitants of Quebec, who believe that they were offered the whole territory and that the Natives own only the reserves that were retroceded to them.

In another case of diverging interpretations, the Innu say that they were promised economic aid, which they never really received, and which was to last for as long as the Europeans used their territory. Adherents of the written tradition affirm that it was primarily military aid that had been promised, and that this was supplied at the appropriate time and place.[3] To the Innu's way of thinking, the agreement was indeed violated and the French were liars and thieves, as are their inheritors in the present day. In the estimation of non-Native historians, on the other hand, the French met their obligations toward the Innu.

A third example of divergence occurs in the case of the interpreters of Champlain's accounts, who are somewhat prone to accept them at face value. The Montagnais are portrayed in these writings as fully complying with the French request to settle on their lands. The authors of one school textbook have even reversed the roles, suggesting that it was the Montagnais who asked the French to come and settle on their lands (Vaugeois and Lacoursière 1976, 46). In the oral version, on the other hand, the Innu were hesitant, suspicious, and not terribly inclined to allow the French to settle, whereas the French are described as being insistent and determined.

This brief sketch of the divergences that can arise between the bearers of written tradition and those of oral tradition underscore how the interpretations of each type spring from opposing ideologies. These interpretations are in part rooted in their respective cultures, but they also testify to how conflicting versions are, respectively, the products of a dominant society and a dominated people. Now, there is nothing to prevent one from offering different versions of the same events in the same course or in the same book. This is in fact an increasingly frequent option. One example of this trend is the book by Jean-Paul Bernard (1983) on the rebellions in Lower Canada of 1837–8, which presents the interpretations of eight historians on these crucial events in the history of Quebec. More recently, Denis Vaugeois has compiled the studies of four historians on General Murray's 'Treaty' with the Indians in 1760, which are far from presenting a consensus on their subject (Vaugeois 1996, 227). Placing potentially irreconcilable interpretations side by side within the same book would perhaps throw light on contemporary political positions and might enable the Innu's interlocutors to understand the basis of their point of view, and vice versa.

The Conceptual Framework

If it is possible to establish correspondences between Native and non-Native versions of history, and indeed to set these versions off with respect to one another, a third obstacle nevertheless arises: that of the conceptual framework within which historical narratives are inscribed.

In the first place, because the events that are narrated fit into a frame of time, it is of the utmost importance to become acquainted with the conceptions of time specific to both the Innu and the other inhabitants of Quebec. From the outset, this entails ascertaining whether both groups divide up time the same way. In other words, we must determine if the periods identified by each group are the same, and, in addition, if the markers used offer a basis for comparison.

For the Innu, historical time begins once the earth became inhabitable, that is, after the heroes of their culture liberated the earth from the cannibalistic beings who once roamed over it. This temporality is divided into three major periods: the time of the Ancestors, the time of the Innu, and the time of future generations (Vincent 1991). The contours of these periods are hazy, and their duration is relative and cannot be measured in terms of years or any other unit of time. Thus, the Innu of today will at some point become the Ancestors to future generations, and the current period will be considered to fit into the period that preceded it.

This elasticity owes in particular to the fact that the phenomena which serve to mark off periods – the phenomena that define their beginning and their end – are not events occurring at a precise date (this or that war, treaty, revolution, or coming to power of a given person), but are instead transformations in the Innu's ways of living. The major turning points of history, as told by the Innu, are ascribed to changes in the degree of Innu self-sufficiency and autonomy. Thus, the period of the Ancestors is characterized by total autonomy. Having distanced themselves somewhat from animals and invisible beings (without, however, being entirely cut off from them), human beings developed, on the one hand, means for communicating and interacting with these other worlds (dreams, drums, songs, sweat lodge ceremonies and shaking tent, etc.), and, on the other, a type of technology and material culture that set them off from other peoples (forms of habitation, clothing, fire-building techniques, canoes, snowshoes, hunting techniques, etc.). The period of the Innu commences when the influence of Western culture became strong enough to create new needs (for guns, flour, canvas, and other goods), and when the imposition of new ways of thinking (the Catholic religion) and political organization (the appointment of chiefs) forced the Innu to live in accordance with two different systems. The period of future generations will be that of a single way of life – either assimilation and the loss of autonomy, or a return to Innu values.

Within these major periods, chronology does not appear to play an important role. Obviously, some narratives recount events that are known to have occurred previous to others, but it is neither essential nor productive to classify them according to their degree of ancientness. The timelines that Western schoolchildren are familiar with could, in the case of the Innu, be replaced by time zones in which the before and after are not particularly relevant, although they could not be totally excluded or proscribed.

Given the preceding, it would be difficult to establish exact, definitive correspondences between Western systems of dating and the Innu division of time. For Westerners, European colonization of the Quebec City region is located at the beginning of the seventeenth century, in 1608 to be precise. In the Innu system, on the other hand, this phenomenon falls within the long period of the Ancestors, an era whose beginning is difficult to pin down with any accuracy and which more or less extends into the middle or the end of the nineteenth century for the time being, and which could extend into the twentieth century in another hundred years. We are faced, then, with relativity in terms of the division of time into periods, and also in terms of the concepts that represent the key to this history. If autonomy is the key concept today, who can predict what it will be tomorrow?

Another obstacle to establishing parallels between these two types of history owes to the fact that while Innu narratives (and Native narratives in general) do recount precise events, they nevertheless acquire relevance not so much from the factual information they convey as from the models or characteristic situations they propose (e.g., in their connection with identity, or in their relationships to territory or rules governing social organization). Thus, students of the oral tradition have attempted to grasp the meaning of the fact that a narrative which relates the exploits of the Cree during the period when they were at war with the Iroquois also circulates among numerous other nations belonging to the Algonquian linguistic family – e.g., the Innu, the Atikamekw, the Ojibwa, the Abenaki, the Malecites, the Mi'kmaq, the Penobscots, the Passamaquoddy, etc. (Trudel 1987, 93; Morantz 2001). This narrative recounts how Iroquois warriors fell to their deaths at the instigation of one or two Algonquians (oftentimes an old woman) whom they had taken captive in order to be guided through territory that was foreign to them. The fact that each nation credits itself with this exploit means that it is quite difficult to locate the event in a precise time and place, and thus the narrative is deprived of its 'historical' dimension. However, it does provide insight into, for instance, the perceptions the Algonquians had of the Iroquois, the impossibility of moving about in foreign territory, how weakness can be occasionally offset by pluck and courage, the symbiosis between the Algonquians and their rivers, and so forth. In other cases, the same actions and deeds can be ascribed to different beings or to representatives of a number of nations, so that these narratives then provide more information about relationships with foreigners than about the real behaviour of a particular group of foreigners at a particular time and in a particular place. It is the notion of the foreigner or foreignness that is the theme of the narrative, not a category of foreigners.

In addition to the difficulties that the fluidity of the oral tradition creates for those who attempt to use it within a framework that is extrinsic to it, these observations also underscore the fact that listening to a narrative is not sufficient for understanding it. It is only in the context of a plurality of narratives, by means of the compilation of the themes common to oral tradition and via the interpretation that the bearers makes of this tradition, that it becomes possible to interpret what a given narrative has to tell. No single narrative can really be understood unless it is placed in relation to the others. As with the relativity of Innu division of time, so too the fluidity of Innu narratives requires us to grasp the Innu vision of the past as a whole in order to understand its individual elements. It is tempting to suggest an analogy here with the Innu understanding of their territory. Mobility is not to be understood by examining one particular place or another but by viewing the hydrographic systems, the portaging trails, and the set of resting, camping, and gathering sites.

It is important to point out another divergence, which arises in connection with the types of events that are considered by the Innu and the Québécois as belonging to the past. Previously, it has been a question of relationships with other peoples. However, the lives of the Ancestors as well as of the parents and grandparents of the Innu of today were interwoven with numerous other events which brought into play all living beings, including animals and beings that are invisible to most people. The struggle with the cannibals; encounters with the guardians of the earth or with various inhabitants of the cliffs, the air, or water; journeys by the shamans to the masters of the animals – all are part of the past as this is narrated, hence all are part of history. If the objective is to harmonize Native and Western versions of history, how are these fundamental aspects of Innu history to be accounted for, without reducing them to folkloristic residues and, ultimately, discarding them?

One final divergence should be mentioned here, which involves methods and objectives. If it is true that both versions of history are alike in ultimately attempting to draw on the past to explain the present, they nevertheless offer no basis for comparison in terms of the type of perspective afforded by the relationship to the past and of the instruments by which such perspective is obtained. The methods used in Western history assume that the current situation is the product of past events according to a series of cause-and-effect relationships. For the Innu, yesterday and today stand instead in a relationship of analogy to one another; listening to the story of what happened sometime in the past facilitates an understanding of what is happening today, and, conversely, knowledge of contemporary events provides a firmer grasp of what the Ancestors lived through. In a way, storytellers draw on current events to organize their materials and construct history (Vincent 1978). The same might well be said of written history, but whereas historians search the body of written documents for elements that make it possible to identify the causes of the present situation, Innu storytellers select narratives from the oral tradition that relate situations which are identical to those of today.

What stands out in the example of the Innu – namely, that knowledge and knowledge forms cannot be separated from the context in which they are produced – will come as no surprise. Historians and anthropologists have already stated their positions on the subject. Michel de Certeau, for example, sees the historical operation as the 'relationship between a *place* (a selection process, a milieu, a craft, etc.) and analytical *procedures* (a discipline).' In his view, 'the historical operation refers to the combination of a social *setting* and scientific *practices*' (Certeau 1974, 20). History is 'configurated by the system in which it is worked out': 'Today as yesterday, [history] is determined by the fact of being fabricated locally at this or that particular point within this system. It is only by accounting for its place of production that historiographical knowledge is able to avoid the obliviousness of a class which was ignorant of itself as a class in its relations of production and which, as a result, was ignorant of the society of which it was a part. The articulation of history in connection with a setting is a condition determining the possibility of an analysis of society' (36).

Although de Certeau does not take up the cultural dimension of the construction of history, the setting in which narratives of the past are worked out cannot be exclusively social in nature, but is, of course, cultural as well. As Geertz has observed, it is not possible to understand what others understand without analysing at all places the symbolic forms (words, images, institutions) in terms of which others define their reality themselves (Geertz 1983, 69–70). As Geertz writes, '[anthropology] has always had a keen sense of the dependence of what is seen upon where it is seen from and what it is seen with. To an ethnographer, sorting through the machinery of distant ideas, the shapes of knowledge are always ineluctably local, indivisible from their instruments and their encasements. One may veil this fact with ecumenical rhetoric or blur it with strenuous theory, but one cannot really make it go away' (4). A major obstacle to harmonizing different versions of history thus derives from the fact that all knowledge of the past is the product of various settings that inform the work of historians, who, in order to represent the reality of the past, devise their own methods for better apprehending it, work out their own ways of providing it with some order, and rely on their own symbols for representing it.

Conclusion

Should the incompatibility between these systems of thought be viewed as insurmountable for all that? Because Western constructions of history open on to a world that differs so radically (in terms of their organization, subjects, and concerns) from the Innu representations of the past, does this mean that there is no way of moving from one to the other?

An answer might well lie in the image of the bridge that was developed by Herodotus and explained masterfully by Hartog. If building a bridge is what it takes to establish a passageway between two spaces sharing no common border (Hartog 1980, 76),[4] is there no way of creating one or more bridges between Western and Native versions of history? I believe that I have shown in the first two parts of this text that several such links might be envisaged. However, it is also my opinion that they will settle nothing. As Hartog commented, it was not enough for Darius to create a bridge between Europe and Asia, and another over the Ister (Danube), in order to reach the Scythians, because the latter occupied not only another space, but also a space of another order – that is, one in which the Persian sense of orientation was of absolutely no avail (77, 79). The links suggested at the beginning of this text provide access to fragments of the history of the others, but they do not make it possible to grasp the internal coherence of that history.

In the third part of this text, I have attempted to show that history as told by the Innu is constructed upon principles of relativity, fluidity, and analogy, among other things. Western historians have no way of coming to grips with this type of discourse, nor are they able to get their bearings within it. This is because relativity, fluidity, and the mode of analogy stand in radical contradiction to the way in which Western history establishes its proofs and certainties; as well, the fact that Innu history and Western history do not share the same concerns or instruments entails that they create different universes. History is a space in which each society invents itself according to its own codes. For that reason, Western historians can gain access to Innu history only by leaving aside their own methodological tools and by adopting those used by Innu historians; likewise, Native historians who are trained at universities must don the garb of their Western counterparts. If it is possible for an individual to move from one version of history to another and explain the history of one group to the other, it remains, however, that reconciling versions of history appears to be an impossibility. There is no more compatibility between Native and Western versions of history than there was between a Persian space and a Scythian space.

I would venture another opinion here. Attempts at harmonizing Native and Western versions of history, which are sure to be made at some time or another, can only lead to the end of history as told by Natives. In effect, there is every reason to believe that such efforts would amount to straitjacketing the Native version within the Western conceptual framework, thus automatically depriving it of its contradictions, its luxuriance, its apparent uncertainties, the questions it provides answers to, its modes of explanation, its symbols – in short, its very nature, and with this, its meaning. Once rendered useless as a means for grasping the past, the Native version would either be simply forgotten or would keep only those aspects that are easy to reconcile with Western history (for example, as narratives woven into a foreign framework or chronology, or boxed off in sidebars; in other words, on the margins of works offering 'true' history [see Vincent 1986]). The bridge is not a panacea. It is also an engine of war to which, according to Herodotus and Hartog, the Scythians responded by resorting to nomadism, thus becoming invisible to the Persians. If the Innu were not subjected to the forces of assimilation, they too could use the same strategy to fend off attempts to fit them within a mould via the harmonization of conflicting versions. To do so, they would have to preserve the fluidity and relativity of their narratives, in short, the aspects of their version of history that make it opaque to Western historians. Such an approach would be in keeping with the desire by the Innu to maintain relations and reach agreements with foreigners, but on the condition that doing so does not interfere with their political or cultural autonomy.

By noting this incompatibility, I by no means wish to detract from the urgency of acknowledging the existence of Native versions of history, to grant them credibility, or to do everything possible to understand them – quite to the contrary. It is these very versions that provide much of the substance of the world view of Natives, in particular the representation that they have constructed of themselves and of Canadians and Québécois.

NOTES

1 Data from 1992 and 1993 were collected as part of a project on the notion of history among the Innu that was funded by the Social Sciences and Humanities Research Council of Canada (SSHRC). Thanks to the financial support of Innu organizations (Institut culturel et éducatif montagnais and the Service éducatif de Mamit Innuat) and a donation from Ms I. Paquin, Josephine Bacon and I have done the translation and presentation of narratives and accounts concerning the arrival of the French in the region of Quebec City (about this, see Vincent and Bacon 1992; see also Vincent 1976, 1982, 1991, 2003).

2 Each person has related this history in greater or lesser detail, adding information that the others did not know about or which contradicted the other versions. There was nevertheless a core of information that was common to all accounts (see Vincent and Bacon 1992; Vincent 2003).

3 Girard and Gagné mention that, according to Trigger, 'the Montagnais could count on "their French allies" when winter hunting brought in insufficient game' (Girard and Gagné 1995, 7). However, Trigger did not see in this economic aid the subject of an agreement, but rather an advantage that the Montagnais enjoyed by virtue of the presence of the French at Quebec City (Trigger 1985, 175).

4 I thank Eric Schwimmer for bringing to my attention the passages in this book in which the author explores the difficulty of moving from one's own space to that of another, and for his insightful comments on previous versions of this paper.

REFERENCES

Bernard, J.-P. 1983. *Les Rebellions de 1837–1838*. Montréal: Boréal Express.
Certeau, M. de. 1974. 'L'opération historique.' In J. Le Goff and P. Nora, eds., *Faire de l'histoire, I – Nouveaux problèmes*, 19–68. Paris: Gallimard.

Dickason, O.P. 1993. *Canada's First Nations: A History of Founding Peoples from Earliest Times.* Toronto: McClelland and Stewart.

Geertz, C. 1983. *Local Knowledge: Further Essays in Interpretive Anthropology.* New York: Basic Books.

Girard, C., and É. Gagné. 1995. 'Première alliance interculturelle. Rencontre entre Montagnais et Français à Tadoussac en 1603.' *Recherches amérindiennes au Québec* 25 (3): 3–14.

Groupe de travail sur l'enseignement de l'histoire. 1996. *Se souvenir et devenir. Rapport du groupe de travail sur l'enseignement de l'histoire.* Québec: Gouvernement du Québec, Ministère de l'Éducation.

Hartog, F. 1980. *Le Miroir d'Hérodote. Essai sur la représentation de l'autre.* Paris: Gallimard.

Le Goff, J., and P. Nora. 1974. *Faire de l'histoire.* 3 vols. Paris: Gallimard.

Lévi-Strauss, C. 1962. *La Pensée sauvage.* Paris: Plon.

Morantz, T. 2001. 'Plunder or Harmony? On Merging European and Native Views of Early Contact.' In G. Warkentin and C. Podruchny, eds., *Decentring the Renaissance: Canada and Europe in Multidisciplinary Perspective, 1500–1700,* 48–67. Toronto: University of Toronto Press.

Parent, R. 1985. 'Histoire des Amérindiens du Saint-Maurice jusqu'au Labrador, de la préhistoire à 1760.' PhD diss. Québec: Université Laval.

Savard, R. 1975. 'Des tentes aux maisons à St-Augustin.' *Recherches amérindiennes au Québec* 5 (2): 53–62.

Sulte, B. 1882. *Histoire des Canadiens-français.* Montréal: Wilson.

Trigger, B. 1985. *Natives and Newcomers.* Montreal and Kingston: McGill-Queen's University Press.

Trudel, P. 1987. 'Les Indiens ont-ils peur des Iroquois? Réflexion sur la xénophobie chez les Algonquiens.' *Recherches amérindiennes au Québec* 16 (4): 91–8.

Vaugeois, D. 1996. *Les Hurons de Lorette.* Sillery: Septentrion.

Vaugeois, D., and J. Lacoursière. 1976. *Canada-Québec. Synthèse historique.* Montréal: Éditions du Renouveau pédagogique.

Vincent, S. 1976. 'L'implantation de l'ITT sur la Côte-Nord québécoise à la lumière de quatre siècles d'histoire montagnaise.' *Actes du XLIIe Congrès international des américanistes* V: 303–10. Congrès du Centenaire, 2–9 September 1976, Paris.

– 1978. 'Tradition orale et action politique: le cas de la rivière Natashquan.' In W. Cowan, ed., *Papers of the Ninth Algonquian Conference,* 138–45. Ottawa: Carleton University Press.

– 1982. 'La tradition orale montagnaise. Comment l'interroger?' *Cahiers de*

Clio. Brussels: Centre de la pédagogie de l'histoire et des sciences de l'homme.

– 1986. 'De la nécessité des clôtures. Réflexion libre sur la marginalisation des Amérindiens.' *Anthropologie et sociétés* 10 (2): 75–83.

– 1991. 'La présence des gens du large dans la version montagnaise de l'histoire.' *Anthropologie et sociétés* 15 (1): 125–43.

– 2003. *Le récit de Vepishtikucian, l'arrivée des Français à Québec, selon la tradition orale innue.* Montréal: Société Recherches amérindienne au Québec; Sept-Îles: Institut culturel et éducatif montagnais.

Vincent, S., and J. Bacon. 1992. 'L'arrivée des chercheurs de terres, récits et dires des Montagnais de la Moyenne et de la basse Côte-Nord.' *Recherches amérindiennes au Québec* 22 (2–3): 19–29.

PART III

Non-negotiated Ontologies: Authoring Selves

According to classical political theory, a society is ruled by a single hegemony that uses many techniques, peaceful or violent, to ensure that all members respect that hegemony and its underlying ontology. This objective is not often fully achieved. In modern liberal societies there is usually agreement, informally negotiated, based on a degree of tolerance by the stronger and a degree of compliance by the weaker. One might call this a successful compliance between incompatible ontologies. When this negotiation fails, as in the case of Algonquians analysed here by Samson and Tanner, Indigenous Peoples are subject to what Samson calls 'policing' by 'advisers, helpers and administrators' who lay down ontologically based 'rules' that are not understood and non-negotiable. When they try to comply with these rules, the result is breakdown of the sense of identity, signalled by sharp increases in forms of social deviance, illness, and suicide. Conflict between ontologies thus has practical outcomes.

Tanner's paper describes traditional ways of dealing with various forms of deviance and particularly illness, concentrating on the broad Algonquian concept of illness, which has no exact Western parallel, and collective forms of treatment. He analyses Algonquian healing movements, which operate in an environment far from government-established settlements. The main technique used is withdrawal and the restoration of a sense of identity, reducing the pressure exerted by an alien ontology. Tanner shows that such authoring of new selves, in addition to having religious value, is effective also as a medico-social practice.

Both these papers show that when Algonquians found that no negotiation was possible between the ontology of the White man and their own, their response always took the form of withdrawal. If we take a more global perspective, however, we note (in Part IV of this book) that in some other societies a degree of mutual comprehension of similar ontologies has been achieved and that this has led to the setting up of alternative institutions founded on minority ontologies, without risk to mainstream society.

Chapter Six

'We Live This Experience': Ontological Insecurity and the Colonial Domination of the Innu People of Northern Labrador

COLIN SAMSON

For a minute imagine this ...

You live in a very fine home, with all the comforts to meet your needs. But I move into your home, and I start selling off your furniture and belongings. I receive say 1000$ for the sale and give you 1$. I tell you how you should live in your house. I tell you what you should think about. I tell you how you should feel and respond to things and when you do act I use my values to judge your actions. I tell you that it is now my house. After a while I suggest that maybe we could 'negotiate' some changes to this arrangement but it will remain my house and I am in control.

... We don't have to imagine this, we live this experience.
Daniel Ashini, speaking on behalf of Shinepestis at a court hearing in 1994

The Innu people of Northern Labrador, Canada, *live the experience* articulated by Daniel Ashini. Until they were made subjects of government-sponsored settlement into two communities, Utshimassits (or Davis Inlet) and Sheshatshit, in the 1950s and 1960s, they were nomadic hunters of the forests, river valleys, and tundra of the subarctic. Their way of life was until very recently relatively independent of European influence as a result of the bypassing of Labrador in the westward drive of colonial settlement. Immediately after sedentarization, the land that they had occupied and used for perhaps millennia was appropriated for industrial projects such as hydroelectric plants, logging, mining, and low-level flight training.[1] Under the colonial legal assumption of *terra nullius* and the self-declared sovereignty of the nation state of Canada, Labrador, like other territories, has been 'claimed,' and the land is now used in accordance with the economic aspirations of the settler population of the province of Newfoundland. The state and developers continue to seize the land without any treaty formalities or consent from the Innu. In the villages, the Innu are regulated by alien social institutions and legal constructs that enforce world views that are in many fundamental respects antithetical to those that had made them such successful inhabitants of the Labrador-Quebec peninsula. The tragic experiences of many, if not most, Innu in Utshimassits and Sheshatshit involving mass alcohol consumption, self-destructive behaviour, domestic abuse, and endemic adolescent gasoline sniffing are judged according to the values and social institutions of Euro-Canadian society.

The kind of trauma that Daniel Ashini describes parallels the various social and communicative processes that Laing (Laing 1960; Laing and Esterson 1964) identified as undermining the integrity of the self, and which he believed were crucial to the experience of patients defined as having mental illness. In *Sanity, Madness and the Family*, Laing and Esterson described the environment of many hospitalized mental patients as dominated by a conflict between their own view of themselves and a diametrically opposed view that was being offered and often forced upon them by a parent, psychiatrist, or other authority figure. Many of the patients who were studied were thought to be confined within particularly closed family systems. These existential conflicts, according to Laing and Esterson, then expressed themselves in conduct or 'symptoms' that were taken to be indicative of mental illness. Terming the expression of these tensions 'ontological insecurity,' Laing and Esterson argued that the patients' actions could not be explained outside the broader social network of which each individual was a part.

Similarly, I believe that the well-documented self-destructive acts and tragic events that have befallen the Innu can be seen as an expression of the conflict between their self-perceptions and sensory observations as Innu and the opposing observations made about their character and identity by the Euro-Canadians who now have power over them. This occurs in a social space in which the opportunities for an exit from the authority structure that generates these dynamics are steadily declining. Many of Laing and Esterson's subjects were denied the autonomy and mental and physical space they needed in order to function as sane human beings.

Correspondingly, while the Innu require both individual autonomy and non-industrialized land to express themselves as Innu, articulations of their culture are rapidly squashed through the varied mechanisms of colonial domination, e.g., confiscation of their land, the doctrine of nation-state sovereignty, sedentarization, and forcible exposure to Euro-Canadian culture. Hegemony is maintained over the Innu through the social institutions established by the state under the universal mandate of Canadian law. With the sedentarization of the people, exits from these impositions are gradually being closed off.

Despite the Euro-Canadian perception of social institutions for justice, correction, welfare, health, and education as beneficial,[2] I will argue that they are far from benign and are themselves conduits for highly transparent contradictions that the Innu experience as disorienting and mystifying. These social institutions are portrayed by the state and by their non-Innu (hereafter referred to as *Akaneshau* – literally, 'English speaker') employees as assisting the Innu, yet they are generally experienced as oppressive and repressive.[3] The varying manifestations of these social processes will be described with examples of the Innu-Akaneshau encounter taken from my fieldwork between 1994 and 1997 in the two villages. In this chapter, I will look at a variety of encounters that establish the context for ontologically confusing and psychologically destabilizing processes.

'Die Indians'

John Poker placed a large wooden cross on a hill overlooking the community of Utshimassits. It symbolizes the collective mourning for the tragedy in 1992 when six young children, left alone for an evening, burned to death in a house fire:

> February 14 is usually a day when one gives a loved one a Valentine's present, message or card. But February 14, 1992 is a day the Innu ... will never forget. It marks the death of six innocent children in a house fire. Helplessly the community stood and watched the house burn to the ground. There was no water to put the fire out. Confused about whether or not there was anyone in the house, men went from one house to another to look for the children. Daylight came, and we saw the bones. All day elders, women and children came and examined the ashes, stood around in the freezing cold and cried. (Rich 1995, xiii)

On the first anniversary of the event, six more children, depressed at the deaths of their friends, and intoxicated from sniffing gasoline, barri-

Figure 6.1   Houses in the community of Davis Inlet, as seen from under the hill where John Poker placed a cross. Photograph by Colin Samson.

caded themselves in an unheated shack in temperatures of minus forty degrees Celsius and threatened collective suicide. So disturbed was the local policeman that he videotaped the incident and distributed the tape to the Canadian news media. Such acts of self-destruction – threatened, attempted, and fatal – are common. One-third of all adults in Utshimassits attempted suicide in 1993 (Wilson 1994). Northern Labrador as a whole, which is populated by both Inuit and Innu people, has twice the Native rate and almost five times the national rate of suicide (Wotton 1986, 141). Between 1990 and 1998 there were eight successful suicides in Utshimassits – equivalent to a rate of 178 suicides per 100,000 population, compared to a Canadian rate of 14 per 100,000. Although there are some Native villages, primarily in the Far North, that have recorded higher rates, this is much higher than the already disproportionately high Aboriginal rate in Canada. Whereas Native people in general are two to three times more likely to be victims of suicide, the Innu rate is nine times higher than that for Canada as a whole.[4] Innu are overwhelmingly dying young, with 62 per cent of all deaths in Utshimassits between 1975 and 1995 being of individuals under thirty years of age. Thirty per cent of the total deaths in the two Innu communities were of infants under the age of five, compared to just 2 per cent for other Canadians. Utshimassits has a infant mortality rate that is seven times higher than that for Canada as a whole, while the rate in Sheshatshit is more than three times higher than the national.[5] Further individual and communal suffering from alcohol use, petrol sniffing, marital violence, the destruction of houses, and the vandalism of community supplies is persistently experienced.

Utshimassits was founded as the government settlement of Davis Inlet on Iliukoyak Island in 1968. Close to the former Hudson's Bay Company's Davis Inlet trading post, at the time of the 2003 relocation to the new village of Natuashish (Sango Pond) it numbered about 700. It is accessible only by air for most of the year. The original village consisted of houses, a store, and a supply depot built by the government for 130 Innu, who had previously been forcibly relocated to the Inuit community of Nutak, further to the north, which is treeless and outside of Innu hunting grounds. The annual reports of Ross King, the director of Northern Labrador Affairs in 1966–7 (Roche 1992), make it clear that a decision to omit the basic amenities of running water and sanitation was made in order to save money. Only a handful of Innu houses, but all of the lodgings of non-Innu workers (teachers, the school principal, the social worker, the priest, and, until recently, the Mennonites), have these facilities. Members of the community believe that they had no choice in relocating to Davis Inlet (see Assembly of First Nations 1993; Innu Nation and Mushuau Innu Band Council 1995), and another relocation to the mainland at Natuashish is now complete. Utshimassits has several services and institutions provided by the Euro-Canadian authorities: two stores, a post office, an electrical plant, an airstrip, an alcohol program, a church, a clinic, and a school. In addition, the community contains the political institutions of Innu Nation, which represents all of the Innu sedentarized in Labrador, and the Utshimassits Band Council, which makes policy for the community itself.

Sheshatshit is a community of about 1,200 Innu in central Labrador on the shores of Lake Melville, an inlet from the North Atlantic Ocean, which is 170 miles distant. It differs from Utshimassits not only in size, but also in its proximity to settler communities and to the large air base at Goose Bay and its satellite settler and military communities. Sedentarization started earlier than in Utshimassits and brought together Innu from an array of different groups who would have constantly traversed the Quebec-Labrador border, which was drawn up by the British government in 1927. All houses have electricity, water, and sanitation. It has broadly the same kinds of services and institutions as Utshimassits. Over the last few years, a profusion of institutions, whose only role is to contain the rampant dysfunctions of village life, have been established. Clinics, solvent and alcohol abuse programs, and 'homes' now provide a major source of paid employment for Innu and non-Innu in Sheshatshit.

Although only a few Innu are employed in settler communities (North West River, Happy Valley–Goose Bay), Sheshatshit's closeness to centres of Euro-Canadian population gives it a different cultural dynamic from Utshimassits. Contact with individual Akaneshau and their institutions is more frequent. By making the relatively short journey by car or taxi to Happy Valley–Goose Bay, Innu can go to supermarkets, stores, the hospital, the court, restaurants and sports facilities. The town also has a number of bars and bingo halls that are frequented by residents of Sheshatshit.

Many Innu regard their contacts with the settler communities with ambivalence. On the one hand, they provide entertainment and amenities and a release from the boredom that many experience in the villages. But, on the other hand, Innu are almost universally subjected to racial hostility from the residents of the towns. This often comes to a head in the form of brawls in the Goose Bay bars, but operates perhaps more destructively in subtle acts of racial taunting ranging from stares to jokes. Racist abuse is felt acutely by a handful of Utshimassits Innu who live temporarily in small apartments, known as '2 Cabot,' owned by the band council in Happy Valley. These families reside in the apartments during hospital or court visits or, as is the case with a few individuals, for longer periods of education, training, or night school. In 1996, one of the apartments was seriously damaged by fire, but no one has yet claimed responsibility. George Rich, former vice-president of Innu Nation, occupied one of the apartments for several months that year. During that period he experienced numerous incidents of racial harassment: he and his family were constantly stared at in restaurants; when applying for an advertised apartment, he had been told that the 'vacant' one had recently been rented, but, miraculously, it was still advertised as 'vacant' on subsequent days; when he took his children to the public swimming pool, he overheard the pool attendants joke to each other that the pool would have to be disinfected after the Innu kids swam in it.

Figure 6.2   Graffiti on the North West River side of the bridge connecting this settler community to Sheshatshit. Photograph by Colin Samson.

Sheshatshit is even closer to the settler community of North West River,[6] from which it is separated by a road bridge, and the Innu must go there for their provisions at the store, the post office, and the petrol station. Despite the almost daily contact, there is a distinct lack of communication between the residents of the two communities. Events on one side of the bridge are rarely attended by residents from the other. Sidewalk graffiti proclaiming 'Die Indians' greeted Innu as they traversed the bridge in 1996. In her ethnography of North West River, Plaice (1990) argues that sedentarization has made the Innu and settlers less interdependent. When settlers earned their livelihood from trapping, they necessarily borrowed and learned from the Innu and adopted many Innu customs, hunting techniques, and even clothing. The founding of two separate communities made each group less dependent on the other. Even the bridge, built in 1980, reduced the cooperation needed to travel from one side of the river to the other. While sedentarization accompanied employment in Goose Bay for the North West River settlers, the Innu were left to survive on welfare in Sheshatshit.

Figure 6.3   Richard Rich outside a tent at a gathering site of Mushuau Innu at Kamesteuishikashish. Photograph by Colin Samson.

Since their sedentarization, Innu have retained the ability and capacity to remove themselves from the communities by going to the country (or *nutshimit*) for long periods of time. Because Labrador, as part of Newfoundland, was a British colony until 1949, the Innu and Inuit did not come under the various Indian Acts, which would have made them a 'federal responsibility,' nor did they sign any treaties to relinquish land. Although rights to the land have not been extinguished through such legal contrivances, the land that they use for the exercise of their hunting culture remains sovereign to Canada under the *terra nullius* assumption. Fortunately for the Innu, the vast hunting grounds of the Labrador-Quebec peninsula have not been substantially developed or settled, although encroachments in the form of logging, the damming of rivers, mining, and low-level flying are increasingly made in the face of Innu protests. The *nutshimit* life, then, is currently viable for all Innu who wish to access it and can gain the funds to do so. It is still oriented around principles of sharing, gender equality, anti-authoritarianism, respect for the environment, and personal autonomy that are customary among the Innu (see Henriksen 1973; Leacock 1994; Ashini and Samson 1996).

Figure 6.4   Joseph Remi Rich with a caribou near Sango Bay. Photograph by Colin Samson.

Policing Amnesia

Despite its origin in colonial domination and even with all its problems of suicide, illness, and alcoholism, the village is almost universally taken by Akaneshau as a fait accompli. A tacit assumption is that 'the community,' as it is euphemistically known, is where Innu are now and where they are likely to be for the foreseeable future. These individuals also observe that the Innu now usually experience the country only in short visits. While they may be supportive and positive about *nutshimit*, it is the job of these advisers, helpers, and administrators to assist the Innu in their various traumas and crises in the community and to encourage adaptation to Euro-Canadian norms of personal conduct within it.

This policing occurs through the auspices of institutions such as clinics, schools, courts, and welfare services, all of which were imposed after sedentarization and have no counterpart in Innu history. The Innu never consciously chose to establish such institutions or to be bound by the particular cultural and legal frameworks that they are predicated upon. As the Innu experience in the community proceeds, the fact that this experience and the institutional forces that shape it have been manufactured from outside is ignored or forgotten by the Akaneshau. It becomes normal, a 'reality' that they assume the Innu must orient towards. More importantly, it becomes a 'reality' for the Innu, but one that is transparently false, especially for the older generation who remember permanent nomadic hunting. For these older people, the sedentary community life represents a kind of degeneration, grimly symbolized by the tragedies. As eighty-year-old Tshenish Pasteen told me in 1997, 'in my past, I used to travel, and this way of life was much better than the way Innu Nation and the band council are running the community ... if young leaders were permanent country people and tried to live the way I live, they would catch up.' For many Innu, the community is an artificial order governed by rules that are meaningless or counter to communal and individual well-being. The younger people, traversing between cultures more fluidly, experience it as both real and unreal. Real, in that the law, for example, will apply to their actions and have consequences, as the vast numbers of Innu youth impounded at the Goose Bay Correctional Centre can attest, but unreal in that, to use the same example, this law is often seen as bizarrely judgmental, un-helpful, and capricious by their parents and grandparents.

In many ways, the teams of non-Innu involved directly on a daily basis in the affairs of the two communities encourage an amnesia of a different and separate way of life. In part this is done through the relatively large numerical representation of Akaneshau in positions of authority over the Innu. In Sheshatshit, Akaneshau are the main teachers and administrators of the school, although there are also aides who teach in *Innu-aimun* ('the Innu language') and the first Innu principal was appointed in 2000. The Social Services department is staffed by both Innu and non-Innu, but the chief administrative posts are held by Akaneshau. There are health clinics in Sheshatshit and North West River, but only the aides and translators are Innu. Doctors, nurses, and administrators are Akaneshau. The hospital at Goose Bay caters to a large catchment area that includes both Innu communities as well as coastal settler and Inuit communities and Happy Valley–Goose Bay itself, which has a population of almost nine thousand. In 1995 there was one Innu nurse and one Innu translator at the hospital. In addition, there are also non-Innu carpenters, accountants, environmental advisers, contract researchers, and until recently a Mennonite family. The most crucial legal and political advice is imparted, often through telephones, faxes, and e-mails, to Innu Nation officials from lawyers and anthropologists living in Toronto and St John's. Although there are some notable exceptions, the vast majority of Euro-Canadians involved with the Innu do not live in Sheshatshit, but in the settler communities. Policing of Sheshatshit is done mostly by Royal Canadian Mounted Police officers from outside the community. Until 1996, the Roman Catholic priest operated between the two communities with residences in each. The last priest, a Ghanaian who lived and served in Sheshatshit, departed under accusations of child sexual abuse, thus continuing a trend of abuse by clerics that many Innu recall occurring regularly since sedentarization.

A similar pattern of Akaneshau dominance holds for Utshimassits. Those with positions of administrative and legal power are not Innu. Because Utshimassits is relatively inaccessible for most of the year, non-Innu must also reside in the community. Even with the close proximity of living quarters, the Akaneshau world in Utshimassits is physically and socially set apart from the larger community. Teachers, nurses, and social workers primarily socialize with each other and largely (although, again, there are rare exceptions) refrain from making gratuitous visits or partaking in community activities. They would not have chosen to live in Davis Inlet, and, for the most part, their work supplies their only reason to be there. They exist in the same kind of liminal space as the transient crews on offshore oil rigs. Teachers and nurses receive special 'isolation pay' for working in Utshimassits. These Akaneshau live in segregated and cosseted style. Their dwellings not only are unique in having water and sanitation, but approximate North American suburban households, replete with items that are rare or unknown to the Innu – carpets, new furniture, the latest home entertainment equipment, kitchen gadgets, specially shipped-in dietary and culinary provisions.

There are, of course, some Innu-run services such as the Alcohol Program and Healing Services operated by Innu Nation. These programs, while they may be considered more legitimate by the Innu, lack the authority that the school, the social services, the health services, and the police operate under. This means that it is always possible for communal conflicts, marital disputes, and health and mental health problems to be processed outside of Innu control by a 'higher' authority. Most of the daily affairs of Innu people, then, are controlled and administered, either directly or indirectly, by non-Innu. Innu must appeal to outsiders for welfare payments, legal counsel, child custody, medical assistance, marriage licences, spiritual advice, and education. *Akaneshau* hegemony is sealed in the final sanction of the Canadian law and sovereignty over their land.

However, the Innu loss of autonomy is evidenced most transparently and in some ways superficially by the overload of Akaneshau administrators. As so many commentators on the colonial situation from Fanon onwards have noted, the internalization of the 'master' culture is the most significant cause of cultural and psychological collapse among colonized peoples. Or pushing this idea further, perhaps Taussig (1987, 5) presents a more apt analogy when he depicts the colonial reality as one in which the transforming culture of the conqueror is bound with that of the conquered. In the process, meaning is lost or confused, signs become detached from their referents, and finally, humans become things and things become human. In the communities, the Innu have become things to administer, while the institutions themselves – schools, welfare offices, and, above all else, the law – are infused with human qualities, actions, and intentions.

Self-determination as Alienation

The continuing national and international media attention that the tragedies in Utshimassits attracted (DePalma 1996; DeMont 1999; Farley 2000) has coincided with the articulation of Aboriginal autonomy and self-determination on the part of Canadian governments and their representatives on the ground. It is the Innu people themselves, their band councils, and Innu Nation that are, in their eyes, responsible. Self-determination provides the colonizers with the rebuttal to the view that they are being told how to think, feel, act, and live in the 'house' that Daniel Ashini referred to. The colonial occupation that has transmuted them into things to be administered finds no recognition from Euro-Canadians or their state. In fact, a prevalent view, espoused by both the state and Akaneshau working in the communities, is the opposite – that the Innu are autonomous.

What makes the appeal to Innu liberty possible is the construct of 'self-determination.' The current system of political representation of the Innu through elected officials occupying positions in Innu Nation and the band councils has replaced direct provincial control under the Director of Labradorian Affairs. These new organizations were funded by Canada after sedentarization because, by the 1970s, it was no longer possible to simply take the land for mining, logging projects, and hydroelectric complexes, as the authorities had done in the past. After the 1973 Nisga'a Supreme Court case, which recognized the concept of Aboriginal land rights, various plans for the appropriation and development of land created a need to communicate with Aboriginal people such as the Nisga'a and the Innu who had not signed any treaties ceding land.

In relation to the Innu, this communication has been channelled through Innu Nation and the two band councils. While the band councils and Innu Nation have been creatively adapted by the Innu and officials in them work conscientiously and doggedly for the protection of Innu rights, as institutions, they are culturally and politically part of the machinery of the Canadian state. At a very fundamental level, all of the negotiations that members of these bodies enter into with the federal and provincial governments are conducted in English, the 'master' colonial language, and the proceedings are guided by protocols and laws that are pure creations of the Canadian state.

Thus, the Innu political bodies have been constituted by the Canadian state in such a way that they are vital to the protection of Innu interests *within* that colonial order. As such, they function to divide Innu from one another within and between the various communities – not only the two in Labrador, but the eleven other Innu villages in Quebec, which are dealt with entirely separately. In allowing a more permanent authority than has been customary among the Innu, the artifice of elections generates bitterness between the few political office holders and their families and the many who are largely silent and feel 'spoken for.' Violating the important values of communitarianism, elections produce 'sides.' They are always accompanied by sessions of heavy drinking, which further aggravate the artificial divisions. Some families deliberately vacate the community by setting up camp several miles away in order to avoid the trouble that occurs around polling day. The posts of 'chief,' 'president,' and the like further reinforce differences of status and material wealth that were cultivated by earlier generations of missionaries, colonial administrators, and traders. In so doing, the fundamental values attached to personal autonomy, nonjudgmentalism, and communitarianism that were so vital to the pre-settlement Innu have been eroded. Although these values are certainly part of contemporary Innu life, the existence of authoritative offices means that the Innu must violate their own principles and provoke hostilities among themselves in order to communicate and negotiate with the federal and provincial governments of Canada.

As these institutions are the only officially recognized outlets for the expression of the wishes of the Innu concerning the most fundamental questions of their land, and hence identity, they necessarily place the Innu in an ontologically insecure position. For example, in relation to the process that has followed from the Nisga'a case, namely, comprehensive land claims negotiations, the Canadian state will only allow the Innu to channel their strategies for the struggle to retain their land, the exercise of their rights, and the articulation of their goals and aspirations through an institution that, while staffed by Innu, is a creature of the colonial process. The Innu response to government plans for their land and communities, and, hence, any notion of 'consent,' is arrived at through alien instruments such as elections, referenda, and research projects, often directed and formulated by Akaneshau advisers.

It is as if, for example, the people of a particular European municipality could only express their opposition to a motorway being built through the historically important city centre containing, say, a medieval cathedral by voicing their concerns in a language outside the Indo-European family. The metamorphosed voices would then be diverted through an association financed and regulated by the company building the motorway. To be more precisely analogous, the association would have to submit to company laws at variance with the most cherished beliefs of the people of the community – in this case, that cathedrals were of no consequence whatsoever, perhaps even 'primitive.' Finally, the issue of the motorway would have to be only one among many such battles that the community would have to face in this way.

Let us look at just one example of such processes. In 1994, commercially significant deposits of nickel were 'discovered' about seventy-five kilometres north of Utshimassits at Voisey's Bay[7] – known to the Innu as Emish – and the area has now become the focus of a multi-billion dollar international mining operation. Emish is prime hunting and fishing territory and rich in cultural and personal associations. Several Davis Inlet people were born in the area, and many of their relatives are buried there. In February 1995, Innu Nation served an eviction notice on Archean Resources and Diamond Fields, two of the companies involved in establishing the mine, and Innu then protested at the site, but preparations for mining continued unchecked.

As well as being concerned about the devastating cultural impact of this development – it would draw young people into the wage economy, it would encourage drinking, it would subject the Innu to racist abuse – many Innu believe that mining will adulterate the land and water with toxins, destroying the habitats of the animals. Without a clean environment the animals will not be able to reproduce, and without the animals, the hunting life of the Innu and the rich culture based on it will be destroyed.

Innu Nation has fought a lone battle against the mining development. Not only must Innu people within it do this through authority structures, hierarchies, and institutions that until very recently were completely alien to them, but they must also subject themselves to Laingian 'double binds' and 'switched meanings.' Thus, although Canadian authorities recognize prior Innu 'claims' to the land, state this to the Innu leaders, and act accordingly by participating in the Comprehensive Land Claims negotiations with the Innu leadership, they simultaneously encourage the sale of land that they are ostensibly negotiating with the Innu over. This is how the land at Emish came to be in the possession of mining companies. The Innu leaders are persistently faced with dealings with officials from the province of Newfoundland who state clearly their 'good faith' and, according to Daniel Ashini, 'act as if they are listening to our concerns over the land,' but then do the opposite by condoning its sale to mining companies and prospectors. After 'discoveries' such as that at Emish, the federal government subjects proposed developments to an environmental impact assessment (EIA). This is mediated by a review panel that exposes proposals to social and natural scientific scrutiny as a prerequisite to final permission being granted for a project to go ahead. The actual environmental review is funded by the 'proponent,' the mining company, and, again, it is a procedure that is created by the Canadian state and incorporates the values and assumptions of that state. Most fundamentally, it presumes that Canada has the right to adjudicate over all of the land, including land that it has not settled claims for. In fact, the guidelines for the environmental impact statement, which were approved in June 1997, specifically rule out any connection between the outstanding land claims and the development of the mine. Furthermore, the EIA embodies a Western scientific approach to the environment. 'Resources' are constituted as being detachable, quantifiable, measurable, and capable of valuation in monetary terms. This is not how the Innu or most other Indigenous people in North America would look at the land. The land and animals are not separate from the people and, as Notzke (1994, 277) points out, provide the major integrative social force of many Native people. What leaders like Daniel Ashini are faced with, then, is a state that claims to be respecting their Aboriginal rights and title to the land, but at the same time invalidates any consideration of such rights when they happen to correspond with the site of a 'discovery' that is now a major commercial interest.

What are the leaders to believe about the sincerity of the Canadian state? What are they to communicate to the people in the communities? In what ways are they determining their own future if they can only do so through highly prescribed procedures that are contradicted and undermined to their detriment by other procedures? How can an 'Innu view' be ascertained and communicated? How can people who are traumatized, living in a kind of perpetual torment, provide consent to anything?[8] Are dealings with the Canadian state so duplicitous that they should pull out, as many Innu believe? Double binds are everywhere. If they refuse to participate then they risk being ignored by the state and industrialists, but when they do participate they are drawn into a confused and confusing process that is fraudulent and ultimately validates Canada's supreme rights to their land through the alleged 'self-determination' of the Innu. In essence, Aboriginal self-determination refers to the ability of Aboriginal people to negotiate within the colonizer's protocol, a future outcome overwhelmingly favourable to the colonial antagonist. The alternative offered by the state is to lose everything.

'Through the Innu People'

It is not just the statements and actions of the Canadian state that operate to spread obfuscation and ontological confusion. These processes are mirrored on the ground within the imposed Euro-Canadian institutions in Utshimassits and Sheshatshit. The non-Innu authorities in the various services who I interviewed often argued that their role was limited to that of facilitators of Innu goals and ambitions. A health service administrator used the metaphor of a vehicle for the role of his services. The Innu could either occupy the front or back seat, but progress on dealing with health problems depended on the Innu themselves. A public health nurse portrayed the Innu culture as one that was 'evolving' and changing as a consequence of the active choices of the Innu themselves.

Others, a priest and a judge, for instance, also used evolutionary metaphors to explain that even if the settlement way of life was not directly chosen by the Innu, its inception would inevitably lead the Innu to prefer what they deemed the more comfortable Euro-Canadian existence. Once they 'get the taste of pop and chips,' the priest in Utshimassits believed, they could only proceed to a different form of society – 'a culture cannot go back.' Importantly, these evolutionary statements, so condescending that they would have never been spoken to an Innu person, are themselves completely mystifying. Akaneshau situate the Innu within a historical process that is conceded to be imposed, yet construed as having an inevitable logic – assimilation is something that would have happened anyway once they got the 'taste' of Euro-American consumer products. Surely what must be most confusing to the Innu is the idea that settlement, which they have experienced to be largely forced and traumatic, is, after the fact, depicted by authority figures as something that they really have no choice in going along with because it is part of an abstract historical process called 'evolution.'

The following incident at the social services office in 1995 illustrates how ontological insecurity of this nature is produced in everyday interaction. Social services is one of several purpose-built institutions in Sheshatshit. The only reception room is cramped and fitted with uncomfortable bench-style seats. Many Innu clients stand outside smoking, waiting, and chatting. A plexiglass barrier separates clients from office workers. Only one trained social worker, the director, an Akaneshau, is on the staff. She states that she acts only in accordance with the wishes of the Innu. Decisions are made by the Innu themselves. All the solutions to the problems brought to her attention are 'through the Innu people.' It is really the Innu workers that I should be speaking to. One Innu assistant is asked to sit with us in the office and many questions are deferred to her. Despite the claim to Innu autonomy, during the course of our conversations, several Innu workers entered the room to seek the administrator's permission or signature for various courses of action, such as authority to grant welfare payments to certain Innu applicants. The Innu, then, were being represented as autonomous, but that imputed autonomy was being exercised, in their presence, not by them, but by the Akaneshau director. Important decisions required the director's signature or permission. In the Laingian sense, a process of mystification was being inflicted: 'The attribution of autonomy to someone who clearly is completely alienated from her autonomous self, by the persons who are perpetuating this alienation, albeit unwittingly, is surely most mystifying' (Laing and Esterson 1964, 186). Autonomy was being attributed to people who could act independently only in the most superficial sense – as messengers between the Akaneshau power structure of the office and the Innu clients. Mystification is routine institutional practice and, as we saw, is a component of the larger process of 'self-determination.'

One of the most important, and controversial, areas that social services regulates is child protection, including child sexual abuse. Significantly, this sensitive area is the sole domain of the province (Shewell and Spagnut 1995, 24). A relatively large number of local men and women have either confessed to abusive acts or been charged with abuse. As a statutory service, the social services department is bound by particular tenets of Canadian law, most pertinently the Child Welfare Act, which conveys powers to social workers to remove children from their families.[9] Any case of abuse brought to their attention must, by law, be reported to the police, and the alleged abuser must face court proceedings. Social services personnel believe that this ensures that the child is protected and the abuser is held accountable. While this may be true, it is also the case that Innu are being held answerable to non-Innu systems of justice, involving a conflictual style of resolution that is ultimately adjudicated by non-Innu. Such a system contradicts the consensual and non-hierarchical methods of conflict resolution favoured by the Innu. Furthermore, according to many Innu it inhibits individuals from dealing with their distress in a less punitive and more communal manner. Social services, then, compel the Innu to accommodate an alien method of dealing with their most intimate problems that is then passed off to them as being 'through the Innu people.'

The Nurse's Story

The fact that Akaneshau are absorbed in the most confidential aspects of the lives of the Innu is just as apparent in the health services. Even though no detailed comparative statistics are kept either in Sheshatshit, Utshimassits, at the hospital in Goose Bay, at the health department in St John's, or with Health Canada in Ottawa, it is obvious to health workers that the Innu have chronic health and mental health difficulties that are massively disproportionate to health patterns in other parts of Canada. Infant deaths, alcohol-related deaths, and suicides all occur with alarming frequency. Doctors and nurses report that diabetes, heart conditions, respiratory conditions, skin diseases, alcoholism, and accidents are also common. Many ailments occur at younger ages than are usually found in other Canadian populations.

Although the unwholesome mixture of inadequate and non-existent sanitation in overcrowded houses, and community stores that almost exclusively stock junk food, is acknowledged when discussing the health of the Innu, health workers focus on the lack or loss of control of individual Innu over their well-being. Almost all health workers are critical of the Innu diet. They point out that unhealthy fare consisting of quantities of pop, chips, candy, and canned and processed foods – signs of inevitable progress for the priest quoted above – are what most consume. Meals are irregular and even more so when parents have been drinking. School teachers complain that children are hyperactive, hungry, and ill prepared for their day at school because of inadequate or inappropriate food. Nurses and doctors additionally point to the role of poor hygiene and dirt.

The underlying causes of these health problems are commonly located in the ignorance of the Innu, their inability or unwillingness to teach their children basic safety requirements, their lack of coping skills, their aversion to washing, and their sexual promiscuity. Physicians and nurses routinely spoke of 'non-compliance' with drug, dietary, and exercise regimes advised for diabetics and other sufferers of long-term illnesses. In 1994 the two nurses running the Utshimassits clinic emphasized the intractability of the Innu themselves. Here is the account of one of them, quoted at length, mostly verbatim and unprompted:

Mothers are not able to look after their babies. They don't know how to keep the bottles clean and they feed babies while their hands are dirty. They do not teach their children how to be clean. But this does not worry them because they expect to get medicine at the clinic and will return time and time again. Innu houses are not well ventilated. Inside you sometimes find all burners on the stove on full blast and the kids put their hands on it. Mothers do not have even a basic knowledge of safety. Kids play everywhere, even on top of roofs. They jump off and the parents do not say anything. In the cold, kids play outside without shirts and shoes. They have no idea of nutrition and give greasy pork, which has a high fat content, to babies. Kids eat irregularly and consume a lot of junk food. Sexually transmitted diseases are common, especially chlamydia, because they start sex very young – as young as eight. The kids go to the top of the hill and sniff gas until very late.

They do not have strong coping skills. They want to take pills over the smallest things. There are many overdoses over trivial issues such as 'someone said something about me.' They are all like kids, but they don't know how to cope. They have no control of the children. Kids can do anything they want. Liberation starts from the age of one. Even the police don't do anything about gas sniffing. There is a twelve-year-old girl who has attempted suicide three times. Once with a gunshot wound through her arm near the carotid artery. She did it because her father was sleeping with someone else and she was addicted to gas sniffing. But everyone gives support. We sent her to Goose Bay.

Parents lie too much to get a free flight to Goose Bay. They say they are sick. The midwives say they have no pain when they have babies. They say they don't want to die, so I think they are asking for help. Often the parents are drinking all night and there is no food. They don't teach young people to cook. In the day they are sleeping. They don't have any values for the children. The government gives them too much.

In my country [in Latin America], people don't have money but they are clean. Bathtubs are available here and are in use all day, but it is only some people who use them sporadically. In my country, children have rules. Here, parents don't control the children. They don't believe in punishment. This happened with the fire [mentioned above, in which six children died; the Innu oppose the prosecution of the parents for manslaughter]. Tents are better than houses. They are more comfortable and not as dirty. The boughs are changed every week. They are okay for the elderly, but not for those who have been here twenty years. They've had white people to teach them, but still they're dirty. It can't be 'identity' for young people. They have to blame someone.

Winter is better. They melt the snow and wash with it. They seem very disorganized to us. I teach them. Then they come back dirty and I have to teach them slowly. Self-help is a good thing. We will have a pajama party and teach the children about sex. We will teach the young mothers simple things that mothers do all over the world. The kids eat everything, even money.

Grown men come to see us even for small cuts. They want antibiotics for everything. Skin diseases, scabies, lice, eczema, these are all hygiene related. We are going to start going to houses with social services and the alcohol program – if they allow us – to teach them how to clean the house. There is garbage everywhere. Kids and dogs play in it. I recently saw a kid with a bleach bottle, drinking water from the ditch.

Children don't speak any English. We have very good personal care assistants who are Innu. There has been some success. Some are clean now. They're like mad cows. They destroy everything in sight. Work is very tiring. We are always on call – every second night. Often we work all night. On the phone, they blame you if you don't come. John Poker refused to take medication for his stroke and high blood pressure. He had a stroke in the country and they couldn't get the chopper in there very quickly. The chief swore at me for not getting it there sooner. They blame nurses for everything. It was John Poker's choice not to take medication. Maybe now he is happy [he died three days earlier]. They want medication for everything. Kids say the whites teach them to sniff gasoline, but sometimes parents also do it, as well as alcohol.

We don't have any time off at all. Even at home they knock on the door or phone. They are very dependent. They cannot do anything for themselves. We had a call on Sunday night for condoms, trying us out. They want everything free. The move to Sango Bay will be the same as Davis Inlet if they don't change. That's bad because this is a beautiful place. We get frustrated. It's like talking to the air. They don't appreciate anything.

The nurses' job is not enviable. It is tiring, thankless, exasperating, and ultimately Sisyphean. The Innu spectacle, the undifferentiated 'they' of the narration that would never be delivered to them, is at once horrifying, chaotic, and anomic. Life is precarious, unhappy, and yet carried out with a kind of wilful abandon. Death is never far away. Dirt is everywhere. Their sickness is of their own making, yet they blame the nurses. Any hint of wider influences on their poor health – the change from living in tents to houses, for example – is quickly banished before it can be considered. They never strike the correct balance – John Poker died because of his refusal of medication, yet they all crave medication for the most trivial complaints; they are recklessly dependent and childish, yet they are demanding of their entitlements at the clinic and elsewhere.

The nurses' story does not concern itself with the recent sedentarization of the Innu or with the courageous efforts to save the Innu way of life or the drastic loss of purpose and occupation in the community or the political and cultural domination of the Canadian state. Like many other accounts that I collected, such factors are at best fragments of history that are now largely inconsequential. This is likewise mystifying, given that expressions of collective alienation from the imposed way of life are observable to even the most casual visitor in the communities and are articulated powerfully by the Innu. Yet, this alienation appears to most Akaneshau only as a kind of unspecified, yet discomforting, presence. The Innu articulations of displacement and pain are reconfigured as evidence of their own weakness and ultimately their complicity in the sicknesses that plague them. As we shall see in the next section, while the Innu largely perceive health in a sociological and political frame and clearly see illness in the context of their own dispossession – what could be a clearer symbol of loss than Daniel Ashini's 'house'? – such perceptions are invalidated under a deluge of blame attributed to them, individually and personally.

'He Will Blame Us'

The diseases confronting physicians at the end of the twentieth century are increasingly long-term chronic illnesses, and this pattern implies the need for a sociological understanding of the context of disease and its management (see Turner 1995, 8). At the same time, the dominant biological orientation in Western medicine still relies heavily on individualized treatments that assume the model of the body as machine. This incongruity, a form of mystification itself, is particularly evident in relation to diabetes, a common disease among the Innu. Even though epidemiologists recognize that 'diabetes is a new disease among Indian people and is the consequence of drastic lifestyle and cultural changes that have occurred since World War II' (Joe and Young 1994, 7–8), there is a tendency on the part of medical practitioners, including those ministering to the Innu, to argue that the disproportionately high rates of diabetes among contemporary Native North Americans suggests that a strong genetic factor predisposes them to the disease (see Brosseau 1994, 47; Jackson 1994, 393–4). Curiously, while genetic influences on diabetes among Native people are stated as fact, it is admitted in relation to the 'thrifty gene' hypothesis upon which this depends that 'it remains unclear in what ways the hypothesis applies to American Indians' (Jackson 1994, 394). When Native North Americans across the continent have been divested of their land and made subject to greatly altered lifestyles that are sedentary and have had their diets drastically changed away from fresh game, agricultural produce, and wild berries and towards mass-produced and inexpensive junk foods that are known to be unhealthy and implicated in diabetes, it is remarkably obfuscating that the research agenda privileges genetic explanations.[10]

Although diabetes was not known to Innu raised in the country, local health professionals maintain that the disease may be genetically inherited and then exacerbated by dietary patterns.[11] In other words, the problem may originate in both the biological make-up and the behaviour of the Innu sufferer. Such a belief has the effect of stopping the search for broader causes and fails to address the social circumstances within which disease and illness develop and recur. This is the case, even though it is well known that the nomadic hunting life, by contrast with settlement life, provides a diet far superior in basic vitamins and nutrients than what can be procured from community food stores (Mackie 1987) and the exercise necessary for survival keeps people in good physical condition. To venture into this terrain, however, is perceived as 'political' or beyond the remit of professionals.[12]

Clinicians situate diabetes and other illnesses within the context of the community, which is uncritically accepted as the essential social reference point for the Innu. Illness is not dealt with as a collective problem of sedentarization. Job descriptions, professional codes, and training would prohibit Akaneshau from acting upon such a notion, even though some may recognize sedentarization to be heavily implicated. It is not for them as professionals to campaign either for the improvement of village conditions or the assertion of Innu land rights, which would enable more concerted and confident expeditions to the country. Rather, their role, apart from attending to medical emergencies, is to impart advice to individual Innu in the situations in which they find themselves. It is up to the Innu, given such a structure placed upon the interpretation of their ailments, to reframe their problems in such a way that they can be remedied by swift and literal adherence to the advice of the professionals. This is what is meant by 'compliance.'

These approaches to health are directly contrary to Innu beliefs about well-being. For almost all Innu, health is synonymous with *nutshimit*. The hunting life is active, vigorous, and, perhaps most importantly, spiritual. Success in hunting as in many other matters is connected to observances of respect for the animals and humility to the land. The single most important determinant in the success of a hunt is how respectful one has been to the animals, rather than solely on the skill of the hunter or the nature of his equipment. Hunting is governed by the powerful Animal Gods, who determine which animals will let the hunter kill them. Respect for animals may be demonstrated in many ways – by killing only what is needed, eating and using as much of the animal as possible, properly discarding anything that is not used, and sharing what is killed.

A successful hunt for caribou is often followed by a *mukushan* feast, in which all of the leg bones of the animals are carefully cleaned of meat and the marrow removed. All of the animal is eventually used and any waste product is either burned or put up on a scaffold to keep away from dogs. The crushed leg bones are then boiled, causing the fat to rise to the top. The fat is left to congeal or harden in a separate container and eaten with bread and meat by members of the camp. This occasion serves to show the Animal Gods the respect that they are accorded by the Innu through their careful use of all of the animal. When food was scarce or individuals fell ill, events such as the *kushapashikan* (shaking tent) were enacted in order to affirm the fundamental relationship between the vitality of the Innu and respect for the Animal Masters.

Andrew and Sarsfield (1984) draw attention to the profoundly *political* nature of Innu conceptions of health and illness. The Innu are reluctant to separate their personal health from the wider ecology. If the social life is altered and the physical environment adulterated, then it should be expected that people will suffer in many different ways. It is painful, but not surprising, to the Innu that there have been so many premature fatalities from alcohol, disease, and accidents in the communities. If *nutshimit* is seen as synonymous with health, the community is, for many Innu, the site of collective sickness. Upon returning from the country, people suddenly abandon the strong spirit of sharing and cooperation. The community becomes the context for drinking, quarrelling, and suicide.

The food available in the communities is vastly inferior to that available in the country. The movement in the 1980s of many Innu in Sheshatshit to spend as much as seven months of each year in the country improved health markedly – '[a]lcohol abuse suddenly stops. A combination of improved diet, a rigorous lifestyle and the stable emotional and social environment offered by a functioning Innu society, make for a startling contrast to life in the villages' (Andrew and Sarsfield 1984, 429). Paul Pone, a young Innu man, told me that 'my self, my identity, my own religion is in the country. I go to my own school there. There are medicines there that I know about. Out there I am a worker, a hunter, a fisherman, an environmentalist, and a biologist.'

The Innu view of health is at once spiritual in its insistence on the connections between respect for the Animal Gods and personal well-being, and political in its essential linkage of the imposed community with illness. By contrast Western medicine is intensely secular and, in a mystifying way, apolitical. Illness is thought to result principally from specific physical pathology, and an indifference is sustained towards the dramatic environmental changes that have been forced upon the Innu and many other similarly situated peoples.

One illustration of the contrasts between the two views of health can be gathered from the reactions of the Innu in the two communities to the development of their land. Logging, mining, and low-level flying, they maintain, alter and pollute the land, rivers, lakes, and sea in such a way that animals, necessary to their physical and spiritual life, die or do not reproduce naturally. In turn, this effects the ability of the Innu to live a healthy life. The focus on ecology as an important aspect of well-being transcends, in its ever wider span, even the broad public-health theories of Western medicine and environmentalism.[13] The differences between the two sets of health beliefs, and even in how categories are constructed, is expressed in this remarkable statement by Edward Piwas of Utshimassits, who here discusses the imposition of the opencast nickel mine at Emish, mentioned above:

There will be no fish, caribou, ducks, geese at Emish after the mining starts. The bear is different. The bear is like the whiteman, but he can't live with them in winter. He will walk around in the Emish camp. He will eat at the whiteman's table because the *Akaneshau* has killed the fish in the river. The white people will keep the baby animals for pets and these animals will starve – they will not know how to hunt for themselves ... Even the moose – he is the brother of the *Akaneshau*. He will walk on the streets of Emish with a tie. The *Akaneshau* has three friends – bear, moose and raven, but he can't be friends with the squirrel because it steals from them. The smog from the milling plant will kill the plants and animals. And it will float into our community. We will not see the smog – it will slowly kill the animals and us. They will probably not just drill in one place – they will drill all around us. The wildlife officer will know when he can't find any animals. *He will blame us* for the lack of them but he will not think about the drilling. (Innu Nation 1996, 38; emphasis added)

The Akaneshau tames and controls wild nature to the extent that the contamination will 'kill the animals and us.' Even the moose will be so domesticated that it will walk along the streets of the mining town sporting a tie. Nature and the human vitality that depends on it will die. In the process, the Euro-Canadians, Edward Piwas believes, will blame the Innu.

Here we can see the anticipation of a process of mystification. Edward Piwas states that the Akaneshau will pollute the land through the mining operation to the extent that the animals will die off. While they are perpetrating this contamination, they will impute autonomy, and hence blame, for any adverse environmental effects to the Innu, who will have been prevented from practising their hunting culture by the mere presence of the mine. By extension, this places the Innu in an ontologically insecure position. What they see with their own eyes in the country around Emish, such as pollution and changes in animal behaviour, will be systematically contradicted by the representations of those Euro-Canadians exercising control over them and their land. Such obfuscation is what many Innu have come to expect of the Canadian authorities. In the 1995 hearings on the environmental impact of low-level flying over Innu territories from the Goose Bay airbase, scientific research contradicted the direct observations of Innu hunters. Biologists' reports that the caribou and other wildlife were actually increasing in number despite low-level flying took precedence over the actual experience of hunters, who witnessed decreases in the number of caribou, diseased caribou, and unexplained animal behaviour. At the same time that these authoritative reports were issued, a concerted campaign was conducted by Labrador settlers and the business-controlled local media to portray Innu hunting as a threat to the environment.

A Spiritual Healing Journey

The problem of alcohol abuse is one that Innu have directly confronted, beginning with the move to intermittent and sometimes long-term sobriety by some of the young leaders in the mid-1980s. Because alcohol abuse and gas sniffing have precipitated tragic acts of violence, abuse, and self-harm in Sheshatshit and Utshimassits, alcohol programs have been established in both communities. On-site counselling is provided and individual clients can be funded to go out of the community for up to six months to treatment programs throughout Canada. A pan-Native therapeutic organization, the Nechi Institute from Alberta, has also established both training and treatment for Innu, and has been funded to run mobile treatment programs in the country. Most, if not all, of those who work for the alcohol program are Nechi trained.

Over the last few years, Nechi (as well as other treatment and training programs) has exerted an increasing influence in the communities, and Innu themselves have gone to Alberta for treatment and training. While many people in both communities testify to having quit alcohol through using Nechi techniques, others believe that Nechi trainees who relapse are more severely affected than they were before training. Some of the older Innu believe that Nechi is an unhelpful presence and, like other non-Innu institutions, also imposes particular interpretations and frames of reference that are contrary to, and undermine traditional Innu practices. The use of the sweat lodge as a therapeutic device in the village, for example, differs significantly from the Innu custom of reserving sweat lodges for medicinal and spiritual purposes, and only in the country. Sweat lodges are now being set up in the village for psychological 'healing' through prescribed rules that have little relation to Innu beliefs and practices. Similarly, other icons of pan-Indian identity, such as the dreamcatchers that now festoon the houses of many Nechi graduates, are imports that bear no relation to Innu cosmology.

Nechi was established by Native people in 1974 and developed primarily in the province of Alberta. It has since grown and provides a range of services to native communities across Canada and even abroad. While the philosophy of Nechi recognizes what it calls 'cultural oppression' and urges its clients to understand their own problems in terms of the history of colonial domination, its main focus is clearly psychological and medical. A Nechi pamphlet on adult children of alcoholics gives a flavour of this:

Today in our healing from the effects of alcoholism and other painful ways of living, we are re-discovering that what we are doing is a spiritual healing journey to be shared for the recovery of all our relations. In this century we have gradually come to know much about alcoholism and its effects. Medical research has shown that alcoholism is a disease with recognized symptoms and named progression. Consequently, we now know a great deal about how this disease can physically destroy people. Psychology has brought insights to the emotional pain resulting from alcohol ... This movement [Adult Children of Alcoholics] is guided by two spiritual principles: self-empowerment and mutual aid. Self-empowerment means that each person has the ability, as well as the basic human right, to direct their own life. Mutual aid states that people have the ability to help each other to grow and to heal. (White n.d., 1)

What we see in this passage (and other elements of Nechi literature could be produced to similar effect) is a particular framing of alcohol and other problems. Like the theories of the bulk of non-Native medical and psychiatric services, as well as Alcoholics Anonymous, these problems are depicted by the Nechi literature as 'diseases.' Following medical approaches, Nechi promotes the idea of treatment for the disease, although the prescription is described here as a 'spiritual healing journey.' Embarking upon this journey is the first step towards recovery. According to Nechi, recovery is a process that involves practical exercises, mastery of handout information, and self-disclosure and confession in order to unblock the pain that lies underneath the substance abuse. Denial, or the inability to freely disclose past and present anguish, pain, and abuse, is considered one of the cardinal traits of members of alcoholic and other 'dysfunctional' families. Many of the handouts require memorization of key terms and definitions and stipulate particular learning and behavioural outcomes, the most important of which is permanent sobriety. Nechi claims high success rates, including the fact that after training specified percentages of its graduates returned to school, increased their income, held program management positions, improved their family life, and strengthened their identity as Native people. These claims, however, assume both a certain degree of assimilation and a structure of opportunities that largely do not apply to the Innu.

Although it has greater legitimacy as an invited rather than an imposed institution, Nechi proposes certain solutions to personal problems of the Innu that derive from discourses of Euro-American popular science and the decontextualized beliefs and practices of more assimi-lated Native people from Western and Central Canada. The notion that treatment for alcoholism somehow relates to pan-Native experience in Canada, yet at the same time the condition is a disease to which every-one is susceptible, conveys a particularly *external* frame of reference to the personal trauma of the Innu. In doing so, it shares a pervasive urban bias with other health, welfare, and drug and alcohol programs operat-ing in rural areas (see Dorn and South 1985). Like other institutions, Nechi provides both the diagnosis and the treatment. Whether or not it is successful for particular Innu (and there is much to suggest that it is for some), Innu remain as clients.

The Nechi literature, although providing a pan-Native historical sweep of oppression, skims over Innu history. In its emphasis on its clients' sobriety, it ignores the role of alcohol in Innu history. Alcohol has long been known to the Innu. William Duncan Strong (see Leacock and Rothschild 1994) in the diaries of his 1927–8 ethnographic visit reports that drinking spruce beer and home brew occurred especially in order to celebrate a big kill. He records no particular adverse effects other than mild chaos. Speck (1977, 92) observed that after particular dreams, hunters would drink whisky to give their soul-spirits a libation to pay for the revelation of a caribou by a river and to induce its fulfilment. Similarly, Henriksen (1973) argues that Innu used alcohol not only to celebrate but, along with drumming, singing, and dancing, to commu-nicate with the Animal Gods. In the early sedentarization phase, alco-hol, along with shamanism and the shaking tent (or *kushapashikan*), was suppressed by the church, and as Henriksen puts it, 'the people were thereby deprived of some of their crucial means to obtain spiritual power' (8–9). Alcohol becomes sin and is stigmatized. Although the Nechi disease theory does not use the word 'sin,' alcohol use is clearly represented as an individual failing.

Although alcohol is sometimes consumed in the country, binge drink-ing and daily drunkenness are primarily associated with village life. Importantly, drinking occurs, then, when the means by which Innu can enact celebratory rituals and interpret dreams connected with the hunt-ing culture has been severely compromised. The meaning of drinking has radically changed. People now drink in separation from the objects of celebration and the activities associated with them. Heavy drinking takes place against a background of chronic boredom, loss of purpose, forced acculturation, and extreme material poverty. While these points may be acknowledged by Nechi and other treatment programs, the programs themselves assume the primacy of psychological causes. By the same token, healing for these ills is attempted largely outside the Innu milieu, particularly that of hunting in the country. This applies to Nechi and obviously to the treatment programs to which the alcohol program makes referrals, and which are often thousands of miles away.

The cultural legitimacy of these programs is reduced still further when we consider that they are supported by Innu Nation only in an indirect way. The funding is provided by Health and Welfare Canada; Innu Nation serves merely as a conduit. Similarly, referrals to Nechi and other alcohol treatment centres far away from Labrador is often made not by the Innu themselves, but as a condition of the sentences of many people in the courts that now claim jurisdiction over the Innu.[14]

The fact remains, though, that despite the efforts of Nechi and the ongoing destruction caused by alcohol, many Innu continuously drink. In the face of this, it is difficult to conceive of alcohol as anything other than a *social* problem.[15] Drinking may be a normal reaction to the extraordinary circumstance in which one perceives a loss of control over one's life and future. In *The Divided Self,* Laing identified a similar situation when he reinterpreted Emil Kraepelin's famous case study of a patient who showed signs of catatonic excitement. After describing the objectification of the patient in the case presentation in a medical lecture hall, Laing offers an understanding of why the patient may have said and done what he did in view of what could be seen as a public humiliation at the hands of Kraepelin. Laing's (1960, 31) conclusion is that '[o]ne may see his behaviour as "signs" of a "disease"; one may see his behaviour as expressive of his existence.' I am arguing here that alcohol is expressive of Innu existence. Attempts to control or banish it through popular psychological theories and techniques potentially in-crease levels of alienation. What the Innu know through their everyday experience – that alcohol occurs in the context of utter domination – is denied and projected as a politically neutral psychological trait. This increases the distance between what is perceived as reality by indi-vidual Innu and what is represented as reality by those who have decision-making powers over their lives. In relation to alcohol and their most troubling experiences, the Innu live in a perpetual space of onto-logical insecurity.

Conclusion

The distinctly non-Innu exigencies of the sedentary life continually burden the Innu. Etienne Pone, an Innu Department of Fisheries worker, helped put this in perspective. It was his job to check the nets of Innu fishermen, ask them how many fish they had caught, and, if necessary, take action against those violating the regulations on catches. The uniform that he was told to wear he likens to a mask. He felt like the scout in the cowboy and Indian films. The government tells him that he is working *for* Innu people, but what he is being told to do cannot be reconciled with the Innu use of fish as a summertime staple. Every government program, he is told, is for *their* improvement, yet the evidence of his own senses tells him this is not the case. And for him it is because of processes like this that Innu are under stress, and why many kids sniff gasoline, others drink, and so many try to harm themselves. Innu are trying to come to grips with these tragedies, then, while wearing masks that fundamentally distort what they see.

Innu, as Etienne Pone pointed out, are told that the involvement of Akaneshau is for their improvement. In the context of the two communities, this means making observations as to what is *wrong* with them and what can be done to help. These evaluations inevitably entail taking village life as a given and, at least tacitly, measuring Innu up to Euro-Canadian expectations as to how people ideally behave in such a community in regard to the law, raising children, rules of hygiene, medical advice, seeking employment, attending school, drinking alcohol, and the like. In these terms, Innu are continually found wanting, even though their villages bear little resemblance to other communities across Canada except for those Native communities that have been decimated by government policies of assimilation.[16]

In effect, almost every day of their lives in the villages the Innu are subject to communications that represent as reality that which is not real to them. This occurs through their contacts with a host of Euro-Canadian institutions. The health services and the Nechi alcohol treatment program assume that ill health is primarily an individual failing, and not intelligible in terms of the calamitous social upheaval that the Innu have been subjected to. At a broader, and more fundamental, level, the various tiers of government that maintain control over the Innu represent policies that usurp Native autonomy. Other institutions such as the church, the school, the courts, and the police, not discussed in detail here, play similar roles. In sum, the government and its institutions in the communities have mobilized a set of procedures, beliefs, and values that operate systematically in favour of an imposed colonial order, and in doing so have devalued Innu values, thus undermining self-esteem and creating rampant disorder.[17] Canadian law, as an authoritative framework and final arbiter of all conflict, presents a 'no exit' situation for the Innu. Literally, there are no other sources of legitimization – certainly not Innu sources – that the Canadian state will recognize. Used this way, the law represents a direct assault on the self, as Svennson (1979) has pointed out in relation to Native Americans in general. It removes the right to be an Aboriginal person.

Canada claims sovereignty over territories that have been home to the Innu for perhaps thousands of years and that are vital to their identity. The federal and provincial governments display contempt for the land in numerous gestures such as the recent expansion of low-level flight training over hunting territory in the face of continuing protests and the sale of the Emish land to mining companies while land claims negotiations with the Innu are in process. The Innu are constant witnesses to the sequestering of their land by means of legalities that they did not consent to. Hardly a day passes without news of some new or deepening encroachment – low-level flying witnessed over new areas, a new military target found in the country, multimillion dollar investments at Emish, a new road, a hitherto unknown commercial fishing camp in the interior.

The relations between the Canadian state and the Innu, then, are blatantly colonial. The process by which they can gain 'self-determination' seem only designed to make the Innu collaborate in the theft of their land and the undermining of their hunting way of life. Colonialism, as Fanon (1963, 250) observed, creates certain psychological dispositions in the colonized: 'colonialism forces the people it dominates to ask themselves the question constantly; "In reality, who am I?"' In reference to Algeria, he noted that the indigenous customs were systematically disparaged and North Africans made to feel that they were lesser human beings than their colonizers. This process in turn led to cycles of self-doubt, self-hatred, dependency, and new social divisions.

The Innu also *live this experience.*

NOTES

Grateful acknowledgment is made to all of the Innu people of Sheshatshit and Utshimassits, and especially to the many who have discussed the issues presented here with me, translated for me (Cecilia Rich, Basil Penashue, and Daniel Ashini), and accommodated me in their homes (Janet Jenkinson, the Ashini family, the Pijogge family) or tents (Daniel Ashini, Sheila Blake and family, Joseph Rich and Christine Rich and family). Dr Michael Jong, Medical

Director of the Grenfell Health Service in Goose Bay, provided valuable co-operation, as did nurses, doctors, social workers, clergy, and teachers in the two communities. Fieldwork was funded by the Research Institute for the Study of Man for a 1995 RISM Landes Fellowship and the Canadian High Commission for an Institutional Research Grant. Initial funding for the project was provided by the Research Promotion Fund and the Fuller Bequest at the University of Essex. Helpful comments on drafts of this chapter have been made by Anthony Jenkinson, James Wilson, Nigel South, Jane Hindley, and Andrew Canessa. An earlier version of this paper was presented at the American Sociological Association conference, New York, 19 August 1996, where Miguel Centeno made helpful suggestions. Drafts of this chapter appear in Colin Samson, 'Healing and Drinking: Reflections on the Lost Autonomy of the Innu,' *Indigenous Nations Studies Journal*, 2 (2) (2002) and Colin Samson, *A Way of Life That Does Not Exist: Canada and the Extinguishment of the Innu* (St John's: ISER Books, Memorial University of Newfoundland).

1 According to one archaeologist (Loring 1988), evidence of Indian and Inuit occupation of the 'far Northeast' goes back at least eight thousand years.
2 Many of the official reports into Aboriginal social problems produced by Canada are couched in the rhetoric of benevolent liberalism. Although injustices are admitted, the solution to problems such as suicide are sought not in a reinvigoration of Native cultures or in the assertion of autonomy from Canada, but in the form of new and improved, albeit Native-led, ameliorative institutions. This is the tone of recent reports by the Royal Commission on Aboriginal Peoples (1995a, 1996).
3 When the Innu themselves attempted to make sense of the tragedies that they have recently experienced, they did so in terms of the loss of control over their lives brought about by the involvement of particular *institutions* – the government, the church, the school, social services, the clinic, the police, and the store. This is presented in Innu Nation and Mushuau Innu Band Council, 1995, *Gathering Voices*.
4 These figures are calculated from the Royal Commission on Aboriginal Peoples (1995a, 1–18).
5 This is calculated from statistics gathered from Roman Catholic Church records, Innu informants, and the United Nations (1993, 414–15).
6 The ethnic identification of North West River residents is complex. Most originated from Scottish and English trappers and fishing families who married Inuit people (see Plaice 1990). Many are members of the Labrador Inuit Association. Recently, perhaps in response to Native land claims

issues and economic development, North West River residents have begun to identify themselves as Metis.

7   According to several Innu, these deposits have been known to them for a long time. Because they did not say anything, they have no rights to them whatsoever.

8   At a meeting to develop an Innu response to the Emish mine, an Innu woman, Mary May Osmond, likened such processes to handing a dying man a menu. Like a menu, the processes are pre-established and change according to the dictates of the restaurant.

9   The law has affected Aboriginal communities disproportionately. Indian children are almost five times more likely to be in care than other Canadian children (Shewell and Spagnut 1995, 25). Stripped of their language and history, several young Innu have gradually made their way back from foster homes in other parts of Canada.

10   Similar genetic arguments are also currently being applied to other historically oppressed groups in North America. While the U.S. African American community has the highest rates of lung cancer and coronary disease and simultaneously has increased cigarette consumption at a time when Whites have quit smoking in large numbers, the top twenty biotechnology firms are concentrating their efforts in the search for the genetic markers of susceptibility to these diseases (Duster 1990, 115–6).

11   Two doctors, a public health nurse, and a nutritionist all made statements to this effect.

12   This is not to say that medical workers have always taken this approach. Scott and Conn (1987, 1653), for example, advocate a public health understanding of the problems of the Innu along the lines of Rudolf Virchow. They believe that the physician must 'educate himself about the historical, political and sociological pathogenesis of disease in the community he purports to serve.'

13   However, a growing disenchantment with scientific rationalism, given its catastrophic implications for the environment, can be detected in science itself, the philosophy of science, and the social sciences. Wright (1992), for example, argues that Western science is intellectually incoherent because it separates itself as a human practice from the environment through the contrivance of 'objectivity.'

14   Having said this, it is important to recognize that in the face of severe and ongoing alcohol problems in the communities, it remains to be seen whether the Innu, many of whom are committed advocates of Nechi, can adapt such techniques to their own benefit.

15   As C.W. Mills (1959, 9) put it, 'When, in a city of 100 000, only one man is

unemployed, that is his personal trouble, and for its relief we properly look to the character of the man, his skills, and his immediate opportunities. But, when in a nation of 50 million employees, 15 million men are unemployed, that is an issue, and we may not hope to find its solution within the range of opportunities open to any one individual.'

16 A close parallel is the Ojibwa community of Grassy Narrows in Ontario. This relocated community also suffers from extremely high morbidity from illnesses, suicide, and alcohol. In her book on the subject, Shkilnyk (1985, 175) states that, 'in the end, the system proved its extraordinary effectiveness in pursuing the objective of assimilation. In the span of only one generation after the relocation of Grassy Narrows, the central institutions of Ojibwa culture, the people's moral values and beliefs, customary social relationships, political organization, and mode of production – all were rendered impotent, useless, even superfluous under the imposed conditions of the new reserve.'

17 Another parallel process can be seen in Gaventa's (1980) study of the imposition of coal mining on the rural mountaineers of an Appalachian valley. Gaventa draws attention to the techniques by which the nineteenth-century residents of an Appalachian valley were colonized and subjected to the degradation of their culture, then acquiesced to industrialization through various exercises of power that I believe are similar to those operating against the Innu.

REFERENCES

Andrew, B., and P. Sarsfield. 1984. 'Innu Health: The Role of Self-Determination.' In R. Fortuine, ed., *Circumpolar Health '84: Proceedings of the Sixth International Symposium on Circumpolar Health*, 428–30. Seattle: University of Washington Press.

Ashini, D., and C. Samson. 1996. 'Out in the Cold: The Survival of the Innu.' *Outdoors Illustrated*: 38–42.

Assembly of First Nations. 1993. *Violations of Law and Human Rights by the Governments of Canada and Newfoundland in Regard to the Mushuau Innu: A Documentation of Injustice in Utshimassits (Davis Inlet)*. Submission to the Canadian Human Rights Commission. Ottawa: Assembly of First Nations.

Brosseau, J. 1994. 'Diabetes and Indians: A Clinician's Perspective.' In J. Joe and R. Young, eds., *Diabetes as a Disease of Civilization: The Impact of Culture Change on Indigenous Peoples*, 41–66. Berlin: Mouton de Gruyter.

DeMont, J. 1999. 'The Tragedy of Andrew Rich.' *Maclean's*, 22 November, 36–40.

DePalma, A. 1996. 'Shedding Ashes of a Canadian Tribe's "Evil Place."' *New York Times*, 22 November A1, A6.

Dorn, N., and N. South. 1985. 'Drink, Drugs and Development Studies: Recreation and Intoxication in Declining and Peripheral Areas within Developed Countries.' *Manchester Papers on Development* 1 (2): 25–48.

Duster, T. 1990. *Backdoor to Eugenics*. London: Routledge.

Fanon, F. 1963. *The Wretched of the Earth*. New York: Grove Press.

Farley, M. 2000. 'Tribe Sends Kids Away to Dry Out.' *Los Angeles Times*, 19 December. http://www.latimes.com/news/nation/20001219/t000120936.html

Gaventa, J. 1980. *Power and Powerlessness: Quiescence and Rebellion in an Appalachian Valley*. Urbana: University of Illinois Press.

Henriksen, G. 1973. *Hunters in the Barrens: The Naskapi on the Edge of the White Man's World*. St John's: Institute of Social and Economic Research Press.

Innu Nation. 1996. *Between a Rock and a Hard Place*. Sheshatshit: Innu Nation.

Innu Nation and Mushuau Innu Band Council. 1995. *Gathering Voices: Finding Strength to Help Our Children*. Vancouver: Douglas and McIntyre.

Jackson, M.Y. 1994. 'Diet, Culture and Diabetes.' In J. Joe and R. Young, eds., *Diabetes as a Disease of Civilization: The Impact of Culture Change on Indigenous Peoples*, 381–406. Berlin: Mouton de Gruyter.

Joe, J., and R. Young. 1994. Introduction. In J. Joe and R. Young, eds., *Diabetes as a Disease of Civilization: The Impact of Culture Change on Indigenous Peoples*, 1–18. Berlin: Mouton de Gruyter.

Laing, R.D. 1960. *The Divided Self*. Harmondsworth, UK: Penguin.

Laing, R.D., and A. Esterson. 1964. *Sanity, Madness and the Family*. Harmondsworth, UK: Penguin.

Leacock, E.B., 1994. 'The Montagnais-Naskapi of the Labrador Peninsula.' In R.B. Morrison and C.R. Wilson, eds., *Native Peoples: The Canadian Experience*, 150–80. Toronto: McClelland and Stewart.

Leacock, E.B., and N. Rothschild. 1994. *Labrador Winter: The Ethnographic Journals of William Duncan Strong*. Washington, DC: Smithsonian Institution Press.

Loring, S. 1988. 'Keeping Things Whole: Nearly Two Thousand Years of Indian (Innu) Occupation of Northern Labrador.' In *Boreal Forest and Sub-Arctic Archaeology*, 157–82. London: Occasional Publications of the London Chapter, Ontario Archaeological Society.

Mackie, M.G.A. 1987. *Nutrition: Does Access to Country Food Really Matter?*

Presentation to the Fearo Assessment Review Panel Military Flying Activities in Labrador and Quebec. Montreal, 7 October.

Mills, C.W. 1959. *The Sociological Imagination*. New York: Oxford University Press.

Notzke, C. 1994. *Aboriginal Peoples and Natural Resources in Canada*. North York, ON: Captus Press.

Plaice, E. 1990. *The Native Game: Settler Perceptions of Indian/Settler Relations in Central Labrador*. St Johns: Institute for Social and Economic Research, Memorial University of Newfoundland.

Rich, K. 1995. Foreword. In Innu Nation and Mushuau Innu Band Council, ed., *Gathering Voices: Finding Strength to Help Our Children*. Vancouver: Douglas and McIntyre.

Roche, J. 1992. *Resettlement of the Mushuau Innu 1948 and 1967: A Collection of Documents from the Provincial Archives of Newfoundland and Labrador and the Centre for Newfoundland Studies*. Sheshatshit: Innu Nation.

Royal Commission on Aboriginal Peoples. 1995. *Choosing Life: Special Report on Suicide among Aboriginal People*. Ottawa: Minister of Supply and Services Canada.

– 1996. *Looking Forward, Looking Backward*. 5 volumes. Ottawa: Minister of Supply and Services Canada.

Scott, R., and C. Conn. 1987. 'The Failure of Scientific Medicine: Davis Inlet as an Example of Sociopolitical Morbidity.' *Canadian Family Physician* 33: 1649–53.

Shewell, H., and A. Spagnut. 1995. 'The First Nations of Canada: Social Welfare and the Quest for Self-Government.' In J. Dixon and R. Scheurell, eds., *Social Welfare with Indigenous Peoples*, 1–51. London: Routledge.

Shkilnyk, A. 1985. *A Poison Stronger Than Love: The Destruction of an Ojibwa Community*. New Haven: Yale University Press.

Speck, F. 1977 (1935). *Naskapi: The Savage Hunters of the Labrador Peninsula*. Norman: University of Oklahoma Press.

Svennson, F. 1979. 'Imposed Law and the Manipulation of Identity: The American Indian Case.' In S. Burman and B. Hurrell-Bond, eds., *The Imposition of Law*, 69–87. New York: Academic Press.

Taussig, M. 1987. *Shamanism, Colonialism and the Wild Man: A Study in Teror and Healing*. Chicago: University of Chicago Press.

Turner, B. 1995. *Medical Power and Social Knowledge*. London: Sage.

United Nations. 1993. *Demographic Yearbook 1993*. New York: United Nations.

White, J.A. N.d. *Adult Children of Alcoholics: From Survival to Healing, Walking the Recovery Road*. Edmonton: Nechi Institute on Alcohol and Drug Education.

Wilson, J. 1994. *The Two Worlds of the Innu*. BBC2 documentary film. Produced by Ken Kirby. 7 August.

Wotton, K. 1986. 'Mortality of Labrador Innu and Inuit, 1971–1982.' In R. Fortuine, ed., *Circumpolar Health '84: Proceedings of the Sixth International Symposium on Circumpolar Health*, 139–42. Seattle: University of Washington Press.

Wright, W. 1992. *Wild Knowledge: Science, Language and Social Life in a Fragile Environment*. Minneapolis: University of Minnesota Press.

Chapter Seven

The Cosmology of Nature, Cultural Divergence, and the Metaphysics of Community Healing

ADRIAN TANNER

Introduction

The notion that there are cognitive barriers to intercultural understanding – exhibited as an inability or unwillingness of people from different backgrounds to find common ways of thinking about issues – although long accepted within, and perhaps even fundamental to, anthropology, is not well conceptualized. The evidence for the existence of such barriers includes the many practical problems that tend to arise in relations between people of different cultures. There are also linguistic indicators, like divergent semantic categories and incompatible grammatical structures. Other possible indicators include the different dominant metaphors used by the cultural groups concerned, and incompatible ideologies characteristic of the different groups. In this paper I want to focus particularly on incompatible metaphysical ideas.

While it may be relatively easy to show that two systems of metaphysical ideas differ, it is more difficult to demonstrate that any particular problem arising between people of two cultures is due to a deep-seated incompatibility between their metaphysical ideas, rather than some other reason. In dealing with cognitive barriers we are concerned with a wide range of transactions that can occur at the interface of two divergent modes of thought. Besides the differences in the actual ontological ideas and assumptions that members of each group bring to the interaction, there are also particular semiotic structures by which each group's ideas are conventionally expressed, and which in turn may lead to communication difficulties, including difficulties in translation. There are also problems arising from the tendency of either side to make ethnocentric judgments about the other, a matter linked to their divergent value orientations. The groups may not themselves see these issues in terms of cognitive barriers, while an outside observer may not have direct access to the metaphysical systems as they occur 'in use.' The barriers with which we are concerned involve not only divergent ideas, assumptions, and values, but also include the wider context of symbolic systems.

The difficulties in identifying and understanding the operation of these kinds of barriers are presumably magnified in stratified multiethnic societies like Canada's, given the hegemonic tendencies of the dominant group and its consequent reluctance to acknowledge or take seriously a subordinate group's metaphysical system, particularly one that is incompatible with its own. Where practical problems are at issue, and both groups share the same perception that the problems exist, any failure to find solutions may not be recognized for what it is – namely, the consequence of cognitive incompatibility – but instead attributed to other factors. In such cases it is frequently asserted that a kind of universal logic of 'common sense' must apply, and that this should be enough to overcome any religious or other metaphysical differences. The blame may be placed on the personalities of those involved or on the divergent political interests between the groups involved.

Despite these practical difficulties in identifying intercultural cognitive barriers with precision, these barriers can be shown to exist. In this paper I examine how such barriers underlie the failure of Canadian public agencies to adequately cope with the serious social problems of formerly nomadic northern Aboriginal people, whose problems result from their rapid settlement into villages. I go on to show how what is known as the 'healing movement' is a local response to this failure. While various programs of alcohol, drug, suicide, family violence, and psychiatric treatment have been started in these villages, the healing movement is distinguished from them by its use of collective ceremonies based on Aboriginal traditions, rather than the individual or small group therapies generally employed by the treatment programs. The movement exemplifies the ideology that social problems can be solved through collective revitalization and affirmation of ethnic identity.

I will examine, in particular, the 'healing movement' among the East Cree and Innu, peoples who speak closely related Northern Algonquian languages, and who both live in the northern parts of the Quebec-Labrador peninsula[1]. The movement is a loosely coordinated set of diverse community activities, sharing a common general ideological focus, but differing from settlement to settlement and from region to region as to how activities are organized and put into practice. Among the movement's main activities are ceremonial 'gatherings' lasting several days at which key symbolic features of traditional life, knowledge, beliefs, and practices are reformulated and publicly presented. These are features that, until recently, had declined in everyday use, as people have tended to spend less time in hunting camps.

First I will briefly demonstrate in practical terms the relevance of the notion of culturally based cognitive barriers to the situation of Canadian Aboriginal people who find themselves caught in the gap between their own understandings and those of the dominant society. I will then outline the main features of the 'healing movement' and look at the main influences on the movement's origins. Following this, I will consider the relationship of the movement to traditional northern Cree and Innu religious ideology. In conclusion, I will show how the healing movement contributes to the incorporation of new realities within an existing Aboriginal perspective at the same time as it tries to exist alongside the Western institutions of health care and social work, asserting the principle of local autonomy.

Intercultural Cognitive Barriers

As Canadian Aboriginal people have come into contact with Euro-Canadians, and as the state has increasingly extended its administrative jurisdiction and control over Aboriginal lands and communities, conflicts based on misunderstandings and failed communication between them and Euro-Canadians have frequently arisen. A few examples will suffice to indicate the kind of problems I am referring to. These are not analysed here in any detail, since my intention is merely to indicate something of the range of the cognitive barriers with which I am concerned.

As is well known, a highly disproportionate number of Aboriginal people get into trouble with the Canadian justice system. While no doubt many of these cases are simply due to acts that are seen as 'criminal' by either group, some are due to discrepancies over notions of personal rights, individual responsibility, and appropriate behaviour. In the cultures of the Northern Algonquian Indians (e.g., Cree, Innu, Mi'kmaq, and Ojibwa) an especially high value is placed on respect for the autonomy of the individual, so that, despite pressures to conform to group norms, there is also a high tolerance for the deviant behaviour of individuals. A high value is also placed on egalitarianism and sharing, which means that the unfettered rights of private ownership are often not strongly supported in practice. Behaviour based on these values and attitudes may lead to the laying of charges by Euro-Canadian authorities. Moreover, when confronted by the police and the courts, another aspect of the emphasis on individual autonomy comes into play, in that a person is expected to accept without question responsibility for his or her actions. Thus, instead of the accused adopting a defensive position and looking for any way out, as assumed by the Euro-Canadian legal system, many Native people simply plead guilty when charged, often without knowing in what way they have broken the law. Even if other factors may also be involved, these differences are, in turn, indicative of deep-seated cultural incompatibilities. Similar conclusions on this matter were arrived at by an assistant crown attorney and former lawyer with ten years of experience in cases involving Ojibwa. He has outlined some basic principles of what he calls 'Indian Reality,' principles he shows as being in conflict with basic Euro-Canadian ideas, and which he concludes are a major cause of problems some aboriginal people have with the justice system (Ross 1992).

Another example can be seen in the health of Aboriginal people, the statistics for which are strikingly worse than for other Canadians. While the problem has many facets, a recent study, also of a northern Ojibwa group, has revealed that the problem is not a simple matter of difficulties of access to quality professional health care services in the remote settlements where these Indians reside. Even when, under a special program, well-trained doctors were brought into this relatively isolated region, no improvements in health statistics resulted. Preventative health programs failed because 'they were not structured to accommodate local customs and sensitivities' (Young 1988, 132). My research in the same region that Young writes about revealed that many of the people have elaborate ideas about health, as well as access to many traditional Ojibwa cures from several types of local healers. While the Ojibwa do make use of Western medicine, many of them also recognize forms of sickness that they believe Western health care professionals are unable to treat, and whose treatment, in their view, might even make things worse (Tanner 1971). Since most of the Western health care specialists had strongly negative attitudes towards these Ojibwa concepts of healing, if they were aware of them at all, an ongoing struggle had developed between patients and doctors over what forms of medical treatment the patients would receive. In some cases patients hid, or were hidden by their parents, from Western doctors or nurses. Despite these fundamental differences between Western and Ojibwa approaches to sickness, few serious attempts had been made by the Western medical professionals to even inform themselves about these Ojibwa notions.

Another example involves the application of environmental impact assessments (EIAs) to industrial projects that are liable to negatively impact northern Aboriginal groups. Granted, some attempts have been made within the EIA process to take account of the distinctive forms of knowledge Aboriginal people have of their environment, and the distinctive kinds of values they place on features in the environment. As a result, most contemporary EIAs affecting Aboriginal lands specify that the 'traditional environmental knowledge' (TEK) of the local Indigenous people must be documented, and the group's 'valued environmental components' (VECs) must be taken into account in the assessment. In practice it has proved highly doubtful, however, if the EIA process, in its current form, can incorporate these concepts in any meaningful way into the decision-making process.[2] Brody provides an example of this kind of problem from the Beaver Indians of northern British Columbia, in which members of a panel investigating the potential impact of a proposed pipeline found themselves unable to understand or take account of the spiritual interpretations of the significance of landscape and maps of the area where the pipeline was planned, as expressed by an Aboriginal witness at a village hearing (1981, 256–70). In other EIA hearings, many of the specific objections made by the Innu of Labrador to low-level military flying over their hunting lands, and by the Cree of James Bay to the flooding and river diversions of the planned Great Whale hydroelectric project, were not addressed in the EIA process (National Defence 1989; Jacobs et al. 1994). In both instances certain of these objections were even misrepresented and reinterpreted by the proponents of the developments and their allies as attempts by the Aboriginal groups to improve their political bargaining position. Given the Euro-Canadian bias of the EIA process, the objections could neither be understood nor incorporated into the findings in the terms in which they had been stated by the Aboriginal people.

My final example is a recent dispute regarding the relocation of several Inuit residential groups in the 1950s (Kennedy 1994; Marcus 1992; Royal Commission on Aboriginal Peoples 1994). Both in the testimony of those involved forty years after the event and through the examination of documents of the period, two entirely contradictory versions of the purpose of the relocation, and the way in which it was conducted, have emerged. The people who were relocated, and their descendants, testified that they did not go willingly, and that various promises made to them about living conditions in the new locations were never fulfilled. They also assert their understanding that the purpose of the relocations was not their welfare, but the protection of Canadian territorial sovereignty. All this is denied by those who carried out the project. The most important analysis of this relocation (Tester and Kulchyski 1994) reveals that this scheme was only one of a number of such projects of the period directed by the government at the Inuit. A common thread among them was that government officials made critical decisions on behalf of the Inuit, possibly with the best of intentions, but often with drastic results, due to their misunderstandings of the Inuit. The disparity in understanding between the officials and the Inuit was so great that in one instance several Inuit, who had alternately been encouraged and discouraged from depending on handouts, starved to death when caribou failed to appear. In their reports government officials, who had failed to heed warnings of shortages, put the blame on the Inuit themselves (272–3). In my view, one reason for these incidents was that various intercultural misunderstandings were based on deep-seated cognitive barriers.

To be sure, other examples could be cited demonstrating the possibilities for crossing cultural boundaries and facilitating intercultural communication, although the difficulties these efforts entail are often underestimated. Indeed, only a few decades ago anthropologists confidently predicted that Canadian Indians and Inuit would soon disappear, through acculturation, intermarriage, and assimilation. Today, however, it is clear that most Aboriginal people did not disappear into the mainstream of Canadian society, despite the enormous pressures put on them to do so. This is yet another indication that there are significant intercultural barriers that are self-reproducing across generations, and that these barriers are cognitive as well as social.

Social Pathology and Collective Healing

One way Aboriginal people in modern states have sought to deal with the inequities caused by intercultural cognitive barriers is by seeking forms of autonomy. Recently, what has become known as the 'healing movement' has emerged in several Indian communities throughout the Canadian subarctic, including among the Cree of the Quebec side of

James Bay and the Innu of Labrador (Adelson 1997; Fouillard 1995; Mackey 1995; Royal Commission on Aboriginal Peoples 1993). One of the main purposes of the movement is the use of local initiatives to address a widespread and intractable set of social problems, including the abuse of alcohol and other intoxicating substances, interpersonal violence, and suicide. From a Euro-Canadian health care and social work perspective, these problems are a linked set of psychiatric symptoms of stress and anomie, the result of recent rapid social changes occurring with the settlement of these nomadic hunters into permanent villages – particularly the legal requirement that they send their children to formal schooling, the imposition on them of what was, effectively, a virtually jobless market economy, and the alienation for industrial purposes of significant parts of their hunting lands. Despite policies intended to mitigate these impacts, the imposed changes have, over the course of a generation or so, transformed the northern Cree and Innu from a self-sufficient, subsistence-based, and largely autonomous people without any significant level of social pathology to a people facing chronic unemployment and welfare dependency, a society in which the youth face limited economic futures, increasingly alienated from their parents and grandparents due to cultural and linguistic discontinuities.

External public welfare agencies have tended to respond to the social breakdown with specialized therapies principally directed at individuals with identifiable behavioural disorders. Initially, these therapies used standard North American professional social work and psychiatric health care approaches, later to be supplemented or replaced by alcohol and drug treatment programs developed and staffed by Aboriginal people. Several centres for these Aboriginal treatment programs were started in southern Canada, catering to many different kinds of Aboriginal clients from diverse cultural and social backgrounds, including northern settlements, southern reserves, the inner cities, and within institutions. Like that of the healing movement, upon which they were to have an important influence, the ideology of the Aboriginal treatment centres includes an emphasis on Aboriginal pride and a return to traditional Aboriginal spirituality, often using a pan-Indian form.[3] But in some ways the Aboriginal treatment programs remained like the Western ones which they replaced, in their use of therapeutic methods designed to bring about changes in the problem behaviour of individuals and families, leaving out the client's social setting. These programs use psychiatric methods addressed at individuals, groups, or families, often in organized groups known as 'healing circles,' with follow-up counselling and self-help community groups once clients return to their own localities[4].

A primary characteristic of the healing movement is that it is village based. While individual returnees from the external treatment programs were a major influence on its beginnings, it has actually developed an approach to social problems that is quite different from them. Central to this difference is that the problem, and thus the solution, is seen as occurring at the level of the social group, while the treatment centres, like the professional therapies before them, generally locate the trouble within the lives of problem individuals and their families. The healing movement, moreover, represents a reaction against dependency on external agencies, asserting the ideal of each local group taking responsibility for the solution to its own problems. In most northern Cree and Innu communities the healing movement began among a few key people, but where it has taken hold it has relatively quickly achieved community-wide recognition and participation. The movement has little or no formal structure, so its success cannot be counted in membership or numbers of people in treatment. Even though community acceptance of the movement has not been universal, some who do not openly support it will nevertheless participate in the movement's activities. This is related to the fact that the movement is directed at the entire village, and not just at the pathological behaviour of certain problem individuals. Thus, at the ceremonials and other social events, the movement's main forms of activity, it is significant that everyone attending is equally involved, and events do not distinguish those with personal or family problems from others.

The activities of the healing movement, while different from a therapeutic approach, are more consistent with the closest indigenous concept to the English term 'health,' *miyupimaatisin,* meaning 'living well' (given here in the East Cree form). Three aspects of this concept should be particularly noted. First, the focus on individuality and privacy, which are intrinsic to Western therapy, is missing from the northern Cree and Innu concept, for whom *miyupimaatisin* (as distinct from curing) is understood to be a public and collective enterprise. Secondly, the northern Cree and Innu notion of health is not based on the kind of positivist, mechanistic, and delimited notion of 'body' that is central to Western medicine. The concept of *miyupimaatisin* assumes that there is a link between morality, religious teachings, and health. For the northern Cree and Innu the conditions for *miyupimaatisin* are based on the maintenance of a harmony between humans and the spiritual forces of nature, an approach that is antithetical to the Western health care model.

In summary, the healing movement, through the use of ceremonials and other social activities, is directed at cultural and religious revitalization, as well as aimed more specifically at the symptoms of social pathology. It has been influenced by pan-Indian religious ideology and ritual practices, as these have been incorporated into the Aboriginal treatment programs of southern Canada. As will be shown in more detail below, the movement involves some reorganization of existing Northern Algonquian religious ideas about animals and the natural environment, while maintaining a continuity of these ideas under changing conditions, as the northern Cree and Innu move from a subsistence-oriented way of life to a more mixed settlement-oriented economic and social existence.

Sources of the Healing Movement

Although the East Cree and Innu have been in contact with Europeans for more than three hundred years, it was not until the advent of Western schooling, which began in James Bay in the 1930s and '40s, and in Labrador in the 1960s, that youth were subjected to prolonged contact with ways of thinking based on entirely different principles of thought from those of their parents. Young northern Cree and Innu now finish high school having been intensively exposed to Western scientific notions of the natural world being subject to physical laws, as well as to Christian moral philosophy. By contrast, they have relatively little exposure to their parents' own religious traditions about nature, animals, and the natural environment. This is because, apart from the activities of the healing movement, most of their time with their families occurs in the settlement, while their parents generally only bring animistic thinking into everyday life and practice when they are living in the hunting camps.

Due to the prevalence of social problems, the move to settlement life has been marked by many personal tragedies, including suicides, homicides, and accidental deaths, events which have marked whole communities. Not only does the resulting social dysfunction further erode participation in hunting; it has led to a neglect of the traditional rules of respect towards animals. For example, in the documentary film *Place of the Boss*, John Poker, a Davis Inlet man, speaks of how in the settlement the bones of caribou are not treated with respect by being put on a bone platform, as required by traditional rules for the disposal of animal remains, and as would normally be done in a hunting camp. Instead they are left as garbage and eaten by the dogs, which is considered highly offensive to the animal spirits. The disrespect shown to the animal spirits is seen by Poker as explaining why the animals are now hard to kill. He suggests, moreover, that this is the cause of the many human tragedies that have occurred in that settlement over the past twenty years (Walker 1996).

The undermining of the hunting way of life has not, however, resulted in a total switch to Euro-Canadian scientific and Christian forms of thinking. On the contrary, as the healing movement exemplifies, there has been a general revitalization of certain traditional religious ideas. The development of the movement has been fed by three religious traditions, although in different proportions in each East Cree and Innu village.

One external influence is the pan-Indian religious ideology and its associated practices. These practices include public ceremonies like the annual powwow (an event principally involving drumming, dancing, and other traditional activities), the sweat lodge, and the pipe ceremony. The form of these rituals is particularly associated with Plains Indians, including the Plains Cree located to the south and east of the forest-dwelling northern Cree. The pan-Indian ideology and its associated activities are employed by a number of Aboriginal treatment programs, particularly those of Western Canada and Ontario. These forms of treatment have, in turn, been introduced into the local village-based treatment programs by former clients of these programs upon returning to northern Cree and Innu settlements.

Compared with the local traditional animism practiced by northern Cree and Innu hunters in which multiple spiritual entities are recognized, the pan-Indian religious ideology is more focused on a single central entity, referred to as the 'Creator' or 'Great Spirit.' While other animist entities are recognized in pan-Indian ideology, there is little emphasis on those spiritual beings that the northern Cree and Innu identify with specific animal species and forces of nature. Instead, more attention is paid to concepts and entities with multivocal and abstract symbolic referents. There is also a greater concern in pan-Indian ideology with healing than is the case with the East Cree and Innu animism, which is more focused on encounters with game animals. This theme of animal encounters does have a place in the pan-Indian religious ideology, however, particularly in the context of the 'spirit quest.' There are other features shared between pan-Indian and northern Cree and Innu religious practice, like tobacco offerings, the sweat lodge, and the shaking tent, although each of these is used in somewhat different ways in each tradition. Other pan-Indian practices, like powwow costume dancing and the associated styles of drumming and singing, and the use of burning sweet grass for spiritual purification, are new to the present-day northern Cree and Innu.[5]

A second important, if indirect, influence on the development of the healing movement, at least among the Cree, although not among the Innu, has been the Pentecostal church. This Protestant sect has gained a significant following over the past twenty years in some East Cree settlements, often effectively dividing villages into factions – converts and non-converts. While the religious ideology of Pentecostalism is totally incompatible with the ideology of the healing movement, both focus attention on the prevalence of social pathologies, in the Pentecostal case totally prohibiting alcohol to its members. Its arrival in a particular settlement has had the effect of focusing public attention, of non-converts as much as of converts, on these social problems. It has also caused some non-converts to question the basis of their own religious beliefs.

Before the advent of the healing movement, a form of 'religious dualism' existed, such that traditional animism was largely confined to the hunting camp, while Christianity (Anglicanism among the East Cree, Roman Catholicism among the Innu) was largely confined to the settlement (Tanner 1979). While Pentecostalism openly sought to stamp out animist practices, including those that remained relatively hidden from public view in the hunting camps, the healing movement has taken the opposite direction, bringing many aspects of the traditional animist religion into the settlement, effectively expanding its social context. The effect of both has been to break down the religious dualism of the past.

Despite its obvious conflicts with Northern Algonquian animism, Pentecostalism as practised by the Cree is not entirely opposed to an animist perspective. In fact, it actually entails a form of affirmation of the animist entities believed to control the forces of nature. Converts to the Pentecostal church are required to publicly dissociate themselves from their former animist ritual practices. It was explained by the first Euro-Canadian Pentecostal ministers that the animist entities were actually forms of the Christian devil, meaning that rituals that involved communication with these entities had to be suppressed. However, the

Pentecostal converts I spoke to some years later said they believed that only certain Cree animist practices involving sorcery and magic actually constituted communication with the Christian devil. While they also had stopped practising other animist rituals, including drumming and singing to animal spirits, and hunting divination, they did this only as a sign of their new Christian status, and also because they now considered it improper to use supernatural assistance in hunting. The issue for the Cree Pentecostalists is thus not one of a Christian-animist ontological incompatibility. There is agreement between Pentecostals and animists over the existence of the animist entities; the disagreement is over whether or not it is acceptable to have relations with them.[6]

Despite there being no Pentecostal influence among the Labrador Innu, the current relationship between Christianity and animist ideas and practices among them has similar implications. Most Innu were converted centuries ago by Roman Catholic missionaries, who, right from the start, were far more opposed to the animist practices than were many of the Anglican missionaries encountered by the Cree. Despite missionary disapproval, for most of the year while hunting the Innu continued their animist practices, and were able to reconcile this, at least to their own satisfaction, with being devout practising Catholics while living in the settlement. In recent years, while the Innu have become more confined to living in the settlements, the objections of the Roman Catholic Church to animism have become more muted. At the same time, even in the settlement context many Innu have become more open about their animist ideas and practices.

For both northern Cree and Innu the shift to life in the settlement has altered the balance of religious dualism, threatening the animist side, both because people spent less time in the bush and because of external Christian, educational-scientific, and pan-Indian influences. Partly as a response to the new Pentecostal and Pan-Indian ideologies and practices, which some reject as not stemming from local Aboriginal tradition, a variety of new village events has been organized that incorporates local traditions in a new form. In some cases these events were a reaction to the fact that young people had turned to the new outside religious influences, complaining they knew nothing of their parents' own Aboriginal religious traditions. This complaint came about because in the past northern Cree and Innu religious practices had not been passed on with any formal apprenticeship; instead, the young were expected to acquire them in the hunting camps through silent observation of their elders. Later, as youths, they were expected to acquire religious knowledge through direct inspiration, in the form of dreams and visions, usually in connection with hunting. The organized events of the healing movement were a new way of passing on traditional knowledge. They also effectively reformulate northern Cree and Innu animist practices, formerly focused largely around hunting, to make them more appropriate to a settlement-based population. These 'neo-traditional' events have also become the means for those who now live full time in a settlement to spend time in bush camp and to share some of the experience of bush living.

Among the James Bay Cree these attempts to include the experience of bush living in modern life now include the alteration of the school year to incorporate a break in the spring, which allows children to live with their parents at goose-hunting camp. In other programs, youth, including those undergoing treatment, are taken to live in a hunting camp in the bush. It has been proposed that such programs be extended to substitute for the corrective detention of convicted Aboriginal criminals.

Among the Cree a number of neo-traditional events, usually lasting from several days to several weeks, are held, often near but some distance outside the settlement, symbolically in the bush. The events generally take place in the summer, and may last from a weekend to several weeks. They are known by such terms as 'gatherings,' 'culture camps,' 'cultural retreats,' or 'healing conferences.' For the Cree of the villages of Waswanipi and Chisasibi they include an annual period of return to a former summer trading-post settlement that is now abandoned. In these events people self-consciously engage in traditional practices, living in the traditional hunting camp types of dwellings, eating traditional food cooked as it is in hunting camps, and engaging in ceremonies otherwise normally held only in the bush. At these events elders demonstrate and explain to the young traditional skills, like preparing hides and medicines. In the evenings, traditional dances and feasts are held. These events are variously explained as efforts to overcome the disincentives to hunting; as forms of education for youth who otherwise experience discontinuities in their exposure to the traditional religion of hunting; or as forms of healing to address social pathologies.

Among the Innu of Labrador, the healing movement tends overall to be a more unified initiative, compared with that of the East Cree. The events are often used by organizers as occasions to advocate, as a core ideological principle, a return to living in the bush. This is not the same kind of ideological issue for the Cree, given the financial support they receive to maintain the hunting way of life, following from the provisions of the 1975 James Bay and Northern Quebec Agreement (Government of Quebec 1991). The initiative of the Davis Inlet band of the Labrador Innu to move its village from Iluikoyak Island, where they were settled by government fiat in 1969, has involved such a 'return to the land' ideology (Press 1995). In practical terms, the move will mean that residents will have easier access to the interior, particularly during the periods of freeze-up and break-up. Symbolically, it will also mean moving to a location surrounded by trees and overlooking fresh water, representing the ideal of being closer to the bush.

A number of similarities can be seen among the three religious influences on the healing movement described above. Pan-Indianism and neo-traditional animism are transformations of the animist concepts once followed by many northern Aboriginal people. Even Christian church services have begun to incorporate traditional animist elements; for example, the public declarations of personal salvation that characterize Pentecostal services sometimes include dream revelations, a basic component of the Algonquian animist religion. Moreover, as noted above, acceptance of traditional spiritual entities may continue after conversion to Pentecostalism, although the position of these entities in the moral universe has changed, as they are now more likely to be seen as involved in sorcery and therefore bad, whereas before they were more often seen as good, in terms of the assistance they provided to hunters.

To summarize, the healing movement, a form of Aboriginal religious tradition incorporating new external influences, has certain key features. It sponsors communal rituals at formalized events, usually called 'gatherings,' which have the therapeutic goal of combating social pathology through local autonomy by bringing about a renewal and rehabilitation of personal pride and ethnic identity. At these events the knowledge, beliefs, and practices, both animist and non-religious, that were until recently confined to bush camps as an adjunct to hunting are reformulated and presented, both to instruct the young and to make aspects of the hunting camp lifestyle accessible to those adults now largely confined to settlement life.

Northern Cree and Innu Animism

For the northern Cree and Innu the activity of hunting has been, and for many still is, both the central practical productive activity for a major part of the year and the central symbolic focus of religious beliefs and ritual practices. As already noted, the hunting way of life continues, but it has been seriously undermined by external pressures to sedentarize, and the community breakdown and social pathology associated with this sedentarization. Nevertheless, the northern Cree group, living from Labrador to Saskatchewan, have maintained an essentially uniform animist religious tradition. The scholarly picture of this religion for the modern period has been confirmed, corrected, deepened, and expanded in several recent ethnographic studies (Armitage 1992; Henriksen 1973; Tanner 1979). Even a number of recent documentary television films (e.g., Markham 1996; Wilson 1994) contain footage in which northern Cree and Innu hunters express, in surprisingly profound ways, some of their distinctive animist religious ideas.

The most recent and important of the new scholarly sources on the religion of the northern Cree group is Robert Brightman's *Grateful Prey: Rock Cree Human-Animal Relationships* (1993). Almost single-handedly, Brightman, in a combination of fieldwork and synthesis of historical sources, has filled in many details of the hunting religion of the northern Cree for the large but heretofore little-known area west of James and Hudson bays, extending the picture of northern Cree animism that, prior to his publication, was emerging in no small measure on the basis of northern Quebec and Labrador ethnographic research. While Brightman's account shows there are some important differences between his region and Quebec-Labrador, for example, a greater emphasis on guardian spirits and antagonistic monsters, and a somewhat different conception of the 'animal masters,' the main outlines are otherwise closely similar. This underlying continuity of the traditional religion of the contemporary northern Cree group that Brightman's study confirms is all the more remarkable, given that the conditions of Rock Cree hunting have deteriorated further than that indicated in recent East Cree studies, in a similar way that it also has among the Innu of eastern Quebec. Much hunting is now conducted by all-male groups, women remaining in the settlement, and not often by multi-family hunting groups, as was the case in the past and still is among many East Cree.

In this section I will summarize some core principles of the Northern Algonquian animist tradition. The particular details vary somewhat from region to region, and to avoid reducing this material to generalities I will focus on my own research with the East Cree of Mistassini (now spelled Mistissini), northern Quebec (Tanner 1979). Maintaining relations with animals spirits and other personified forces of nature involve hunters and their companions in a set of religious rules and moral constraints. If hunters treat animals with respect, obeying rules and taboos during the hunt, dealing correctly with the animal corpse, and properly disposing of the inedible remains, they can expect animals to act as their friends, allowing themselves to be killed by these same hunters. As well as being spiritual beings themselves, animals are also, either as species, or as groups of species, under the control of unseen entities, commonly referred to in the ethnographic literature as 'animal masters,' who can also either allow their animals to be killed or withhold them. Still other unseen entities influence natural phenomena like weather. All of these entities can be subject to human influence.

A brief survey of religious practices regarding weather control is a useful entry point to the Northern Algonquian animist cosmology of nature – the systematic interrelationship among cosmic phenomena, principally between humans and 'other-than-human persons' (Hallowell 1954; Preston 1975, chapter 7), the latter including entities associated with natural forces, astronomic and terrestrial features, and animals. My own knowledge of this cosmology is no doubt incomplete, as it is primarily based on observations of religious practices that were ancillary to hunting, rather than from any systematic investigation into the entire system. In general, a strong association is recognized between particular weather conditions and the prevailing wind direction, the latter being controlled by one of four entities, each associated with one of the cardinal directions.

However, most weather-control rites deal with one of two directions. The Mistissini Cree see the year as divided between two primary seasons, which we may for convenience call 'summer' and 'winter,' with a more detailed secondary division of these. The 'north wind person,' or *ciwêtinsû*, brings colder weather, and is more generally associated with winter weather features such as snowstorms and low temperatures, while the 'south wind person,' or *saawensuu*, brings warm weather, and is generally associated with the opposite summer-weather features. Most Mistissini weather-control techniques I observed were directed at *ciwêtinsû* and were intended to bring cold winds and snow, which are considered good weather conditions for winter hunting. Less frequently, rituals are directed to *saawensuu*, to bring warmer weather.

Beyond being connected with particular weather phenomena, *ciwêtinsû* also has a special association with a particular class of animals, as well as with a particular class of people. *Ciwêtinsû* is spoken of as having a special affection for and influence over 'winter animals,' a group of species that do not hibernate or migrate, but remain active in winter (e.g., caribou, wolf, porcupine, hare, beaver, most lake fish, ptarmigan, raven, and owl). Offerings are made by hunters to *ciwêtinsû* to ensure help when they are hunting any of these species. In addition, *ciwêtinsû* has a special relationship with people who were born in the winter season. Only such a person can perform the key action in those weather-control rituals intended to compel *ciwêtinsû* to send a north wind, in order to make the weather colder or bring a snowstorm. Winter-born persons can even accidentally set off cold weather and storms by unintentional acts, for instance, by pointing to certain sacred mountains, since pointing is generally considered offensive to spiritual entities. *Saawensuu* has a special connection to people born in the summer, in that a person born in the summer is needed to perform the key action in rituals designed to compel the south wind to make the weather warmer or less stormy.

Each animal has a spirit (*âtacâkw*), as do all objects, whether naturally occurring or manufactured. The form of communication between humans and the *âtacâkw* of animals or any of the other phenomena used in rituals mark some particular *âtacâkw* as being special. For instance, in a ceremony that initiates the winter hunting season, bear fat is smeared on certain objects. While smearing fat on guns is fairly self-evident as an offering to the *âtacâkw* of these tools of particular importance in hunting, bear fat is also spread on the doorposts and on the wall above where a person's head lays at night. The former is intended to ensure hunting success for people leaving the dwelling, and the latter to bring propitiatory dreams at night. The *âtacâkw* of animals are in many ways analogous to humans. They live in social groups, and human communication with them of various special kinds is possible, including ritual songs, prayers with standardized phrases asking or enticing, and material offerings. Humans and animals are also united by moral rules. For instance, the various rules of respect the hunter and his companions must show towards animals are in essence reciprocal moral obligations, rather than magical forms of control. At the same time, magical techniques may also be used to control animals and the unseen entities, but these are less frequently encountered, and their use is sometimes frowned upon.

Intellectually, relations between Northern Algonquian hunters and game animals take place within a religious tradition that is both animist and 'shamanistic.' As I use it, the latter term has two implications: first, it denotes a system in which the shaman, or religious specialist, is a part-time role only, such a person otherwise engaging in the same activities as any other hunters; secondly, this shaman is not just a mediator between the human and the spiritual levels, but also makes direct contact with animist entities, for example, in the shaking tent ritual. This is an important and infrequently held event in which spiritual entities of various kinds are called on to reveal themselves publicly. Shamanistic skills are not learned by means of an apprenticeship or through formal instruction. A hunter is said to receive instruction, either in a dream or by inspiration, and has no option but to obey the impetus, however reluctantly. In my own research I encountered only shamans who had practised divination, which includes the shaking tent, although shamanistic healers are well known among the neighboring Ojibwa, and I was told that such specialists existed among the East Cree in the past. There is evidence from within the context of the healing movement that a new generation of such healers may now be emerging (Adelson 1997).

Given that some of the animist entities are always relatively close at hand, in the territory through which hunters move and where they have everyday encounters with animals, the spirit world of the Mistissini Cree is not distant or unfamiliar. Not only shamans, but most ordinary hunters, have some shamanistic skills, in the sense that they are able to mediate between the human and non-human realms. For example, all adults conduct many of the simple forms of divination; they engage in dream interpretation, and make various kinds of offerings to the spirits. Some, but not all, hunters have their own songs with magical power, acquired by inspiration, and sung to animal spirits and other non-human entities, to the accompaniment of the drum. Women acquire through their dreams such sacred knowledge as the patterns for the decorations they put on clothing and moccasins, and these also give hunters magical power.

Since humans, game animals, and spiritual entities are all understood to be bound by a single set of moral principles, there is no Northern Algonquian concept of, or equivalent term for, the Western idea of 'nature,' in the sense of a realm beyond human influence, a realm where, from a human perspective, events occur spontaneously. The northern Cree and Innu do recognize a concept with some of these qualities, in that, alongside those animals with whom they have positive relations, there is another sub-category of animals that are useless to them and with whom they do not have human-like relations, and which includes insects, amphibians, and certain small mammals.[7] The term *nôcimîc* (East Cree form) is often translated as 'the bush,' and refers to the relatively familiar landscape beyond the limits of the settlements and the hunting camps where hunting activities occur. It is a realm where every lake, stream, and hill is named, either in relation to its history or as a recognizable geographic landmark from the hunter's perspective, an area criss-crossed with named and familiar old trails, portages, and former campsites. Whatever controversies still exist among scholars about the private or collective 'ownership' status of the Northern Algonquian hunting territories, or the degree to which hunters are understood to exercise management over these blocks of land, it is clear that this is an environment that is socially constructed by the East Cree and Innu, every bit as much as is the farming landscape in Western societies.

Nôcimîc is thus familiar territory, 'domesticated' in the sense that its animal occupants, like humans, live in domestic family groups, have leaders, act with intention, want to be dealt with respectfully, and follow rules of reciprocity. This view of animals as understandable primarily in terms of their fundamental similarities to, and relations with, humans also applies to the differences between species. Different species have different domestic arrangements and different patterns of leadership, and different hunters relate to these different species in their own ways. In the same way that the autonomy of the individual is acknowledged, and that the most socially relevant differences among humans are their personalities and personal preferences, differences between species are dealt with not simply as fixed and objective forms of adaptation and specialization, as in Western science, but as personality preferences, equivalent to those exhibited by different humans. Moreover, rather than utilizing a fixed human/animal relationship, the northern Cree and Innu acknowledge diverse relations between humans and animals.

Given the nature of these human/animal relations, *nôcimîc* is both the homeland of the animals and the 'domesticated' space of the northern Cree and Innu. But there are still clear differences between animals and humans, and between the territories of humans and of animals. *Nôcimîc* can be seen as primarily the homeland of the animals, and secondarily that of the northern Cree and Innu, since the latter must transform it for themselves, by establishing campsites that introduce culturally standardized patterns to the environment, imposing order with the specific location, orientation, and internal arrangement of their dwellings. This ordered domestic space owes less to conceptions about the animal inhabitants of *nôcimîc* and more to a more distant cosmic order, involving entities beyond the horizon – the winds, the rising sun, and a sun-wise movement.

In summary, the northern Cree and Innu hunters' animistic religious beliefs and practices provide the basis of a distinct cosmology of nature, even though no concept directly equivalent to that of 'nature' is recognized. It is a philosophy that complements the northern Cree and Innu's highly developed empirically based understanding and explanations of the normal phenomena of their material environment, which includes knowledge of normal animal behaviour as well as accounts of their own hunting successes and failures. But northern Cree and Innu religious philosophy also gives a second, more profound level of meaning to these same phenomena, beyond a phenomenological way of thinking about the successes and hardships of their everyday work of hunting. A major part of what Western people see as 'nature' is understood by the northern Cree and Innu to be a complex organization of 'persons,' who include animals, terrestrial features, and non-human forces. These 'persons' have human-like intentionality, and hunters must respect them as they do their own elders; they, in turn, expect hunters to maintain relations of reciprocity with them, and can become antagonistic if hunters fail to do so. This way of thinking, which underlies much of northern Cree and Innu hunting ritual, does not impose a monolithic structure of knowledge ordained and controlled by specialists, but instead encourages individual speculative understanding, and contributes to the aesthetic appreciation of a hunter's everyday experience.

Algonquian Metaphysics and Practical Problems

The healing movement adapts aspects of this animist philosophy to modern settlement life, in order to restore harmony to these northern villages that have been so disrupted by social problems. The movement draws on the Northern Algonquian cosmology of nature and associated ceremonials as its primary ideological inspiration. In the past, animist cosmology and ritual practices were part of a hunting way of life, and were effectively excluded from the settlement, the domain of Western Christian cosmology and of the Western positivist approach to social problems. Both religious and magical thought is based on the logic of analogy. Lévi-Strauss distinguishes the two basic forms of this analogical thought, one involving the 'humanization of nature' that is used in religion, the other involving the 'naturalization of man' used in magic (1972, 221). As I have shown above, Cree and Innu hunters use both religion and magic in this sense, in that the personified animals and forces of nature are dealt with socially, with gifts and entreaties, at the same time as they use magical formulas to compel persons, both other humans as well as animal persons, to do a shaman's bidding, on the analogy of physical cause-and-effect. The cosmology of nature expressed in northern Cree and Innu animism gives primacy to the relationship (often expressed in myths as metamorphosis) between humans and 'other-than-human persons,' mainly animals, but also including personalized natural forces and 'mythic' entities like the winds, monsters, underwater creatures, and other beings with some human characteristics. This way of thought is a combination of hard-nosed empiricism and a complex series of metaphors (Scott 1989).

In these metaphors, models taken from humanity are extended to animals, that is, familiar notions about human society are applied to more distant, less familiar beings. Other-than-human persons are understood as living in social groups that, depending on their species or other characteristics, have habits of social behaviour analogous to those of humans. Some, like caribou, live in large social groups that therefore have leaders, while others, like bears, live a solitary existence, and are said to have no other leader but themselves. Social relations among the different other-than-human persons are understood as being similar to relations that exist within human society. For example, among the Mistissini Cree there is a 'mythic' creature called *memeguesu* that is human-like, covered in hair, and lives in rocky cliffs bordering on lakes. Curiously, the bear, which is otherwise especially revered as powerful because it is the one species that has only itself as spiritual 'master,' is considered subordinate to the *memeguesu*. To mark this subordinate status, the bear is always identified as the 'dog' of the *memeguesu*. The relationship between humans and their domestic animals is extended by analogy to represent a relation among different animals.

A similar set of analogies is applied to the next level of generality, that of either whole species or groups of species, seen as being like human tribes or nations. Some individual species have their own leader, or 'animal master,' while others are grouped into sets of species sharing some common feature (for example, fish, beaver, and muskrat, all water creatures), which share one 'animal master' between them.

I do not, however, interpret the above material as suggesting that human society is seen by Northern Algonquians as simply and automatically a part of nature. That would be to confuse the metaphor with its referent. Humans can be part of nature, in that they can be tied to animals by reciprocal obligations, but these obligations are not automatic and may be neglected, if at a price. Thus, the world of nature is treated by the northern Cree and Innu as to some extent external to, and joined by complex relations with, human society. Yet in this conception of nature it is a sphere that humans can enter and become part of, but only of their own volition. In order to do so, northern Cree and Innu hunters must learn, understand, and follow the rules of this cosmology of nature, rules that are not of their own making. They acquire knowledge of these rules not primarily by the teachings of the elders, but by living close to and having encounters with animals, that is, through the practice of hunting. The more that hunting is conducted in accordance with the rules acquired from the experience of previous hunting encounters, the more hunters participate in the harmony and the power of this nature cosmology.

The rituals and ceremonies based on this cosmology, associated with the conditions and requirements of the hunting way of life, are now being transformed and used as the inspiration to promote communal healing, restoring harmony to human society. Such a use of a traditional religion in a new context is only problematic if the cosmology is seen as narrowly and uniquely dedicated to the specialized needs of hunting. While much northern Cree and Innu religious representation of animals and other aspects of nature does indeed reflect environmental knowledge that is also of great practical use in hunting, it does not mean that this knowledge is to be used for only such a purpose.

Previously, I have criticized the functional interpretations that other anthropologists have used to explain certain religious practices of Northern Algonquian hunters, including interpreting the practice of foretelling the outcome of hunting expeditions by divination as a way to improve the chances of hunting success, or to maintain the social cohesion of the hunting group (1978). I concluded instead that, given that animals are spiritual persons, the significance of this divination is to draw attention to a second dimension of hunting, beyond that of economic production. At this level animals are sacred and spiritual beings, as revealed in the detailed narratives of encounters between hunters and animals. To the extent that Northern Algonquian animism reaches beyond the pragmatic perspective of hunting, it builds from its existing cosmology a philosophical basis for other ways of living, beyond economic imperatives.

Instead of assuming these religious ideas and practices are narrowly functional and adapted solely to the requirements of hunting, we need to adopt a conception that is closer to the Northern Algonquian perspective. In this cosmology animals are seen as part of an interrelated and ordered system that includes both living beings and spiritual entities, a system characterized by its totality, its order, its harmony, and its inclusion of a concept of power. As Descola has pointed out regarding other non-Western cosmologies (1996), the northern Cree and Innu do not categorically exclude human society from 'nature,' following a universal culture/nature opposition. Humans are seen as *potentially* a part of nature, linked to other species by obligations of reciprocity. Animals give themselves as gifts – they allow themselves to be caught – providing that the hunter treats them before, during, and after the hunt with respect, that is, by following rules and taboos, some of which are general to all animals and others particular to each species. If these rules are not obeyed, the result may be anything from a short period of hunting failure to the disappearance of whole species for several decades. These ideas underscore the understanding of this, as with any other conception of 'nature,' as a culturally constructed system.

The analogical thought underlying Northern Algonquian animism, as exemplified in the rituals associated with hunting, is grounded in a certain conception of humanity, and extended by analogy outward to animals and the entities associated with other phenomena of nature. The hunting rituals and ceremonies, the songs sung to the animal spirits, the offerings of food put in the fire for the animal spirits, the honour shown to the animal victims through the tokens brought back to camp, and special treatment of the slain animal, including the proper disposal of the inedible remains, are all done to ensure that a certain kind of order, one that is in essence moral, exists outside human society. In hunting, where animals are seen as 'persons,' hunting failures are indications of neglected obligations. Thus, the state of the cosmos is always contingent; it can be disrupted sometimes only in a minor way, affecting only one hunter for a short period, but also potentially with more widespread and long-term consequences for a whole group.

The healing movement builds on the analogical basis of the humanization of nature, but its focus is not on the contingency of nature.

Instead, it uses a cosmology of nature to address the state of human society, which has become disrupted. This use of cosmological thought to address the situation with human society is not something entirely new, in that traditional northern Cree and Innu animism has always demonstrated this concern with human society. For instance, divination was exercised not only to foretell the outcome of the hunt; it was also used to find lost objects, communicate with distant people, and foretell if visitors from another camp were about to arrive. Neither does this use of the cosmology of nature by the healing movement involve the kind of magical operation involved in Lévi-Strauss's concept of the 'naturalization of man,' referred to above. Bringing cosmic order, as conceived in hunting rituals, into (or near) the settlement is an attempt to extend that order to the human group, bringing with it harmony and order. But the cosmic entities involved are still dealt with on the analogy of human social interaction, rather than by magical cause-and-effect compulsion. At the very time hunting is receding in significance from people's lives, an idealized and ritualized version of the hunting way of life is brought back into everyday human experience, to recreate the communal social order associated with small, multi-family hunting groups.

The similarity in the logic of these two kinds of analogical thought, that of hunting and of that of social healing, is deeper, in the sense that both have a moral purpose. Previously, I have said that animals can be obligated to supply themselves regularly to humans as food, when humans undertake to respect the same principle, since the rules of reciprocity, moral in nature, include humans together with animals. Now I would add that this achievement is more than simply metaphoric. The rules of reciprocity entailed in the religious ideology of hunting apply not only between a hunter and the particular animals he hunts, but also between hunters. It is an offence to the animals to waste their carcass, and this gives religious support to the social rule existing between hunters, requiring the sharing of game by the fortunate hunter and the forbidding of hoarding. By including animals within these rules they become reflected back and extended beyond those other hunters who can be held accountable by direct reciprocity, that is, the members of a single hunting group, to a wider range of humans, to all the members of one band, and ultimately across the whole subarctic. Moreover, rituals previously used in hunting that are introduced to the settlement context bring a more general northern Cree and Innu cosmology of nature, which was originally appropriate to relations between humans in small hunting camps, into the wider context of the social life of settlements, represented within the structure of the nation state by Aboriginal political organizations.

Conclusion

Within anthropology, the assertion that cultures are socially constructed ways of approaching the world such that, in principle, each may base itself on different ontological assumptions, has largely been taken for granted, since the adoption of the doctrine of cultural relativism in the last century. Today we have deconstructed the idea of a world divided by 'cultures,' showing them to actually be ideal types, rather than discrete and internally uniform systems. We can point out that the myriad aspects of culture – language, ontological assumptions, knowledge, values, and practices – may each have their breaking points at different places, dividing social groupings that otherwise share aspects of culture into classes or regional variants. However, given our empirical knowledge of the often harsh consequences of failures in intercultural understanding, this perspective does not dissolve the issue of cultural boundaries. The postmodern perspective merely demonstrates that the phenomenon we are dealing with is more complex than the idea of 'cultures' suggested.

In what ways do the differences between culturally based systems of thought constitute practical obstacles to understanding? Attempts to provide a rigorous theoretical grounding for this perspective have been under way since at least the time of Whorf and Sapir. For these scholars the differing structures of languages were indicative of the underlying incompatibility between ways of thinking, and thus of the fundamentally different experiences of reality between cultures. Yet a clear verification of this approach has remained elusive. One objection to this assertion is that anthropologists (even Whorf and Sapir themselves), whose own languages have a different logical basis from the people they study, are able, nevertheless, to comprehend to a significant degree the ideas of these people. If such ability exists, it would suggest there could be bridges to some deeper and universally valid basis of human cognition and intercultural communication. Moreover, just as people can acquire competence in several languages, can they not also learn to accommodate several incompatible modes of thought?

However, it is one thing to assert that it is possible, with considerable effort, to overcome the incompatibilities between one's own cognitive system and a culturally different one. It is quite a different matter to state that two groups with incompatible cognitive systems, who may see little reason to make the efforts required for mediation, will not experience problems and misunderstandings when dealing with each other. Given two groups with cognitive systems involving incompatible conceptual principles, it is to be expected that people will encounter practical problems of understanding and communication.

Maurice Bloch has put forward an argument regarding theories of cognition that is of relevance to this notion of intercultural barriers (1989a). The argument is complex, parts of his position being found in several papers dealing with the work of many other theorists, but Bloch concludes by distinguishing two forms of cognition, practical and ritual thinking, asserting that the former is universal, while the latter is culturally specific. Each employs different underlying principles. Practical thought is non-ideological and grows from the practical experience of the individual, while ritual thinking is ideological and derives from historical processes. Ritual thinking is widely variable between different societies, involving 'systems of classification of such things as animals, plants, colours, and which, in various ways, link these systems of cognition to social structure' (1989b, 6–7). Practical thinking is universal in which 'colour, plant, animal and even human classifications are based on identical criteria and produce identical classes and sub-classes varying only in degree of elaboration' (7). Bloch asserts that the former type, which is specific to each culture, is used for only one specific form of communication that he labels as 'ritual in the broad sense of the term: greetings, and fixed politeness formulas, formal behaviour and above all rituals, whether social, religious or state.' The other kind of thinking is constrained by nature and used in situations of direct contact with nature, that is, practical activities like productive labour (11). It is only in ritual thought that culturally specific metaphysical and abstract ordering principles are made explicit. One implication of this view is that intercultural barriers may be avoided by limiting the usage of different systems of thought to their specific appropriate contexts.

A major part of Bloch's theory derives from the work of developmental psychology on how children learn by constructing categories on the basis of experience, and only later selecting appropriate cultural terms for these categories. However, with maturation this experience comes, more and more, to be dominated by the experience of, and in the language of, others. Thus, over time there is a growing interpenetration between experience and peer correction. Moreover, Bloch's account does not show how the second form of cognition, involving historically derived influences, as also received from peers, could be kept entirely separate from categories derived from individual experience of the environment.

Bloch is, however, partially right. In religious thought ideological positions are generally asserted in a form that is difficult to debate or argue against. However, the positions do overlap into practical issues, and are used to support particular interests against others. Thus, differing forms of ritual thought may actually involve disputes at the practical level. One implication of Bloch's model is that there cannot be intercultural cognitive differences at the level of practical thought, an assertion that needs to be questioned. In my view, his argument that practical thought is universal (and thus, by implication, so are the ontological bases of such thought) because all humans share the same experience of the environment is incorrect, for two reasons.

First, practical relations between human groups and the environment differ, both because people's environments may differ widely and because their interest in their environment, that is, the parts of the environment that they see as their resources, their techniques of appropriation of resources, and the social forms of labour used in this process, are anything but universal. Bloch thus oversimplifies the basis of the imputed universality of practical thought.

Secondly, when Bloch claims that Berlin and Kay's data on colour classification, or Chomsky's account of universal grammar, indicate universal forms of thought, he is mistaken. What is universal is not the actual syntax or classificatory principles used by real people; what is universal is the highly abstract and, in principle, unconscious structures underlying the diversity in these forms of thinking. Grammar (as the analogue for these structures) is an analytic concept, unconscious in use, and it should not be treated as a form of thought.

At the level of thought, in the sense of consciousness plus articulation, there can be ontological diversity even regarding pragmatic issues, despite any common underlying abstract structures. This is not to say that we do not need a theoretical account for any apparent universal potential of intercultural communication. However, in addition to looking to systems of thought, some account is needed of the place of emotions in the explanation for whatever universal consciousness exists among humans, a matter not alluded to by Bloch.

One could further question Bloch's assertion that there are universal structures of thinking based on the universality of nature. Even if we assume a common perception of shared external reality, as soon as any such individual perceptions are communicated, it is entirely plausible that they would become subject to pressures to modify the account of them, both in response to any pre-existing perceptions and to a speaker's knowledge of the cognitive expectations of those with whom the communication is taking place. In other words, there is no reason to suppose that cognitive enculturation does not occur as much with practical as it apparently does (by Bloch's own account) with ritual thinking. A process of structuration of individual perceptions may well occur because, in order for communication between individual perceptions to occur, any initial differences must be smoothed over and some level of cognitive conformity created. This structuration process need not itself depend solely on any shared empirical reality.

Even arguments supporting the permeability of boundaries do not deny the usefulness of making a fundamental distinction between religion and other kinds of thinking. For Marx, as for Bloch, this distinction was identified with the difference between infrastructure and superstructure, between practical thought and ideology. For me, what makes religion different, apart from its ideological nature, is its dependence on analogical principles of thought, in contrast to other kinds of logic. As Scott (1989) has pointed out, analogical and non-analogical forms of thought are often used together in a complementary relationship. Since religious thinking is based on analogy, it is to be treated as a logically derivative or secondary form of thought, in the sense that it is based on the prior existence of non-analogical forms of thought. However, these are often the basis of cosmological ideas and other concepts that are every bit as real as any other notions, and which can therefore form the basis of cognitive barriers.

Where distinct cultures are in contact, conflicts can arise for many reasons: social inequality based on race or ethnicity, differences in cultural values, or imposed legal differences. An Aboriginal group may have interests different from those of the majority. Cultural minorities within powerful states feel themselves under pressure to get across their political message by employing innovative forms of rhetoric, which may emphasize ethnic difference, particularly where the state can be accused of past moral failures. Other factors may at the same time draw minorities, often unwillingly, towards employing the idioms of the dominant group, for example, in their utilization of popular North American symbols of 'Indianness.' Talented orators may vie for attention, and in doing so may shape their demands in those forms that they feel the majority can best understand.

An obvious feature of the modern world is cultural diversity and the need for, and indeed prevalence of, intercultural communication. While this diversity is now self-evident, it is not just a feature that only recently emerged in modern multicultural societies. It has long been in the nature of societies to have some external social relations, including intermarriage, with neighbouring alien peoples. Thus, humanity is not by nature intrinsically confined to living within a single culture-bound frame of reference. People can acquire cultural codes other than the one they grew up with, and can develop the ability for cultural 'code switching.' This potential would appear to be especially relevant for groups like the northern Cree and Innu, minorities living with more powerful cultural groups within a multi-ethnic nation state. In such cases, where it is easy for the majority to overlook the implications of social changes on minorities with different assumptions and values, there is a need for 'treaties' or other such legal agreements that provide formal acknowledgment and acceptance of ontological diversity. The possibility of culturally based cognitive boundaries as a source of problems must be acknowledged, even while the analysis of it needs to be made with considerable care.

In this paper I have examined the evidence for cognitive boundaries not in specific linguistic features or in the dominant metaphors of the cultures concerned (Salmond 1982), but on the metaphysical level that is implicit in cosmology. The relevance of metaphysics here is that, in order to be able to think about the world, certain underlying ontological assumptions must first be made, and these assumptions are not universal. If made explicit, these assumptions constitute a significant part of a group's basic metaphysical beliefs. These beliefs may take the form of a set of abstract principles, a repertoire of explanatory myths, or a cosmology representing the world as an ordered system, in a form that systematically details and accounts for that order. In many cultures the myths and cosmologies that embody the group's metaphysical principles are inseparable from its system of religious beliefs. It seems to me that this is an especially important area for the study of cognitive barriers.

To account for the acceptance of the healing movement as a means of appropriately addressing the underlying causes of the social problems of Cree or Innu communities, I have found it useful to consider intercultural barriers. Therapy programs, unlike the healing movement, have difficulty in overcoming a conceptual barrier between cultural modes of thinking. The two approaches can be seen to embody divergent cultural codes, each founded on different, culturally specific, conceptions of reality, and on different representations of the place of humanity in the universe. The social movements based on 'healing' (in the sense of renewal, either bodily or social) are grounded in traditional Aboriginal spiritual ideas. They make a connection to the Northern Algonquian world view, and to modes of understanding already familiar to northern Cree and Innu villagers.

More than this, the healing movement involves a subtle reformulation of Northern Algonquian spiritual ideas. They entail a reworking of the animist ideas of formerly nomadic hunters to better suit the contemporary, more sedentary, and market-oriented way of life. Having located the source of the pathology within society, rather than within the individual, they direct their attention to the rebuilding of the Cree or the Innu social order. Both the Cree and the Innu have considerable experience with government efforts to rebuild their societies along other lines. In the case of the Cree of Quebec, twenty years' experience living with the James Bay and Northern Quebec Agreement, whatever its benefits, has not achieved one of the primary objectives that was hoped for by the Cree at the time of the signing: a secure place in the economic and social order of Quebec. The Innu of Labrador also have considerable experience of their growing social marginalization within an emerging multi-ethnic Labrador society (Tanner 1993). Under these circumstances, the healing movement represents a focus inwards, on communities, on ethnic identity, and on cultural renewal. Social pathologies come to be seen in terms of the rebuilding of Cree or Innu society and collective identity.

The healing movement is an ideological refocusing on what has been referred to as a 'cosmology of nature.' It can be represented as a continuity with the ideas of the past, but it also involves a shift in perspective, from that of autonomous hunters controlling, through practical and spiritual relations with animals, many of the key factors affecting their own lives, to that of an ethnic group establishing itself within a complex Canadian or North American economic and political context, and seeking a more satisfactory way of life.

NOTES

My thanks to the Innu of Sheshatshit and Utshimassits (Davis Inlet), Labrador, and the East Cree of Mistissini, Quebec, where I have conduced research over several years. For preliminary reconnaissance work on the Healing Movement in Mistissini starting in 1996 I am grateful for the financial support of the Native Mental Health Group, directed by Dr Laurence Kirmayer, with funds from the Conseil québécois de la recherche sociale, Government of Quebec. Comments on an earlier version of this paper, 'Environmental Boundaries and Moral Knowledge of the East Cree and Innu of Quebec-Labrador,' given at the colloquium 'Les Obstacles ontologiques dans les relations interculturelles' at Forêt Montmorency, Quebec, October 1996, were given by Clifford Moar, Mary Coon, John Clammer, and Sylvie Poirier. I am also grateful for the detailed comments and suggestions of Eric Schwimmer, and those of my colleague at Memorial University, Jean Briggs.

1 The East Cree and the Innu (who are also known in the ethnographic literature as the Montagnais-Naskapi) are closely related to each other, linguistically and culturally. Together they are part of the widespread Northern Algonquian grouping, which also includes the Ojibwa and the Plains Cree. Because historically the Quebec East Cree and the Labrador Innu came under different administrative regimes, and also because of local dialect variations, they do not use a common standardized term of self-reference. Thus, while in Labrador and adjacent Quebec they call themselves, in their own language, 'Innu' (literally, 'person'), among the East Cree (allowing for both dialect shifts and the various orthographic conventions in use) the same term appears as either 'Iyiyu' or 'Iyinu.' In general, my use of the term 'Cree' should by understood as a shorthand form of 'East Cree.'

2 For a recent indication of the scepticism with which many in the environmental assessment profession view these requirements, see Howard and Widdowson 1996.

3 Pan-Indianism, as will be outlined below, refers to a set of cultural features common to many North American Aboriginal peoples, practices particularly suited to urban situations, and public ceremonies like the powwow, where there are people of North American Native ancestry from many different tribal backgrounds. Activities include the pipe ceremony, dancing, drumming, the sweat lodge, the sweet grass ceremony, and ceremonial dress; symbolic elements include the medicine wheel and North America as 'turtle island' (Frideres 1988, 283–5; Sun Bear, Wind, and Mulligan 1991).

4 For a critique of one such follow-up program among the Labrador Innu, see Samson's paper in this volume.

5 According to some East Cree with whom I have spoken, the northern Cree are now simply recovering their former ritual practices, shared by all of the Cree during the pre-contact period, but maintained after contact only by the Plains Cree.

220   Adrian Tanner

6 For a similar point regarding relations between Christian and 'pagan' Kwaio of Mailaita, Solomon Islands, see Keesing (1992, 142–4).
7 Descola makes a similar observation, in reference to the Achuar of the Amazon Basin (1996, 64).

REFERENCES

Adelson, N. 1997. 'Gathering Knowledge: Reflections on the Anthropology of Identity, Aboriginality, and the Annual Gatherings in Whapmagoostui, Quebec.' AGREE Discussion Paper Number 1. Montreal: Aboriginal Government, Resources, Economy and Environment, McGill University.
Armitage, P. 1992. 'Religious Ideology among the Innu of Eastern Quebec and Labrador,' *Religiologiques* 6: 64–110.
Bloch M. 1989a. *Ritual, History and Power: Selected Papers in Anthropology.* London: Athlone Press.
– 1989b. 'The Past and the Present in the Present.' *Ritual, History and Power: Selected Papers in Anthropology.* London: Athlone Press.
Brightman, R. 1993. *Grateful Prey: Rock Cree Human-Animal Relationships.* Berkeley: University of California Press.
Brody, H. 1981. *Maps and Dreams: Indians and the British Columbia Frontier.* Vancouver: Douglas and McIntyre.
Descola, P. 1996. 'Les cosmologies des indiens d'Amazone.' *La Recherche* 292: 62–7.
Fouillard, C. 1995. *Gathering Voices: Finding Strength to Help Our Children.* Vancouver: Douglas and McIntyre.
Frideres, J.S. 1988. *Native Peoples in Canada: Contemporary Conflicts.* Scarborough: Prentice-Hall.
Government of Quebec. 1991. *James Bay and Northern Quebec Agreement and Complementary Agreements.* Quebec: Les Publications du Québec.
Hallowell, A.I. 1954. 'The Self and Its Behavioral Environment.' *Explorations II* (April).
Henriksen, G. 1973. *Hunters in the Barrens: The Naskapi on the Edge of the White Man's World.* St John's: Institute of Social and Economic Research.
Howard, A., and F. Widdowson. 1996. 'Traditional Knowledge Threatens Environmental Assessment.' *Policy Options* November: 34–6.
Jacobs, P., P. Lacoste, and G. Moisan. 1994. *Joint Report of the Conformity and Quality of the Environmental Impact Statement for the Proposed Great Whale River Hydroelectric Project.* Montreal: Great Whale River Public Review Support Office.

Keesing, R. 1992. *Custom and Confrontation: The Kwaio Struggle for Cultural Autonomy.* Chicago: University of Chicago Press.

Kennedy, G. 1994. *Arctic Smoke and Mirrors.* Prescott, ON: Voyager Publishing.

Lévi-Strauss, C. 1972. *The Savage Mind.* London: Weidenfeld and Nicolson.

Mackey, M.G.A. 1995. *We are Healing Ourselves: Healing Efforts of the Mushuau Innu Since 1992.* Prepared for the Musuau Innu Renewal Committee and Mushuau Innu Band Council, August.

Marcus, A.R. 1992. *Out in the Cold.* Copenhagen: International Work Group on Indigenous Affairs.

National Defence (Canada). 1989. *Goose Bay EIS: An Environmental Impact Statement on Military Flying Activities in Labrador and Quebec.* Ottawa: Department of National Defence.

Press, H. 1995. 'Davis Inlet in Crisis: Will the Lessons Ever Be Learned?' *Canadian Journal of Native Studies* 15 (2): 187–209.

Preston, R.J. 1975. *Cree Narrative: Expressing the Personal Meanings of Events.* Ottawa: National Museum of Man.

Ross, R. 1992. *Dancing with a Ghost: Exploring Indian Reality.* Markham, ON: Reed Books.

Royal Commission on Aboriginal Peoples. 1993. *The Path to Healing: Report of the National Round Table on Aboriginal Health and Social Issues.* Ottawa: Supply and Services.

– 1994. *The High Arctic Relocation: A Report on the 1953–55 Relocation.* Ottawa: Supply and Services.

Salmond, A. 1982. 'Theoretical Landscapes. On a Cross-Cultural Conception of Knowledge.' In David Parkin, ed., *Semantic Anthropology,* 65–87. London: Academic Press.

Scott, C. 1989. 'Knowledge Construction among Cree Hunters: Metaphors and Literal Understanding.' *Journal de la Société des Américanistes* 75: 193–208.

Sun Bear, W. Wind, and C. Mulligan. 1991. *Dancing with the Wheel: The Medicine Wheel Workbook.* New York: Simon and Schuster.

Tanner, A. 1971. 'Ideology and Sickness among the Ojibwa Indians of New Osnaburg, Ontario.' Unpublished report to the Sioux Lookout Project on the Delivery of Health Care to the Indians in Northern Ontario, Department of Social Relations, University of Toronto.

– 1978. 'Divinations and Decisions: Multiple Explanations for Algonquian Scapulamancy.' *Yearbook of Symbolic Anthropology* 1979: 89–101. Montreal: McGill-Queen's University Press.

– 1979. *Bringing Home Animals: Religious Ideology and Mode of Production of the Mistassini Cree Hunters.* London: Hurst Publishers; St John's: Institute of Social and Economic Research; New York: St Martin's Press.

- 1993. 'History and Culture in the Generation of Ethnic Nationalism.' In M. Levin, ed., *Aboriginality and Ethnicity*, 75–96. Toronto: University of Toronto Press.

Tester, F.J., and P. Kulchyski. 1994. *Tammarniit (Mistakes): Inuit Relocation in the Eastern Arctic, 1939–63*. Vancouver: UBC Press.

Walker, John (Dir.). 1996. *Place of the Boss*. Montreal: National Film Board of Canada. Videocassette.

Wilson, J. (Dir.). 1994. *The Two Worlds of the Innu*. London: Channel Four. Video-cassette.

Young, T.K. 1988. *Health Care and Cultural Change: The Indian Experience in the Central Subarctic*. Toronto: University of Toronto Press.

PART IV

Negotiating Ontologies, Making Worlds

A great deal of negotiation between Indigenous and mainstream groups has been going on for some time in many democratic societies, but it has mostly been limited to the interpretation of specific and exclusive legal provisions laid down by Whites and applied to indigenes. It is only very recently that a principle of legal pluralism, as Melkevik calls it, began to be applied to Indigenous societies, in Canada or elsewhere. Legal pluralism refers to the establishment of alternative systems of law, based on the diverse ontologies present in each country. Melkevik's paper sets out the social philosophy of legal pluralism, of which he has practical knowledge by studying the Sami of Norway, while Schwimmer describes the pattern of negotiations conducted by minorities, like the New Zealand Mâori, as they struggle to have a principle of legal pluralism applied to their own people.

This account of the Mâori case reveals a people with both a modern lifestyle and profound roots in Polynesian ontology. Schwimmer partly explains this apparent paradox by a brief recall of a step-by-step development of concepts relived and reshaped by each generation of Mâori leaders and thinkers, who are inventive but still draw fundamental ideas from Polynesian cultural resources. Their process of reshaping and reappropriation is extremely complex as some revered institutions need transforming from generation to generation to ensure that their essence will not fade away in the course of negotiations.

Negotiation can produce what Holland et al. (1998) call co-development. The Mâori case illustrates the watchfulness and the analytical skill of leaders who are responding to mainstream assimilative pressures, who sense hidden implications and seek consensus in debates and symbolic performances, until they (or their ancestors, appearing in dreams) find countermoves that solve problems and keep the mainstream at bay. As long as good responses keep coming, assimilative pressures in advanced societies are resistible, and seemingly incompatible ontologies can negotiate their common survival. Co-development goes beyond salvaging individuals in difficulty and helping them to author their lives; it sets up structures that have been negotiated with the majority but are managed by minorities, permitting alternative ontologies to develop and endure with a minimum of conflict over the generations.

REFERENCES

Holland, D., W. Lachicotte, D. Skinner, and C. Cain. 1998. *Identity and Agency in Cultural Worlds.* Cambridge: Harvard University Press.

Chapter Eight

The Customary Law of Indigenous Peoples and Modern Law: Rivalry or Reconciliation?

BJARNE MELKEVIK

The aim in writing this article is to reflect upon and to discuss the relationship between the Aboriginal Peoples' customary law heritage, in Quebec and Canada, and legal modernism.[1] We strive to discern the way in which each represents an 'ontological' obstacle to the other. Rather than simply establishing a rivalry between these two notions, we will also offer our reflections on a negotiated political reconciliation, respectful of both. This reconciliation is, we feel, both possible and desirable, within the very conception of legal modernism. It is best to underscore that our reflections are born of a preoccupation with the law and with the project of legal modernism. We should also clarify the basic trends of this project, from an occidental standpoint, in the face of the quantifiable methods of scientists. Working from a conception of law as a perpetual intersubjective mediation, it follows that the law is always discerned on the basis of logical methodical proceduralism, i.e., the discourse followed to determine the law. From this point of view, the law is not something ready made, neither on the side of Aboriginal nor on that of non-Aboriginal people, but rather a project of mediation, as flexible as required by the infinite possibilities of particular social contexts. In fact, the law maintains a detached relationship with facts, be they natural, cultural, anthropological, sociological, political, or otherwise. The law does not relate to the facts, but holds them at a distance, or puts them in parentheses, to better determine the meaning of intersubjective relationships, or, more specifically, social mediation between individuals. The law is not preoccupied with facts, it is concerned with the intersubjective relationships and the possibilities involved in such relationships. These preliminary remarks lead into our initial reflection on traditional Aboriginal law from a legal and philosophical standpoint, which will be followed by a determination of how 'ancestral rights' have been defined by the Supreme Court of Canada. Lastly, we will reflect on a conception of modern legality that is not antinomical to a policy of recognition of the customary law heritage of Aboriginal Peoples.

The Traditional Aboriginal Philosophy of 'Law'

First of all, a clarification of our use of the word 'philosophy,' as it refers to Native people in Quebec and Canada, is in order. Traditional Native philosophy is not of Hellenistic inspiration. The occidental conception of philosophy, in so far as it is without a doubt of Hellenistic origin, is structured as an interrogation based on reason available for organizing human experience. Occidental philosophy, in its Greek origins, abandons ancient mythology and subjects it to three questions: What is True? What is Just (and Good)? What is Beautiful? Socrates is synonymous with this questioning, as his 'crime' was refusing to teach the ancient customs, legends, and mythology before he had accomplished the initial process of self-understanding. Occidental philosophy is, in this way, inherently bound to a conception of rationality as this self-understanding serves to understand the world as an emanation of a rational thinking self.

Traditional Native philosophy is not structured on a Hellenistic basis. It is not a bearer of rationality and social, legal, or political differentiation, nor is it responsible for their concrete implementation in the large and broadening public space of rationalized cultures. The fact that we do not make, or reduce, traditional Native philosophy into an avatar of Greek philosophy does not prevent us from considering each philosophy in its own right. Here, we define philosophy simply as being the question of 'meaning,' available for social, legal, and political experience.

Philosophy, taken in this specific role, refers to the production and the transmission of 'meaning' in North American Native cultural contexts. It produces and transmits a philosophical conception, or a traditional philosophy, that structures and asserts available meaning within the customary law heritage of Native people.

The customary law heritage is manifold and differs considerably from one Native Nation to another. As such, each heritage stands for itself and should be studied concretely on its own merit. We will analyse a common denominator, a modern political expression, of the customary law heritage that is intended to establish it on the basis of 'equality' with state law. The 1980 Declaration of the Assembly of First Nations, with respect to the 'rights' and the 'narrative origin' of the customary law heritage, could be approached as an expression of Native legal philosophy :

> We the Original Peoples of this land know the Creator put us here.
>
> The Creator gave us laws that govern all our relationships to live in harmony with nature and mankind.
>
> The Laws of the Creator defined our rights and responsibilities.
>
> The Creator gave us our spiritual beliefs, our languages, our culture, and a place on Mother Earth which provided us with all our needs.
>
> We have maintained our freedom, our languages, and our traditions from time immemorial.
>
> We continue to exercise the rights and fulfil the responsibilities and obligations given to us by the Creator, for the land upon which we were placed.
>
> The Creator has given us the right to govern ourselves and the right to self-determination.
>
> The rights and responsibilities given to us by the Creator cannot be altered or taken away by any other Nation. (Imai et al. 1993, 77)

The ethno-nationalistic reference to the Native Nation is here more a modern borrowing from the natural law discourses the sixteenth and seventeenth centuries than an Aboriginal phenomenon.[2] Setting this aside, however, we can insist that it describes the modern political essence of the Native peoples' customary law heritage as it 'can be found in stories voiced through generations' (Turpel 1991, 517). Using this affirmation as the modern philosophical keyhole to our under-standing of the Native customary law heritage, it reveals to us the formation of a 'Narration of Origins,' structuring this heritage and bringing it to the forefront. What we observe, in fact, is that the custom-ary law heritage is determined by a narrative discourse of origins, of Creation. It is a narration that teaches us that all human beings, and specifically the Aboriginals, must submit to a cosmogony encompass-ing equally Nature, animals, and human.[3] This cosmographical Cre-ation is attributed the status of being the Great Law, or the Law of Nature. This symbolism of Creation brings to light an account of foun-dations, explaining the place occupied by both extrahuman and human reality, and their relation to each other (Sioui 1995). It is a cosmological account that serves to ensure a common understanding and a knowledge of the Great Law's significance for humankind (see Ross 1992; Lyons 1984, 1985).

In this way, the narration of the Great Law sets down two fundamental teachings: first, an absence of differentiation between the elements of Creation, where all beings and all realities are equal; and secondly, the Cosmic Law, seen as being circular, as a harmonious cycle or a quadruple logic, that returns without fail to its departure point. We will examine these two teaching more closely.

First, concerning the absence of differentiation, we observe within the customary law heritage the establishment of a holistic and spiritual philosophy of Nature, in which Nature has a spirit. It is 'alive' in the sense of a communion or dialogue between human and non-human. Nature, like humankind, has a spirit and responsibility. As Nature and humankind are sister and brother, if not mother and child, their dialogue is reduced to a question of 'family,' of responsibility, respect, and sharing. It is an aesthetic dialogue outside of, and opposed to, any linguistic constraint. Nature, as a spiritual being, comes to humankind aesthetically, in the form of 'Beauty' and 'Truth.' Each person, according to his or her development and spiritual awareness, receives the spiritual message as an integral part of his or her being (Monture 1991, 351).

Secondly, the Law of Nature must be understood in the contemplation of its cyclical expressions, which poses the question of openness of the human experience. We discover that the available 'time-experience' is restrained by the fact that time itself is modelled after the cyclical rhythm of nature. Actually, the cyclical rhythm of time (spring, summer, autumn, and winter) moves and combines with space (east, west, north, and south). This encompasses the question of time and space within the very narration of what the Law of Nature is and what it should be, according to the Aboriginal cosmology, which explains the impossibility of a conceptual differentiation of rights.

Briefly returning to Hellenic philosophy, we can, within an occidental natural law perspective, see humankind as being engaged in a logic of transcendence with respect to justice; justice is the end, and law, courts, rights, and the like are means to reach it to settle an affair. In the Aboriginal legal cosmology, on the other hand, the Aboriginal person becomes the Law of Nature, personifies it, and there is no possibility whatever of transcendence. Consequently, when North American Natives, on the basis of this cosmology, are able to assert themselves and their state of being (ontologically speaking, the Law of Nature), they situate and see themselves as trustees of a Narration of Origins. Thus, in respect of their 'essence' or authenticity, they perpetuate the Narration of Origins on a personal level.

In this way, with respect to cosmology and on the level of customary law, historical narration of the foundation story binds individuals to one another and creates a feeling of intersubjective sharing. It is the community, the Nation, as trustee of the Great Law of Nature and as the direct emanation of it, that is in charge of, and responsible for, the origin narration, and that must assure the individual learning process of personification and socialization of Native youth. If we examine this micro-narration, we can see that it metamorphoses the origin narration within an authentic narration in historical time.

There are two things to be said concerning the continual narration of the members of the Native community. First of all, the initial narration becomes true, authentic, and real through the process of renarration. The origin narration indicates the place (at once spiritual and physical) that the Aboriginal Peoples have or should now have, today. Then the renarration situates the different individuals within the confirmation process of the origin narration. This is a powerful form of narrative construction where the individual is bound, in a religious sense,[4] at once to the origin narration and to the narrating community (the Native Nation).

The question of the narration, in historical time, must be accompanied by an interpretation of the latter. We can approach this second aspect of the Native North American Nations' legal customs heritage by underscoring the fact that the furnishing of meaning is necessarily historical (temporal). What we have been able to ascertain through our analysis thus far is that even if the renarration passes through each individual, the interpretation down through generations is supposed to be limited to those people who have the necessary spiritual capability and the closest access to the origin narration. This role is filled by spiritual leaders, but more often, as a general rule, by the elders of the community. The elders become the 'oracles' of the origin narration, and, often, the only ones who can legitimately interpret it under the new conditions. Even the elders are not free to alter the narration, for they are obliged to transmit an unaltered, authentic narration to new generations. In short, the interpretation of the origin narration must always be limited to a confirmation of the 'origins': it must relate to the origin narration. The narration encompasses all possible human experience, including, obviously, law.

It is important to underline that one consequence of a lack of autonomy in interpretation is that North American Native Peoples quickly sheltered their customary law culture from non-Natives through their strategy of renarration of the encounter between the two. As of the sixteenth century, it was the theme, the myth, of the 'two row wampum' that consecrated this strategy. The theme of the 'two row wampum' differs depending on the source, but we may quote one version that found great favour: Two canoes float side-by-side down the River of Life; the Native canoe carries the Native heritage, while the non-Native canoe carries its own. This image, repeated for centuries, confirms that there are, and should be, two independent cultures, independent legal systems, and independent political institutions (see Dickson-Gilmore 1991; Delisle 1984). It is the product of a counterstrategy, and a counter-myth, with respect to policies on acculturation. And the message is clear: there is nothing that can be shared.

Turning now to an evaluation of the construction of the Native legal philosophy, we can highlight two aspects. First, the Native customary law heritage is above all 'spiritual,' as opposed to material or empirical. It is a spiritual system, referring both to the personification and the socialization of Natives within customs, traditions, and such ideologies that can ensure the performance of community authenticity. Authenticity is thus affirmed to be the boundary of all customary law experiences. Secondly, the customary law heritage brings to the forefront a logic of communion between the cosmos, Nature, animals, and humankind. Natives say: 'We are the Law of Nature,' which, practically speaking, implies a logic of non-differentiation between humankind, the cosmos, Nature, and territory. What is more, it introduces the conception of a circular legal temporality as the only one available for legal experience. It is a customary law system condensed into a very strong community logic, legitimizing only community experiences.

The result, from our perspective, is that there exists no affinity or dialogue with the other in this philosophical customary law formula. What we have found is a complete explanation of a Native authenticity where the non-Native has neither place nor existence. As the non-Native does not exist, he is excluded through not having a place in the origin narration. A consequence of this non-existence is that any dialogue becomes impossible. The origin narration sets up any non-Aboriginal person as an 'ontological obstacle.' This is confirmed by the aforementioned 'two row wampum' myth, in so much as there is nothing that can be shared, and no participation.

For the purpose of legal reflection, it is also important to underline that the origin narration confers the role of aesthetic spectator on Aboriginal and non-Aboriginal alike, where modern law cannot operate except on the basis of arguments and reasons to be honoured by all parties. There is no possibility of argument and reason in this model, and above all, no argument that can be brought forth by a non-Aboriginal. The narration becomes, in this way, an 'ontological obstacle' to any intercultural relationship worthy of the name.

The Ghettoization of North American Native Culture

Where is the customary law heritage of the Quebec and Canadian Native Peoples and Nations today? We would like to emphasize the fact that the affirmation of this heritage has been transformed into a ghetto logic by a succession of decisions from the Supreme Court of Canada (Kulchyski 1994) – a ghetto that encloses, imprisons, and mounts 'ontological obstacles' at every turn. We may ascertain that the recognition of rights provided for in the 1982 Constitutional Act has become a trap. To support our assertion, we will analyse how the Supreme Court of Canada (in *R. v. Van der Peet*) undertakes to define existing rights, recognized and confirmed by Article 35(1).[5]

Let us briefly review the facts. Dorothy Van der Peet, a member of the Sto:lo Aboriginal Nation of British Columbia, sold ten salmons caught under the protection of a native food fishing licence. As the British Columbia Fishery (General) Regulations Act prohibits such a sale, Van der Peet was accused of the offence. In her defence, she argued that the law contravened her existing right to sell the fish. It is the first case in Canadian jurisprudence explicitly concerned with defining the significance of Canadian Aboriginal Peoples' constitutionally protected 'existing' rights.

Concretely, what Van der Peet actually did was to refer to the expression of existing Aboriginal rights protected in the Constitution. In article 35(1) it is written that '[t]he existing aboriginal and treaty rights of the aboriginal peoples of Canada are hereby recognised and affirmed.' We should also mention that the legal claims of, and indeed the strife experienced by, the Native Nations in Quebec and Canada from 1982 on have stemmed from their struggle to obtain and protect recognition of their pre-existing rights (Sanders 1989; Clark 1991). These rights have been reclaimed as 'inherent' and have, in Native political discourse, regrouped all claims so as to give structural coherence to the purport of a Nation-to-Nation relationship (Jhappan 1993) rather than one of individuals to the state.

The method used by the court in deciding the meaning that should be attributed to the existing Aboriginal rights was, however, rather surprising. It decided that instead of referring to the English expression 'existing aboriginal and treaty rights,' reference must come from the French constitutional expression 'droits existants – ancestraux ou issus de traités' (existing rights, ancestral or resulting from treaties). In the not negligible distinction between 'existing' and 'ancestral,' the court relied on 'ancestral' as the sole meaning to be given to the rights described in article 35(1). Even though the court could have, more conventionally, conjugated the English expression, speaking of 'existing aboriginal and treaty rights' with the French expression, which would have produced a more subtle reflection, it instead affirmed that it was the word 'ancestral' that best summarized the interests of Native Nations protected constitutionally. Thus, the Supreme Court of Canada, in favouring the term 'ancestral,' can easily affirm with respect to the interpretation '[t]hat the purpose of s. 35(1) lies in its recognition of the prior occupation of North America by aboriginal peoples is suggested by the French version of the text.'[6] The meaning of the constitutional protection of Article 35(1) now comes of a pre-Columbian logic, to be found in ancestry, and not in that which is 'in existence.'

On the basis of this pre-Columbian logic, the Supreme Court of Canada passed into a second phase in the specific defining of Aboriginal rights. Here, too, the Supreme Court had different choices. In this case, its choice was to ponder what interests were protected by Article 35(1). In responding that the ancestral rights derived from the existence of distinctive Aboriginal collectivities, occupying 'the land as did their ancestors for centuries,' as stated in the *Calder* case,[7] the court considered the interests involved in the two cases to be connected. The court introduced a method of interpretation founded on the image of 'fixed rights,' in connection with Aboriginal practices. This means that to be recognized as an ancestral right, an activity must be an element of custom, practice, or tradition that is an integral part of an Aboriginal Nation's distinctive culture, since the pre-contact era. It must be a fixed right that cannot be interpreted as 'evolvable' or 'political.'

We can observe this when the court discarded the use of a 'social test' in defining rights. In her defence, Van der Peet felt that it was necessary to understand the constitutionally protected rights of the Aboriginal Peoples in their context and in relation to their social repercussions.

This argument was accepted by dissenting Justice Lambert, of the Appeals Court of British Columbia, but rejected, promptly, by the Supreme Court. It is a reasoning that the Supreme Court expressly refused in the following terms:

> The social test casts the aboriginal right in terms that are too broad and in a manner which distracts the court from what should be its main focus – the nature of the aboriginal community's practices, customs or traditions themselves. The nature of the applicant's claim must be delineated in terms of the particular practice, custom or tradition under which it is claimed; the significance of the practice, custom or tradition to the aboriginal community is a factor to be considered in determining whether the practice, custom or tradition is integral to the distinctive culture, but the significance of a practice, custom or tradition cannot, itself, constitute an aboriginal right.[8]

At stake in this affirmation is the fact that ancestral rights are seen through their empirical interpretation. We can see this again with respect to the criteria for ancestral rights of the Supreme Court:

> This aspect of the integral to a distinctive culture test arises from the fact that aboriginal rights have their basis in the prior occupation of Canada by distinctive aboriginal societies. To recognise and affirm the prior occupation of Canada by distinctive aboriginal societies it is *to what makes those societies distinctive* that the court must look in identifying aboriginal rights. The court cannot look at those aspects of the aboriginal society that are true of every human society (e.g., eating to survive), nor can it look at those aspects of aboriginal society that are only incidental or occasional to that society; the court must look instead to the defining and central attributes of the aboriginal society in question. It is only by focusing on the aspects of aboriginal society that make that society distinctive that the definition of aboriginal rights will accomplish the purpose underlying s. 35(1).[9]

In sum, ancestral rights refer to the legal inscription of an Aboriginal ethno-cultural particularity into customs, practices, and traditions. This is the supposed 'essence' of aboriginalism in so much as the rights seek the affirmation and the protection of customs, practices, and traditions, defined by a pre-Columbian logic and as being an integral part of the distinctive cultures of the first occupants of the territory.

This singularly important decision permits us to make several observations about the method used to define these rights and also to accentuate the fact that these rights have become an 'ontological obstacle,' if not a ghetto without a future.

We can, in fact, observe that the Aboriginal heritage from the pre-contact period has become the very essence of aboriginality. It is an 'archaic law,' ancestral and fixed, petrified and stratified, and it in no way corresponds to the challenges facing the Aboriginal Nations of today. The court has, in refusing to give the notion of existing Aboriginal rights a contemporary meaning, naturalized the sociality of Aboriginal culture and heritage. The existing rights are confined to practices and usages that were integral to pre-contact aboriginality, but which do not correspond to any social, economic, or political reality. This legal naturalization of Native Peoples proposes the protection of a 'true' or 'authentic' aboriginality from the non-Native standpoint. But more properly, it transforms all anthropological knowledge of pre-contact Native society into a theory of Aboriginal purity.

It is law that places the Aboriginal reality in a ghetto logic. Incapable of evolving and adapting to new living conditions, and without a hold on the social contexts of the Aboriginal Nations, who, it must be remembered, no longer live in a pre-contact society, the ancestral right confirms the Aboriginal societies within a naturalized logic of subsistence. Subsistence economics that, furthermore, in no way respond to the economic conditions of the Aboriginal societies and their relationship with non-Aboriginals.

Legal Modernism and the Aboriginal Peoples

In the relationship between the law and the Aboriginal Peoples, the question of legal modernism was, is, and always will be a stumbling block. This makes it necessary to say a few words on legal modernism. We can affirm that there are many formulations of such modernism. We can privilege two of them: the first, liberal, is based on an abstract universality and refuses any recognition of legal customs, and the second, based on the concept of communicative intersubjectivity, leans toward a negotiated recognition.

As a matter of fact, the refusal to recognize the Native customary law heritage, or, at least, the refusal to attribute a broad, open interpretation to the concept that we witnessed in the aforementioned Supreme Court of Canada decision, is primarily issued from a philosophically liberal ideology. Indeed, it is the direct result of a liberal legal philosophy.[10]

The logic confirming this conception of Aboriginal rights, and which reveals the underlying aspirations, appears in this same judgment of the Supreme Court of Canada:

> In the liberal enlightenment view, reflected in the American Bill of Rights and, more indirectly, in the *Charter*, rights are held by all people in society because each person is entitled to dignity and respect. Rights are general and universal; they are the way in which the 'inherent dignity' of each individual in society is respected ...
>
> Aboriginal rights cannot, however, be defined on the basis of the philosophical precepts of the liberal enlightenment ... aboriginal rights must be viewed differently from *Charter* rights because they are rights held only by aboriginal members of Canadian society. They rise from the fact that aboriginal people are *aboriginal*.'[11]

We can thus confirm that we have on one side a right to 'dignity and respect,' and on the other, an ancestral right that perpetuates a pre-Columbian reality. As argued by the Supreme Court, *ancestral* rights cannot be defined by applying the principles of liberal philosophy.[12] But can these rights arise from 'facts,' as the Supreme Court supposes, or are they only, as we can presume, a political forging of second-order rights?

This judgment, in fact, turns 'ancestral rights' into second-order rights – rights that cannot stand the test of universality, a privilege exclusively accorded to rights issued by the state, i.e., state laws. If, in fact, the court understood correctly that 'existing rights,' or 'ancestral rights,' refers for Aboriginals to a 'statutes' logic, it has turned this status into a moral insignificance. As Milton Gordon reminds us, the liberal idea of law is characterized by 'the absence, even prohibition, of any legal or governmental recognition of racial, religious, language or groups as corporate entities with a standing in the legal or governmental process, and a prohibition of the use of ethnic criteria of any type for discriminatory purposes, or conversely for special or favoured treatment' (Gordon 1975, 105). In this way, when the Supreme Court seeks, as we have seen, to reduce the 'existing rights' of Aboriginals through interpretations within a logic of exclusion, it follows a tradition where universality is attached uniquely to state law. The Aboriginal society and its rights cannot help but be different. By being 'different,' they are also, consistently, morally insignificant.

By referring to legislative history, it is possible for us to determine more precisely how this point of view of legal modernism constitutes an 'ontological obstacle' for the Aboriginal customary law heritage. In fact, constitutional recognition of existing Aboriginal rights was extracted from the Canadian government after a horrendous battle. Canadian prime minister Pierre Elliott Trudeau's 1969 project was meant to abolish all Aboriginal rights, powers of reserve, and laws concerning Aboriginals, in an effort to bring about equality with all other citizens (Weaver 1981, 108–21). If Trudeau was not able to attain his goal; if he backed down in the face of Aboriginal opposition; and if he was obliged to recognize existing Aboriginal rights, it still remains true that he succeeded in affirming a state ideology, namely, the moral insignificance of Aboriginal rights, hence the idea of their long-term abolishment. It is this ideology that is expressed in the recent Supreme Court decision. Aboriginal rights, seen in this light, become morally insignificant, and it is logical, within such a conception, that they would meet with 'ontological obstacles' to bar them from a Western society.

We are, however, inclined to accept a different way of understanding legal modernism – our conception of it is 'communicative.'[13] According to this conception, modern legality is viewed as being attached to the question of communicative intersubjectivity. In this way, we no longer have a need for any metaphysical analysis of the individual, be it Kantian or other, nor of any antinomy between the individual and the policy constructed as a mediation between abstract and concrete dimensions of power and institutions. Neither, as was the case of the Supreme Court, is there need for a pre-established moral vision of rights. Communicative intersubjectivity should constitute the very essence of modernism in the concrete and real sense of individuals being reciprocally the authors and the addressees of the selection discourse for legal norms and institutions (Habermas 1996, 38, 104–5). In this way, everyone, Aboriginals included, should be seen, pragmatically, as being engaged in a (quasi-transcendental) process that confirms them as authors and addressees with respect to their legal norms and institutions. Dignity and respect are not the quality of 'rights,' as held by the Supreme Court, but the starting point of relations individuals share reciprocally in a process of self-legislation in matters that concern them.

Assuming that the individual represents the unsurpassable horizon of legal modernism, we propose, in an effort to remove him from modern metaphysics, to think of him in his intersubjectivity. More precisely, to think of the individual, the modern subject, in his interaction with others. In this way, we can consider intersubjectivity as the actual, and not the metaphysical, expression of modernism that, through speaking out and taking a position, assures the subject a place symbolizing the modern project of self-legislation. Individuals who, seen intersubjectively, exercise a real and concrete autonomy, and the desire to see themselves as authors of legal norms and institutions. We will now clarify our affirmations by referring to the question of political autonomy, and follow with the question of identity.

The concept of political autonomy is, in fact, double-sided. It is a notion that accompanied the construction of nationstates from the seventeenth through the nineteenth centuries, the struggle for the decolonization of the Third World, and national restructuring within nations and in the order of nations (e.g., the former Soviet Union), just as much as Aboriginal Peoples struggle today within the framework of established states. The very notion of political autonomy, as conveyed by modern thinking, implies a moral requirement that must be honoured. It is up to each individual to ensure a concordance between moral requirement and policy elaboration. On the other hand, how can we keep this idea restricted to a single nation state, when the composition of these states is so heterogeneous, composed as they are of different peoples that can each claim a history and a culture tied to territory? This attachment becomes that much stronger as international law, based on this same legal modernism, has constructed a set of norms so that Aboriginal Peoples can benefit from a right to live according to their own culture, in their own language, and according to the religious beliefs of their ancestors.[14]

If we look more closely at Aboriginal law from the perspective of legal modernism, we can see that the search for a compromise between the first wave of this modernism (represented by the building of nation states, and the quest for universality by which it is characterized) and the second (the challenge to recognize the Aboriginal fact) represents an enormous task as much for jurists as for politicians. Examples of this search are the fierce issue of individual versus collective rights as well as the very concept of political autonomy (McDonald 1991, 217–419; Baker 1994; Kymlicka 1995). The sources at the disposal of legal modernism might indicate the direction being taken to find an answer, respectful of universalist requirements, while confirming the individuals (whether Aboriginal or citizens of a modern democratic and pluralistic state) as the authors and addressees of legal norms and institutions.

Let us now consider the question of identity. As we know, Aboriginal

Peoples in Quebec and in Canada, as elsewhere around the world, seek recognition of their identity (Brøsted et al. 1985; Berger 1991; Goehring 1993). We know that this search encounters opposition from liberals, who do not wish to recognize Aboriginal identity, seeing only an immoral request in this claim, a regression, if not an invitation to implement an unjust and harmful system. In our conception of modernism, however, things look quite different, our perception of modernism being connected to identify as an expression of individuals who proclaim and see themselves as authors and addressees of legal norms and institutions.

Going back to our definition of modernism, that is, the concrete individual who produces, intersubjectively with others, his norms and his public institutions, the Aboriginal claims are not shocking. They express the desire to produce the norms and institutions that give them shape. As these norms and institutions affect them directly, they speak out, on the basis of one conception of legal modernism, as the authors and addressees of the rights that they would see attributed to themselves. The pertinence of this conception of legal modernism, with respect to our understanding of what Aboriginal rights could be today, is in its granting the values of 'dignity' and 'respect' to all individuals. It reverses the Supreme Court's expressed philosophy, by emphasizing that Aboriginals can, and should, assert a place in politics and law that could continually allow them to produce and select cogent and sound legal norms. Indeed, it introduces a perspective which allows that if legal modernism consists primarily of individuals who mutually assert themselves as the authors and the addressees of law, nothing keeps us from seeing these authors and these addressees as embedded in the narrative and interpretative contexts giving a sense to their existence and their desire to continue to live and to recognise themselves as Aboriginals.

On the other hand, common norms and institutions should be negotiated in concert. In this way this conception of legal modernism advocates a continual 'judicial' negotiation of what Aboriginal legal rights can mean today and how they can be accommodated with Aboriginal legal heritage. It is a political and democratic conception of law as opposed to the liberal moral vision of law. Obviously, this conception of modern legality does not solve all possible problems, but the world is made up of often overlapping legal jurisdictions. The relationships between them have always been politically negotiated. Only human rights can constitute firm ground for the legal imagination.

Conclusion

Aboriginal leaders know that crucial choices must be made; they know that their communities must accommodate themselves to new and altered patterns of existence. The new political narrative of Aboriginal legal culture works, as we see it, to ensure a basis of identity and authenticity in this difficult process. It builds a bridge between the new existence of Aboriginal Peoples and the inherited legal cultures. The task confronting Native Nations is to rewrite the narration, the origin narration, to respond to and anticipate new and altered sociological, economic, and political patterns. Cultural survival can only be assured when this rewriting is undertaken.

Legal modernity, as seen in its communicative version, insisting on individuals seen as authors and addressees of legal norms and institutions, represents the inescapable horizon to any sound recognition of Native legal custom. We should, in this way, see a recognition of Native legal customs as an ideal where the cultural heritage of individuals is no longer the opposite of universality, but as fundamentally tied to it as a mountain spring is to a mountain. The basis of any recognition is human rights as they are described with respect to Aboriginal Peoples within new international law (Otis and Melkevik 1996).

Our reflections lead us to the conclusion that the function of law is not to express identity, but to permit identities to freely express themselves. Its task is not to dictate identities, but to negotiate the relationships between them. Permitting legal modernism is, so to speak, a way of overcoming ontological, naturalizing obstacles.

NOTES

1 We would like to specify that our use of capitalization for the terms 'Aboriginal' and 'Native' is out of respect for the Aboriginal people in the same way as references to specific peoples are capitalized in the cases of 'Quebecer' or 'Canadians.' See Goehring (1993).

2 See Thomas (1994). Concerning ethnonationalistic discourses, see Levin (1993).

3 See Hultkrantz (1987, ch. 2).

4 Let us remember the etymology of the word 'religion': that which 'binds' or 'joins.'

5 *R. v. Van der Peet*, [1996] 2 Canada Supreme Court Reports (S.C.R.), 507.

This decision is followed by *R. v. Gladstone*, [1996] 2 S.C.R., 703; *R. v. Pamajewon*, [1996] 2 S.C.R., 821; *R. v. Côté*, [1996] 3 S.C.R., 139; and *R. v. Adams*, [1996] 3 S.C.R., 101, which confirm the conclusions laid down in *R. v. Van der Peet.*

6   *R. v. Van der Peet*, 539.

7   *Calder v. Attorney General of British Columbia*, [1973] S.C.R. 313.

8   *R. v. Van der Peet*, 552.

9   Ibid., 553.

10 Kymlicka (1990) suggests a liberal reconciliation with cultural communities.

11 *R. v. Van der Peet*, 534.

12 Ibid., 534–5.

13 We are here inspired by, if not rigorously following, the work of Habermas (1994a, 1994b, 1996). On Habermas and law, see Deflem (1996) or Melkevik (1996).

14 Otis and Melkevik (1996), Capotorti (1979). See also article 27 of the *International Covenant on Civil and Political Rights* (1966).

REFERENCES

Baker, J. 1994. *Group Rights*. Toronto: University of Toronto Press.

Berger, T.R. 1991. *A Long and Terrible Shadow*. Vancouver: Douglas and McIntyre.

Brøsted, J., J. Dahl, A. Gray, H.G. Gulløv, G. Henriksen, and I. Kleivan. 1985. *Native Power: The Quest for Autonomy and Nationhood of Indigenous Peoples*. Bergen, Norway: Universitetsforlaget.

Capotorti, F. 1979. *Study on the Rights of Persons Belonging to Ethnic, Religious and Linguistic Minorities*. New York: United Nations Documents E/CN.4/Sub.2/384/Rev.1.

Clark, B. 1991. *Native Liberty, Crown Sovereignty: The Existing Aboriginal Rights of Self-Government in Canada*. Montreal and Kingston: McGill-Queen's University Press.

Deflem, M. 1996. *Habermas, Modernity and Law*. London: Sage Publications.

Delisle, A. 1984. 'How We Regained Control over Our Lives and Territories: The Kahnawake Story.' In L. Little Bear, M. Boldt, and J.A. Long, eds., *Pathways to Self-Determination: Canadian Indians and the Canadian State*, 141–7. Toronto: University of Toronto Press.

Dickson-Gilmore, E.J. 1991. 'Resurrecting the Peace: Traditionalist Approaches to Separate Justice in the Kahnawake Mohawk Nation.' In *Proceedings on the 6th International Symposium of the Commission on Folk Law and Legal Pluralism*, 260–83. Ottawa.

Goehring, B. 1993. *Indigenous Peoples of the World: An Introduction to Their Past, Present, and Future*. Saskatoon: Purich Publishing.

Gordon, M. 1975. 'Toward a General Theory of Racial and Ethnic Group Relations.' In N. Glaezer and D.P. Moynihan, eds., *Ethnicity, Theory and Experience*, 84–110. Cambridge: Harvard University Press.

Habermas, J. 1994a. 'Three Normative Models of Democracy.' *Constellations* 1 (1): 1–10.

– 1994b. 'Human Rights and Popular Sovereignty: The Liberal and Republican Versions,' *Ratio Juris* 7 (1): 1–13.

– 1996. *Between Facts and Norms: Contributions to a Discourse Theory of Law and Democracy*. Cambridge, MA: MIT Press.

Hultkrantz, A. 1987. *Native Religions of North America*. San Francisco: Harper Collins.

Imai, S., K. Logan, and G. Stein. 1993. *Aboriginal Law Handbook*. Toronto: Carswell.

Jhappan, R. 1993. 'Inherency, Three Nations and Collective Rights: The Evolution of Aboriginal Constitutional Discourse from 1982 to the Charlottetown Accord.' *International Journal of Canadian Studies* 7–8: 225–59.

Kulchyski, P. 1994. *Unjust Relations: Aboriginal Rights in Canadian Courts*. Don Mills, ON: Oxford University Press.

Kymlicka, W. 1990. *Contemporary Political Philosophy: An Introduction*. Oxford: Clarendon Press.

– 1995. *Multicultural Citizenship: A Liberal Theory of Minority Rights*. Oxford: Oxford University Press.

Levin, M.D. 1993. *Ethnicity and Aboriginality: Case Studies in Ethnonationalism*. Toronto: University of Toronto Press.

Lyons, O. 1984. 'Spirituality, Equality and Natural Law.' In L. Little Bear, M. Boldt, and J.A. Long, eds., *Pathways to Self-Determination: Canadian Indians and the Canadian State*, 1–13. Toronto: University of Toronto Press.

– 1985. 'Traditional Native Philosophies Relating to Aboriginal Rights.' In M. Boldt, J.A. Long, and L. Little Bear, eds., *The Quest for Justice: Aboriginal Peoples and Aboriginal Rights*, 19–23. Toronto: University of Toronto Press.

McDonald, M. 1991. 'Collective Rights.' *Canadian Journal of Law and Jurisprudence* 4: 217–419.

Melkevik, B. 1996. 'Habermas et l'état de droit.' In J. Boulad-Ayoub, B. Melkevik, and P. Robert, eds., *L'Amour des lois. La crise de la loi moderne dans les sociétés démocratiques*, 371–87. Paris: l'Harmattan; Québec: Les Presses de l'Université Laval.

Monture, P.A. 1991. 'Reflecting on Flint Woman.' In R.F. Devlin, ed., *Canadian Perspectives on Legal Theory*, 351–66. Toronto: Montgomery.

Otis, G., and B. Melkevik. 1996. *Peuples autochtones et normes internationales*.

Analyse et textes relatifs au régime de protection identitaire des peuples autochtones. Cowansville, QC: Yvon Blais.

Ross, R. 1992. *Dancing with a Ghost: Exploring Indian Reality.* Markham, ON: Octopus Books.

Sanders, D. 1989. 'Pre-Existing Rights: The Aboriginal Peoples of Canada.' In G.A. Beaudoin and E. Rathushny, eds., *The Canadian Charter of Rights and Freedoms,* 707–38. Toronto: Carswell.

Sioui, G.E. 1995. *For an Amerindian Autohistory: An Essay on the Foundations of a Social Ethic.* Montreal and Kingston: McGill-Queen's University Press.

Thomas, N. 1994 *Colonialism's Culture.* Princeton: Princeton University Press.

Turpel, M.E. 1991. 'Aboriginal Peoples and the Canadian Charter: Interpretative Monopolies, Cultural Differences.' In R.F. Devlin, ed., *Canadian Perspective on Legal Theory,* 517. Toronto: Montgomery.

Weaver, S.M. 1981. *Making Canadian Indian Policy: The Hidden Agenda, 1968–1970.* Toronto: University of Toronto Press.

Chapter Nine

Making a World: The Mâori of Aotearoa/New Zealand

ERIC SCHWIMMER

For Pita Sharples

It is now thirty-five years since I left New Zealand for Canada and Quebec. Before leaving, and just after, I wrote some books and articles about biculturalism in New Zealand. Since then, Mâori culture has changed profoundly; so has the toolkit anthropologists use to study cultures. When I decided in 1997 to do a restudy of biculturalism and went to New Zealand with a sketch plan, I was unaware of the gulf separating my project from my scientific 'object,' based on changes in Mâori culture since the Treaty of Waitangi Act of 1975 and the Amendment Act of 1985.[1] It became obvious during my 'fieldwork' that the legal provisions had not only transformed the New Zealand social universe, but also obliged me to rethink my methodology in the light of decolonization. My immediate reaction, while still in the 'field,' was to assume the role of an amanuensis to a compassionate Mâori leader, Pita Sharples, whose guidance initiated me in the ethnography of Mâori regeneration.

Like most of my other projects, this one was concerned with the consequences of conquest and the process of decolonization. Apart from the Mâori, I have studied this theme among the Indonesians, the Canadian Indians, the Québécois, and the Basques. The problem facing all of these groups is to reshape their images of collective identity. One solution, in New Zealand as elsewhere, is to identify with the conquerors' society. To some elite individuals, this is satisfying in itself, but there has also been a tendency, especially since the Second World War, to develop decolonization movements, involving claims to land and forms of sovereignty (linguistic, economic, political), all aiming at recognition, co-development, and self-liberation.

The Mâori term for such objectives, *mana motuhake*, is virtually untranslatable. Both Mâori and *Pâkehâ* authors have offered translations into English, but the ontological status of the translation varies with the mother tongue of the translator. If the 1975 and 1985 acts allow equal validity to statements of collective objectives whether stated in Mâori or English, they still leave Mâori with some discretion in choosing the English words in which Mâori terms are to be stated. Accordingly, my glossary of Mâori terms is based on the one published by Mâori author Ranginui Walker (1990, 295ff),[2] who offers the following entries: *mana* = authority, power, prestige, psychic force; and *motuhake* = discrete, separate, independent.

If we couple each of the three English adjectives, in these glosses, with each of the four English nouns, we have twelve expressions, ranging from 'independent authority' to 'discrete psychic force.' All these correctly express some aspect of what is implied in *mana motuhake*. This example may illustrate the difference between cultural ontology and creative construction. In Mâori ontology, phenomena are described synthetically, whereas Pâkehâ ontology tends to describe them analytically. Thus, the choice between twelve available English renderings is a matter of construction, interpretation, and negotiation. It is not suggested that ontologies cannot change, but only that Walker's glossary cannot help translating synthetic terms into analytical ones.

Many contemporary states (Belgium, Britain, Canada, Norway, Spain, New Zealand, etc.) are seeking ways of symbiosis with citizen communities exhibiting such ontological diversity. They have opened negotiations and offered forms of cultural autonomy and redress of grievances while at the same time strengthening common denominators between peoples cohabiting in the same national space.[3] The possibility of combining these two objectives is increasingly recognized by politicians as well as social scientists (cf. Eriksen 1998, 187).

Thus, following the Treaty of Waitangi and Amendment Acts (1975, 1985), many new Mâori management, consultancy, and service roles were officially recognized in central state apparatuses and in their decentralized, privatized, devolved, autonomized administrative functions. Many of these roles were vested in representatives of what were taken to be traditional units of Mâori social organization: *iwi, hapû, whânau, rûnanga,* trust boards, etc.[4] Fields of activity thus recognized include health, education, employment, justice, environment, and culture. In addition, land and fishery claims and a vast range of local Mâori development projects germinated in the Mâori periphery were presented to official agencies by a widely distributed range of officially recognized deliberative bodies operated by active, well-educated Mâori voluntary workers.

In one way or another, many thousands of Mâori are now involved in these activities. Certainly, such communitarian concerns are by no means new in the Mâori world. But in the 1950s, when I was first able to observe these involved Mâori: their number was smaller, their knowledge of the Pâkehâ world was more limited, and above all, they had far less officially sanctioned access to decision makers. Moreover, some Mâori activities – notably in education and health – have remarkable resonance among the population at large. Even now, Mâori people meet with many obstacles and are often unrewarded, but their legitimacy is recognized, and, if they are wronged, they have more remedies. In recent years, the central government has tried to streamline their abundant efflorescence, but when some doors close, others tend to open up.

Did this process lead to a 'cultural' transformation? Some researchers, including at least one Canadian, concluded somewhat hastily that Mâori are 'retribalising.' This term (based on the translation iwi = tribe) has many possible meanings; the statement is true in the sense that descendants of the same ancestor are increasingly concerned to share in his *mana* – his authority, power, prestige, psychic force. Yet Mâori thought of the nineteenth and twentieth centuries has greatly modified the range and scope of this *mana*, along with other parts of their 'figured world,'[5] as documented by the thought of some Mâori thinkers (e.g., Te Matorohanga, Te Rangikaheke, Te Kooti) who noticed the threats to the future of Mâori collective identity and offered their own interpretations of Mâori ontology, named gods and ancestors as exemplars for common action, and laid down a system of values for Mâori to follow in the new age.

Mâori Figured Worlds

These interpretations were, in part, tacit responses to British colonialism and missionary activity. They were addressed to Mâori, even though Te Rangikaheke was amanuensis to Governor Sir George Grey, who asked him to write a Mâori mythology (which Grey published in Mâori in 1854 and translated into English in 1855). Te Rangikaheke knew that Grey would make comparisons with Greek mythology (see Curnow 1985). The Mâori writer thus sketched a vision of an ancient Polynesian civilization that fitted the Victorian era and eventually became New Zealand's greatest best-seller, with editions still regularly appearing after more than 140 years, and read by Mâori and Pâkehâ alike. This book was an ontology, a figured world, presented through characters, meanings, and values with which Mâori continue to identify.

Te Matorohanga told a different history, to a group of Mâori scholars, around 1860. He introduced a doctrine of a universal God, Io, presiding over a monotheistic cosmos. These teachings did not appear in writing (in Mâori and English) until Percy Smith (1913). Te Matorohanga starts by noting the collapse of the traditional *mana* of the Mâori: 'Gods of the old type exist no longer – their divinity has been brought down to the level of lizards, stones and trees.' Io is the pinnacle of a system of spirit beings, human and non-human, hierarchized by their degree of moral purity. Some propensities, especially love, are close to Io, others more distant, as appears from the positioning of different classes of beings after death. Io is otherwise almost an otiose god, intervening only once in human affairs in order to offer man (hence, Mâori) three hierarchized baskets of knowledge, but leaving him otherwise responsible for determining what values he will pursue and how.

Te Kooti, after a missionary upbringing, led an anti-colonialist uprising modelled on the conduct of war in the Old Testament, and finally became the founder of the Ringatû Church. He has had a commanding influence on the construction of the figured world of the Mâori today, especially due to his vision of the *whânau* community's morality, sacredness, and aesthetics; to his Io-inspired ontology, applied to Mâori political autonomy; and to the defence of Mâori rights against Pâkehâ encroachment.

Te Kooti's teachings survive not only in communities of Ringatû faith, but as stories widely remembered and retold *sub rosa*. It was only after 1975 that the Mâori/Pâkehâ struggle could be approached by Mâori-initiated bicultural negotiation, without crypto-assimilation to the New Zealand mainstream. It was only then that strands of ontological thinking such as those outlined above surfaced as openly professed Mâori views of their collective identity. When we compare the difference between Te Kooti's ontology and the sense of Mâori identity since 1975, we note that it flowed directly from the change in Pâkehâ response to Mâori claims. Te Kooti's doctrine was that the god Taane, with Io's blessing, received the emblem of divine justice (as also did King David and the Queen of England, by the grace of Io).[6] Yet Pâkehâ courts, in Te Kooti's day, continued to maintain that the Treaty of

Waitangi was a legal nullity. Only after the New Zealand legislation of 1975 did the treaty became part of the national ontology.

Historians such as Walker (1990) rightly explain this legislation by improvements in the power position of a much more numerous, highly educated, urbanized Mâori population and international pressures in the postcolonial era. If changed power relations can lead to a major change in Mâori figured worlds, one may well argue, with Bourdieu and Foucault, that power relations are fully determinative of figured worlds. This view is defended by talented scholars close to the Mâori scene and has to be studied in some detail.

Positional Identities

The practical question that arises is whether a Mâori local community can enter into cross-cultural contracts and freely adopt a bicultural 'positional identity' without betraying the Mâori collective self-image.[7] This possibility is firmly denied by Elizabeth Rata in a notable doctoral thesis. In her view, biculturalism leads to the rise of what she calls 'tribal capitalism,' the 'fetishisation of the commodity relation and concealment of an exploitative class relation by the process of neo-traditional reification' (1996, 246). She argues that even though kôhanga reo do reproduce Mâori cultural resources, they imprison pre-school education in an 'exploitative class relation.' A similar critique was heard recently when the European Community planned to write a charter of linguistic rights for regional peoples.[8]

Elizabeth Rata certainly succeeds in showing that any policy of constructing a revitalized Mâori world must entail bicultural negotiations and that any Mâori conducting such negotiations may serve contradictory interests. But it is less evident that Mâori bicultural actors must then become objective allies of the Pâkehâ ruling class. They could well become the authors of a new form of discourse,[9] composed of several voices and used in addressing different types of interested parties, while remaining staunch objective allies of their natal whânau. If we study particular cases, it is mostly the balanced sharing out of loyalties that makes Mâori bicultural agents effective. If they lose the trust of their natal whânau, this becomes known and their mana is short-lived. If they lose the trust of a Pâkehâ agency, at least their mana among Mâori may survive.

A concept like Bourdieu's 'symbolic capital,' then, is perfectly capable of explaining why Mâori bicultural leaders maintain their Mâori identity, but it is less capable of explaining why the constituencies of these leaders continue to insist on it, not only as a rhetorical display, but on the profoundest level. Constituents likewise appear to practise a division of identity into distinct compartments, the sum total of which is their figured world. This compartmentalization is expressed not only in different behaviour in different social contexts, but also in a heteroglossic identity uttering a heteroglossic discourse.

Authoring Selves

In order to understand how biculturalism and Māori revitalization are interrelated, I consulted many texts written and published by Māori authors. These state the contradictions of biculturalism but find ways to create an authorial self stylistically by speaking in several voices. One example is Merata Mita's account of her early teaching career, which prepared her for her later, better-known vocation as a film-maker. She describes herself in her memoir (1986; see also Ihimaera 1993a) as being of 'very humble' Māori rural origin, her childhood language and culture having been Māori. She went through teachers' college in Auckland only because her home people obliged her to. At Kawerau College, she was given a troubled and disadvantaged class to teach: 'The headmaster said he did not care what I did as long as I kept them out of trouble' (Mita 1993, 281).

Merata Mita responded in three voices, all characteristic of talented Māori bicultural agents: (1) the *whānau* spirit – 'I treated them like a family, a *whānau* where I was friend, tutor and mother. I had a real concept of *aroha* which didn't fit easily into the classroom' (281); (2) the professional educationalist – 'I'd take them to the bush and we'd do painting and social studies up there and I related the maths and everything else to what they were familiar with' (281); and (3) the universalist initiator – 'I first used a movie camera at that school. Instead of writing an essay, they had to write a script, act it out, film it, edit it' (281). The conceptual universe made up of these three voices is deeply heterogeneous, but each is an aspect of Merata Mita's bicultural persona. The first voice establishes a link with the local universe (the *whānau*); the second maintains a plausible relation with a national mainstream institution (the school system); while the third initiates the group in a new universe (cinema), transcending the contradiction between the first two.

Merata Mita's personal story is no doubt a success for biculturalism.

Her award-winning films *Bastion Point–Day 507, Patu!* (1983), and *Mauri* (1988) are important in New Zealand film history. The awards they received were won according to international criteria, not negotiable within Pâkehâ/Mâori relationships. Her cinematic language leaves the contradictions of biculturalism behind, as Mâori film-maker Barry Barclay (1990) argues, in part because there are no adequate public or private means for films addressing Mâori only, but also because Mita's work addresses universal issues.

In spite of the new *legitimacy* of the *whânau* under the bicultural dispensation, their status stops short of equality. That dispensation gives what Sir Apirana Ngata asked for in 1931: recognition of the legitimacy of Mâori culture and a closer *approximation* of equal status. While this is the position of Mâori pupils at Kawerau College, Merata Mita's status in the New Zealand film industry has fewer ethnic constraints. There is a sharp split between the two modalities of bicultural space in New Zealand culture. In the figured world of *traditional Mâori* social space (*iwi/hapû/whânau*), Merata was proud of her community identity. It was only later, in mainstream social space, that she acquired a *positional* identity, due to her talent as a film-maker and her expert knowledge of Mâori culture. As success in each position demands great social-interactional and social-relational skill and effort, bicultural agents are heavily burdened. Hiwi Tauroa's grim picture of their conflicts, rivalries, ambitions, jealousies, and financial sacrifices is probably not overdrawn.[10]

This analysis posits two social spaces but three voices. The arts are not confined to any social space. As a cultural artifact, they have 'potential for the liberation of human capacities' (Holland et al. 1998, 64). The first of these voices is the author's, the second is the listener's, but the third is the voice 'heard in the word before the author comes upon it' (Bakhtin 1986, 121). The utterances in which films such as *Patu!* and *Mauri* recollect them are not classifiable as 'traditional Mâori' or 'Pâkehâ' but recall many other voices flowing in continually from all over the world. All creative art is addressed to a shadowy someone, whom Bakhtin calls the 'super-addressee whose absolutely just responsive understanding is presumed' (126), for example, God, a tribal ancestor, or the universe. But it is not only artists who speak to a super-addressee. This figure is invoked also by bicultural agents, for instance, in the administration of Mâori public health. Heteroglossia in administration is a major sociopolitical device of Mâori leadership. Mâori leaders abound in references to Mâori ontology, and these are far more than rhetorical flourishes. Pâkehâ negotiators, who are well able to detect and discard such flourishes, may be convinced if they encounter a genuine, profound, clearly expressed alternative world view. So far, many Mâori leaders have been able to communicate not only their commitment but also their ontological knowledge and experience.

This emerges clearly from a book such as *Whaiora* by Mason Durie (1994). It treats of many challenges in the administration of Mâori health, such as bicultural skills and behavioural styles of personnel and the concept of Pâkehâ-Mâori partnership. Nine years after publication, some details need updating, but Durie's profound discussion of bicultural health agendas gives the book enduring value. The New Zealand Ministry of Health issued a new 'bicultural' agenda in 1990, partly in response to vigorous Mâori criticism in the 1980s (see Ministerial Advisory Committee on Mâori Health 1990). Durie's book is his riposte, offering an ontological Mâori agenda.

Mâori critiques of the 1980s all included the same kind of ontological elements. In Durie's schema, health is a 'house' with four 'walls,' or basic elements: spiritual, mental, physical, and the *whânau.* He quotes (chap. 5) other Mâori schemata, all committed to a more comprehensive model of well-being than biological medicine: 'Essentially they sought to widen understandings of health, to translate health into terms which were culturally significant, and to balance physical and biological approaches with cultural and sociological views' (Durie 1994, 78). All these schemata drew on Mâori esoterics and the Greek New Testament.[11]

The 'bicultural' elements in the Department of Health Agenda of 1990 were drawn, in part, from the WHO constitution and from Mâori views and writings. But as Durie writes, 'Generally, however, Mâori health perspectives were consistent with new orientations and global · trends: general systems theory, family psycho-therapy, the community health movement, primary health care, and calls for de-medicalisation of the human life cycle. The NZ Board of Health advocated five principles: holism, empowerment, social and cultural determination, equity of access and devolution, equitable and effective resource use' (Durie 1994, 79). The WHO constitution was acclaimed by Mâori health professionals, who thought it reflected their views, and the government did not contest that interpretation.

On a closer look, however, Mâori ontological models of health do not contain elements like devolution or effective resource use, while the Pâkehâ agenda implies a basic dichotomy between the biological and religious (*taha wairua*) aspects of healing, setting aside the latter as beyond its competence. As the *taha wairua* does not treat the mind and body as inseparable, the two agendas are ontologically incompatible. The New Zealand guidelines skilfully papered over differences, as the terms employed, like holism, empowerment, and cultural determination, may or may not refer to a *taha wairua*. This vagueness served to legitimize the ministry's authority for both peoples.

Gradually, a truly bicultural system was developed to handle irreducible ontological discrepancies. Since 1993, *iwi*, *rûnanga*, and trust boards have controlled many financial operations as key players in skills training, education, economic development, and *matua whângai* as well as health.[12] For these purposes, *iwi* may use their own resources or those provided by contracts or devolution from public or semi-public sources. Apart from their routine management and delivery roles, they may appoint personnel, make policy, do their own planning, compete with other service providers, and initiate action to meet urgent needs in holistic fashion. Durie commented that 'They have in common a commitment to integrate development – cultural, social, economic – based on Mâori tribal structures. Their distinctive feature is the inclusion of health programmes as part of a total package rather than as an isolated medical venture' (1994, 167). Mâori health status statistics have improved significantly under the new regime.

Mason Durie's discourse has three voices similar to Merata Mita's. His first voice describes *mana* and health in terms of a neo-classical Mâori figured world. His second voice expresses the positional identity of the university-trained doctor, psychiatrist, or health administrator. His third voice is attuned, above all, to a super-addressee, a blend of Mâori, Christian God, and WHO constitution. This may surprise, but for many years a Mâori doctor defending a holistic theory of medicine could be classified as a harmless mystic by his Pâkehâ colleagues. The Mâori doctor would thus be heartened by the support of many respected world authorities. Processes like globalization, decentralization, and privatization opened the way in due course for tribes of Aotearoa to become accredited providers of all the services contained within the four-walled house of health.

Should this be described as 'retribalization'? Yes and no. Before the tribes took control, statistics show that Mâori felt uncomfortable with medical services and underused them due to communication difficulties. The advantage of the reforms was that their 'alternate care plans' improved communication. How? Durie just remarks that, for the improvement of health outcomes for Mâori, one should not rely too much on 'the acquisition of bicultural skills by a predominantly Pâkehâ work force' (1994, 193). Illness sharpens spirituality and awareness of hidden dangers. Such notions link biological disease with all that may have gone wrong in life, from ritual faults and social relations to material life and self-identity, to illness. Durie favours a number of *mana*-restoring devices, such as ceremonially creating a *whânau* atmosphere in clinics. This change in health delivery, showing official recognition of ontological differences, seems to have helped to improve statistics of Mâori health status.

On the other hand, Mâori health professionals are committed to the positional identity they share with their Pâkehâ colleagues. Though Mâori traditional healing no longer meets with official opposition, it has not become a field of lively bicultural activity among Mâori health professionals. The on-the-ground relations of power do not permit this. The newly bureaucratized 'tribal' administrations are in the same bind. In a more recent study, Durie (1997) no longer views direct transmission of a Mâori figured world as a task for the 'tribes'; it must be left to the intimacy of extended families, or *whânau*. His tersely balanced account of the costs and benefits of *whanaungatanga* for individuals presents the latter, in many types of situations, as facing a choice between a Pâkehâ and a Mâori value system, each with its attractions and drawbacks. His table 6 (1997, 21) 'highlights the ongoing tension' as Mâori move backward and forward between these two value systems, each of which may at times offer better prospects for mental health. Durie therefore thinks it is essential for access to both systems to remain open. To this end, natural *whânau* 'deserve greater state support' and, above all, 'more consistency.'

Durie's survey does not mention all the *whânau*'s strengths. The institution has maintained its basic historical ontology, is re-establishing *te reo*, and co-opts most children born from mixed marriages, while geographical mobility and consumerism have hardly strengthened informal interethnic networks. Contemporary Aotearoa, like the Pacific Ocean, is made up of small Mâori social islands linked to one another by seemingly indestructible bonds of telephone and motorcar communication.[13]

Mason Durie's health data show that Mâori and Pâkehâ are ontologically far apart but also that excellent symbiosis between them has proved possible.[14] He appears to take the view that this symbiosis, for which Eriksen (1998) has coined the term 'common denominators,' is best maintained if ethnic differences are recognized and respected, and that symbiosis may turn into assimilation unless Māori institutions make deliberate efforts to cultivate an autonomous culture. *Whanaungatanga* institutions do not exclude individualism, but, in Durie's view, should be in balance with it. His table 6 is a supra-ethnic dialogic cost-benefit calculus, showing how each *whānau* balances its own world to satisfy its own ancestral super-addressee.

Authoring Selves in Māori Literature

The study of Māori literary texts is indispensable if we wish to plumb the depths of Māori figured worlds. The field is very rich, but we have space to consider only one author. I chose Patricia Grace, as some of her novels greatly deepen our knowledge of the ontology of the *whānau*, a key topic in this essay. As Elizabeth Deloughrey (1999) perspicaciously remarks, the topic of Grace's novel *Potiki* (1986) is a Māori community's genealogical and cultural identity, while its hero 'fulfills the destiny that in turn was foreshadowed by the ancient narratives of Christ and Māui.'[15] Rather than rejecting Christian elements introduced by European occupation of the Pacific, Grace reincorporates this narrative and localises it in a way where it becomes a living *Pakehā* myth reinscribed in Māori terms' (Deloughrey 1999).

In formal terms, this means that Grace's novels resemble meeting-house oratory, where characters tell their stories in turn. There is no 'authorial voice'; each character says his or her part of the truth and the author acts as secretary. Few characters are sure which version of a story is the true one. 'My making father,' says the hero, 'could be a ghost, or a tree, or a tin-can man, but it does not matter' (*Potiki* 1986, 42). Each of these paternities (Māui, the wood-carving, the derelict) is part of the truth. If *Potiki* presents the ontology of the contemporary *whānau*, the novel *Cousins* (1992) provides Grace's classification of the types of positional identities that may be found in it. The three cousins of the title, taken together, form a microcosm of *whānau* relations. The first cousin, Makareta, represented as the *puhi* (Grace 1992, 202–3), has become a typical member of the bicultural elite, whose range of figured worlds is extensively documented in Witi Ihimaera's six-volume anthology. In Māori writing, authors as well as characters often rediscover their Māori identity due to an initiatory experience and become immersed in a great Māori cause. The second cousin, Missy, is mainstream rather than elite. She is lauded as an investment (229), inconspicuously consolidates alliances between chief families of the *whânau* community, promotes its unity, and becomes the kingpin of what Metge (1995) called 'the *whânau* which comes first to mind.' She incarnates the myth of *whânau* solidarity, deflated by some and honoured by others in Ihimaera's anthology. The third *Cousin*, Mata (95, 201, 241), is 'she who sought nothing, walking, going nowhere.' Keri Hulme immortalized that type in *The Bone People* (1983). Its representatives abound in Ihimaera's anthology, but often recover their Mâori identity. *Whânau* members of every type are as aware as the characters in *Potiki* of their prototypes in myth and story, as a meeting place of living and dead. While Missy ensures the reproduction of the traditional *whânau*, the others enter the bicultural vortex, as sacrificial victims or creative actors.

In this tripartite Mâori figured world,[16] Makareta is the favourite. Can Missy become like Makareta? In Grace's novel, this is one of Missy's dreams: 'The me that I couldn't see was in love with the me that was Makareta' (223). Can Mata become like Makareta? That is a big question. In Ihimaera's voluminous anthology, Makareta probably represents the favourite *puhi* of the contemporary Mâori imagination. Some authors who started life like Mata describe how they coped with their identity problems, often by taking a figure like Makareta as their exemplar. The Missy type, much honoured in the literature of the 1970s, is given some rest in the Ihimaera anthology.

It is not, in the end, the literati who make new worlds and find 'the dynamic uniting the intimate and the social sites of cultural production' (Holland et al. 1998, 235). The figured worlds, life ways, and practical needs of each of Grace's three types differ so much that, in the vicissitudes of elite debate, they are sometimes presented as adversaries competing for the same resources, such as income from fish, about with legal battles were fought in the 1990s.

Obstacles to Making Worlds

Te Ohu Kai Moana (literally, the Seafood Working Bee) is a vast fisheries consortium Mâori were able to set up due to a settlement under the Treaty of Waitangi Acts. Financially, it is the flagship of New Zealand biculturalism. This paper deals only with one aspect of its operations: the allocation of its profits, which has given rise to much litigation on the part of Mâori interests. The discourse of these disputes speaks in three voices: first, tribal voice – its chairman, Sir Tipene O'Regan (one-time lecturer in Mâori studies at a teachers' college), consistently bases his identity on the culture and history of his Ngâi Tahu tribal ancestors, on which he writes brilliantly; second, a mainstream voice – Sir Tipene is a recognized expert in the efficient management of big business assets; and third, a *pan-tribal* voice – Sir Tipene considers the concept of Mâori nationhood to be 'a Pâkehâ transplant.' He is 'suspicious of pan-Mâori operations because they invariably collectivise the majority to tyrannise the minority.'[17] These views and their implications caused much anguish among urban Mâori.

Who owns Te Ohu Kai Moana? On paper, there is a simple answer: all Mâori own part of it and the allocation of the yield is administered by *iwi*. But this answer turns out to be problematic. Under company law, proceeds can be disposed of only to a list of shareholders. Te Ohu Kai Moana invented brilliant, ingenious, but contestable devices to draw up a list of *iwi* whose 'membership' would be determined by genealogy. The Privy Council, when consulted, asked, What is an *iwi*? It was an unsettling question, but met the corporation's wishes in a second judgment.

Like all Mâori questions, these ones were fated to be discussed in many heterogeneous voices. Pâkehâ New Zealand's Mâori policy is inspired by one chief principle: reducing what are called 'glaring economic disparities' between two founding peoples. By this principle, if Te Ohu Kai Moana has distributable assets, these should be applied to those disparities. The money should go to the deserving poor and reduce the burden on the taxpayer. The intention of TOKM was to apply the assets to the financing of Mâori enterprises, whose managers invariably know their genealogies. If Mâori were united on such a policy, Pâkehâ might accept this, but Mâori are far from unanimous. Nor is there a clear, unambiguous definition of the *iwi*.

On this point, most anthropologists are agreed: Kawharu (1975) decribes the system as being made up of two complementary moral principles (*whakapapa* and *whanaungatanga*), and my own research supports that view (Schwimmer 1990). Metge (1995, chap. 3) brings out a similar heterogeneity when analysing Mâori discourse on the *whânau*. The two sides, confronting each other in their affidavits for the Auckland High Court hearings of 1998, defended opposite sides of the same contradiction, the same complementarity. TOKM limited its list of shareholders (or beneficiaries) to those who could establish descent from listed tribes. Most Mâori urban organizations represented at the

Auckland High Court hearings did not need genealogical information from their clientele (beneficiaries) nor would they ever have questioned a prospective client's claim to 'be Mâori.' The group Te Whânau o Hoani Waititi Marae, for instance, accept Pâkehâ as long as they go through a Mâori language immersion course. These recruits are simply incorporated in the *whânau*.

The latter, however, rely on another, equally basic, principle, – *whanaungatanga*. By that principle, in certain contexts, Mâori may practise the broadest conceivable kinship recognition based on genealogical or any other grounds. The principle often used to be invoked to justify the absorption of migrants. Viewed from that angle, there is nothing new (except judiciary forms) in the dispute between TOKM and the urban organizations. There has always been tension between the generous tendency for Mâori communities to incorporate migrants and their occasional moves to counter the resulting social entropy by strictly enforcing the principle of *whakapapa*. The same tension exists today between the leaders who signed the fisheries agreement (whose *whakapapa* are egregious) and urban organizations that are wide open to the *môrehu*. Not only are both *kaupapa* equally Mâori, but the ardour of their contention is very Mâori as well.

Comparing this dispute to Patricia Grace's model of the *whânau*, we recognize the type of Makareta, *te puhi,* in TOKM, and the type of Mata, *te môrehu,* in the urban organizations. The reproductive forces in Mâori social life, symbolized by Missy, are less involved in the dispute. Interviewing an official of the Mâori Congress, which represents these forces, I was told in Wellington that the Congress was keeping out of the argument, as the two sides were still too far apart. The Congress hoped the dispute would end in compromise. If this happens, the basic principles of Mâori social organization will emerge unscathed. This will mean that Mâori culture today, though united on some issues like *te reo,* continues to speak in at least the three voices of the cousins in Grace's novel. All new models of Mâori life ways today are apt to shift, on occasion, from representing Makareta to representing Mata or Missy.

Left to themselves, Mâori would no doubt be able to find a balance between these contradictory interests. However, these divisions tend to be exploited by Pâkehâ interests seeking to restrain Mâori power. As long as Mâori maintain their usual relational and many-voiced ontology, they do not need or desire to subordinate their exchanges to a single authority speaking in one unified voice. As Rangihau (1975) suggested, the deepest level of their culture would be endangered if they abandoned tribal identity. On the other hand, they might need a unified design to counter Pâkehâ symbolic takeover bids encouraged by Mâori tribal divisions. It is in that unifying spirit that they opened a great internal debate about *te kaupapa Mâori*.

During the past decade, several great meetings were held in Mâori communities in the hope that elders and experts could find a pan-Mâori definition of such a concept, but each meeting produced its own version, coloured by its local or sectional interests. This is not surprising. *Kaupapa* is primarily the floor of a meeting house, but it can also be the ground of any design in mind. Now, a meeting house or other Mâori design has not only a general end but also a local reference – history, place, social bonds. As all acceptable *kaupapa* fuse general and intimate perspectives, they vary from place to place, from one sectional interest to another. So the search for a *kaupapa* will reproduce relational social spaces more easily than it will create national uniformity, even though all *kaupapa* I have seen have a strong family likeness. They re-make figured worlds by study, identification, and reinterpretation. They take into account the ambiguities of the Mâori position in bicultural New Zealand by speaking in several voices,[18] whose co-development may create a new autonomous Mâori tradition that is sensitive to global perspectives and connections with other Indigenous Peoples.

Making Worlds: A Field Inquiry

Local *kaupapa Mâori* may arise in larger 'traditional' *whânau* or local *hapû* occupying a culturally autonomous space, where daily life, values, institutions, knowledge, and creative activity are reproducible. But most Maori cultural space tends to be scattered in small conjugal units that may be intimate, warm, and joyous, or conflictual, but that are surrounded by Pâkehâ, so that the quasi-natural reproduction of an autonomous cultural space is often difficult to achieve. Mâori have responded to this predicament by creating modern institutions such as *kôhanga reo*, half school, half family, whose local operators are increasingly professional. To some extent, *whânau* may become nests planned for the transmission of language and culture – virtual institutions.

This gave me the idea to study a frankly non-traditional *whânau*. Non-residential, this *whânau* reproduces the language, cultural and religious values, the intimate *whânau* sign system, and some branches of special knowledge by continuous educational and ceremonial activities, professionally conducted with superior practical, theoretical, and artistic skills. Moreover, this *whânau* had found a *kaupapa* in which the perspectives of Makareta, Missy, and Mata were suitably in balance. I was fortunate in being introduced to such a group by its leader, the educationalist Dr Pita R. Sharples. Te Whânau o Hoani Waititi Marae is situated in Glen Eden, fifteen kilometres southwest of Central Auckland, in a spacious park owned by Waitakere City. Most of its buildings were erected by the Marae Society and included a carved meeting house, a dining hall, a *kôhanga reo*, primary and secondary schools, a centre for post-secondary programs, a training centre for dance and related performances, and land set aside for a university and polytechnic, which are beginning to take shape. The *marae*, though not residential, contains six private houses for *kaumâtua*, whose role it is to provide ceremonial and advisory services and create the social setting of a *whânau*.

The architecture is mostly simple and unpretentious, but the carved house was Pine Taiapa's last masterpiece. A great deal of thought went into the landscaping and pathways of the different sectors, and the two highest modern buildings – a reception hall and the *kôhanga reo* – are distinguished by fine woodwork and vast panels of incised glass whose pattern reminds one of *tukutuku* as well as European minimalism. The message given by the *marae* environment is one of cultural blending in the modern parts and of classicism in the ceremonial parts.

This marae was the first (in the early 1980s) to institute the *kura kaupapa Mâori* system of education at all levels up to university. All teaching is in Mâori, but this linguistic choice is only a first step in creating a special learning environment, representing the values and style of the *whânau*. These values are identified as Mâori but attached above all to the *whânau* community, whose intimacy and trust sustains its members in any adversity. Whatever life may bring, members thus acquire worth, security, strength, and balance. The exacting training given in body culture symbolically represents these qualities. Emphasis is less on formal knowledge than on shaping bodies and minds able to sustain the rigours of the New Age. On the Mâori side, this requires an ability to read complex signs, movement, rhythm, physical control – qualities systematically taught in East and South-East Asia but not in the West and not to or by Pâkehâ.

The latter are no doubt struck by the exotic boldness of such an educational enterprise. They may even wonder about its rationality. But these alternative programs undergo the same scrutiny of professionalism and efficiency as others and the same national quality tests. In the face of strong competition, their enrolment continues to be adequate. Programs like those at Hoani Waititi Marae are not meant to supplant others, but to bring success to many whose lives are difficult.

This status is partly due also to the total role the *marae* plays in Greater Auckland. The *marae* organizes sports events; *kura kaupapa Mâori* teacher training courses; national and international conferences; Mâori programs sponsored by the Waitakere City Council, the Auckland Warriors, and the University of Auckland, experts in traditional Mâori medicine; the National School of Ancient Mâori Weaponry; a Mâori Justice program; three groups in Mâori performing arts; and an emancipatory self-employment student program aimed at the 'pre-training' of long-term unemployed Mâori people. There are courses on self-management, social and cooperative skills, work and study skills, and 'Second chance education and training.' These activities illustrate two aspects of the *whânau* – its network and status in Greater Auckland and the Mâori world, and its commitment to traditional culture and the needs of disadvantaged Mâori. Its principal remedy is by improvement of values and knowledge.

Those setting up an urban non-traditional *whânau* with a largely educational agenda depend not only on their own intimate knowledge of the institution they mean to transplant, but also on high pedagogic skills and exemplary control of some fields of subject matter. In the time at my disposal, I tried to learn some of the main constructs and methods of some transmitting agents on the *marae*, but my coverage is not a full ethnographic survey. More study needs to be done on value and knowledge transmission within the *whânau* community on and off campus, and a cost-benefit analysis of *whanaungatanga* as suggested in Durie (1997).

Voices for a New Age

The object of this *whânau* community is the creation of a Mâori identity for the New Age (*te ao hou*). This concept is as polysemic as many others, varying from one speaker and from one occasion to another. At TWOHWM, at least three fields need to be considered. The first is reproduction and perpetuation of the basic relational and metaphysical values of the traditional *whânau*, even if often in non-traditional forms. The second is negotiation of the ontology of this *whânau* to ensure a kind of symbiosis with the Pâkehâ ontology. This negotiated Mâori ontology has to keep its fundamental values, especially its relational principle. A third field of this new figured world, less often considered, is an increasing tendency to learn about cultures and languages beyond New Zealand. This is increasingly part of New Zealand's being-in-the-world. For Mâori, there are two additional aspects. First, it has long been the practice, as part of the decolonization struggle, not only to fight Pâkehâ, but also to 'learn to be like him, think like him, act like him'[19] and study 'English, French, Italian and Russian,' the art of fencing, etc. Secondly, more recently, Mâori are learning about non-European cultures (Indigenous, Third World, Asian) with values supporting a relational world view. Such knowledge could be turned to emulating the dominance of Pâkehâ *mana*.

Though non-residential, the *whânau* takes responsibility for the off-campus lives of its members. Any Mâori of Greater Auckland and *a fortiori* families involved in campus activities are potential *whânau* members. If they are in trouble, they are helped. If they die, the *whânau*, if approached, will *tangi* for them. The *whânau* will contribute a *koha* to the bereaved. Salaried staff members, like other beneficiaries, are expected to contribute to the cost of discharging *whânau* life crisis responsibilities.

The style of *whânau* life fuses Mâori religious sensibilities with ceremonial observances and school routine. Pupils take an active part in all of them, especially in singing the *waiata* at the end of *whânau* leaders' ceremonial speeches.[20] The crucial aim of *kura kaupapa Mâori* is not just to teach *te reo* but to raise children in an environment where the *whânau* bond's communitarian values prevail. This bond and mutual support may protect individuals from failure and self-depreciation and may offer the best chances of success in a perilous world. This concept is not anti-competitive, but sets up competition among groups rather than individuals. Members of Te Whânau o Hoani Waititi Marae derive their self-respect from the usually very creditable outcomes of inter-group competitions. I attended one of these – a national *haka* contest – where our *marae* won a trophy. The outcomes of such competitions are never free from ambiguity. Tastes in the Mâori world being heterogeneous as well as changeable, the winners are those who catch the trends of majority fashion. If belief in local *kaupapa* remains intact, the competitive setback of an entire *whânau* is more easily borne than that of an individual. In the *whânau* studied, apart from the common language and intimate sign system, cohesion was deepened by a religious Io-based philosophy and a body culture made up of forms of *haka*, *taiaha*, wrestling, and traditional medicine.

Negotiating Ontologies

In a world where most resources are Pâkehâ, how can the group life of such a *whânau* survive? Its core activities include a wide range of programs in education, health, employment, and justice, financed under current government policies. These pay for the salaried staff while adult members following evening programs have regular employment. Some staff are employed by other institutions and work part-time, unpaid, on the *marae*. Funds for emergencies, ceremonial activities, excursions, and diverse *koha* are scratched together by a devoted administrator.

As most of the subsidized activities are not exactly mainstream, one may wonder how Te Whânau o Hoani Waititi Marae managed to have them funded. The one I looked at in detail was called *manaaki tangata* (self-management). Its premise is that some young Mâori think so negatively about themselves that nobody who sees them would give them a job and that standard training courses do not help unless they also change the learners' self-perception. It is not just for ideological reasons, then, that 'decolonization' programs are set up, with state support, to help them earn a living.

Manaaki tangata courses are an invention of TWOHWM. Professionally conducted technical training in preparing job applications is combined with an initiation in *te reo* and the general culture of *marae* and *whânau*. Those taking these courses give much time and energy to becoming adopted as members of the *whânau*. Statistics show that students at these courses often succeed in finding jobs, even though less time is allotted to imparting technical information. Because of this meritorious outcome, they are being funded on the same basis as their mainstream equivalents.

Manaaki tangata courses, however, have to satisfy formal criteria of the New Zealand Qualification Authority and Training Support Agency. Courses are delivered under contract by Te Toi Huarewa,[21] a semi-private agency. As the course plan includes learning a *haka pôwhiri*, evaluators assess whether words, hand and foot movements, rhythm, and unison are correctly learnt. In addition to tutor and student assessments, authorities inside and outside the *marae* join in quality management. This example shows how biculturalism is negotiated: in exchange for state approval of the teaching of a *haka pôwhiri* in a training support course, where *haka* quality is to be judged by strictly correct Mâori criteria, TWOHWM adopts a state control mechanism.

On the level of mediate goals, such cooperation seems to work smoothly. The *whânau* is gaining numbers and status and strengthening Mâori culture, while the state buys good quality training support and economic development. The sharp divergence in ultimate goals does not trouble either side. Biculturalism in action seems to aim at comfortable symbiosis rather than comprehension.[22] But is this model a panacea for the Mâori situation, with each side living in one of two best possible worlds?

No, alas. Te Whânau o Hoani Waititi Marae is on the front line of a harsh pan-Mâori struggle against unemployment, economic failure, poor housing, ill health, delinquency, and suicide. Is Dr Pita Sharples's struggle aimed at salvation or salvage? Salvage in the guise of salvation? Salvation in the guise of salvage? All three models of *whanaungatanga*, as connoted by Patricia Grace's *Cousins*, are present at Hoani Waititi Marae – the staff are like Makareta and *manaaki tangata* is for those who may once have been like Mata. Missy's kind of *whânau* is deeply respected as exemplar and, when feasible, in the flesh. These types are like cousins, none of whom abandons the others. Makareta could give up Mata and be assimilated, but she would then no longer be the *puhi*. The fabric seems to hold. In order to explain why, we have to go to a higher order of analysis than the biculturalism concept.

The Mâori reforms of the 1980s and the Mâori literature that accompanied them certainly authored a new concept of Mâori identity and instituted new educational programs, but such moves do not suffice for the making of an alternative world. Te Whânau o Hoani Waititi Marae has always been aware of this. It is necessary also to transform the minds of the membership by co-development activities and practices that gradually internalize the new *kaupapa*. This process begins with forms of 'initiation' and is maintained by rituals that will turn into habitual social actions, attitudes, and skills. These skills may require arduous physical training. Concomitantly, slowly, bodies and ontologies change; minds delinquish the figured world of colonization.

A Trans-national New Age

From the outset, British colonialism and its missionaries opened a wider world than New Zealand to the Mâori. The most influential mid-nineteenth-century Mâori ontologies had, as was shown earlier in this essay, important trans-national features. Appeals were made to the Queen in England. Te Kooti defended a universal concept of sacred justice, which also informed his Ringatû religion and his aesthetics of village communities. Te Rangikaheke's mythology was, from the start, a trans-national creation. This tendency became even stronger after 1975.

One of the first Mâori moves in the decolonization era, in 1984, was to send the major classical art exhibition *Te Mâori* to New York and other U.S. cities. More recently, when the New Zealand Court of Appeal effectively ruled that profits of Te Ohu Kai Moana should be devoted to Mâori social welfare, that corporation sought and perhaps found relief at the Privy Council in London. Mâori never ceased to believe in an ultimate authority, transcending quarrels between Mâori and Pâkehâ, that would define their real position in the universe. At the very least, as in the universe of Hone Tuwhare's *Mihi*, which is divided into categories of masters and victims, all victims, human and non-human alike, exchange messages among one another and symbolically unite to face their masters. Mâori have been very active in international congresses of Indigenous Peoples. The first major work by a Mâori on the epistemology of decolonization addressed these peoples and was published in London (Smith 1999).

All such pathways meet in Dr Pita Sharples's thought and the work of Te Whânau o Hoani Waititi Marae. Inspired by Mâori values, it enthusiastically advocates feminism, environmentalism, the anti-smoking campaign, and clean administration. Its work in disseminating body culture based on Mâori models is a form of initiation that resonates among other Indigenous Peoples and internationally, as many movements question the Judaeo-Christian doctrine of radical separation of spirit and body and find ways to explore the 'labyrinth' (Mendez 1998) of the body. When I asked Pita to explain his program, he hesitated, saying the *whânau* lacked means for developing theory. But some teachers gave me ideas, based on the three baskets of knowledge of the Io religion (Best 1976, 103, 397–8; Buck 1949, 449; Smith 1913, 449; Tuhoto-ariki 1907).

A triangle like the pattern incised in the windowpanes of some *marae* buildings illustrates the wrestling teacher's *kaupapa*. The triangle's two upper sloping lines represent contrary forces, 'fight' and *rongoâ* (remedy),[23] between which *mamau* (wrestling) forms the connecting base line, establishing a balance. The wrestling teacher taught his course on that principle, as it is an exercise of two *whânau* members whose fight serves a common end. I asked the *taiaha* teacher whether his *kaupapa* is the same as the wrestling teacher's. It is not. Love, peace, and balance are great gifts, contained in Io's *kete aronui*, but the art of the *taiaha* needs different stuff. Its practitioners learn to kill or be killed. The teacher, like Zen teachers of swordsmanship, has to help students to acquire 'an unknown power that comes to one from nowhere' when facing an enemy, a readiness to give or to receive death (Suzuki 1959, 94, and chaps. 5, 6 passim). This gift is part of *kete tuatea*, another of Io's baskets, exposing the nature of dissension and strife. The distinction made here is the classical one opposing the gods Tû and Rongo, each making their own physical demands, necessitating at least two disciplines of physical training. Mainstream New Zealand high schools similarly teach rugby and army drill with less explicit metaphysical underpinnings.

All such programs aim to build a sense of physical identity, but *taiaha* training meets with special difficulties. In classical times, a boy could see men like his father handle the weapon, execute the intricate foot movements, and develop an overall bearing suited to *taiaha* movements, whether choreographic or martial. Children still imitate their elders' body movements, but these are usually no help in handling the *taiaha*. So if, in early adulthood, they take up *taiaha* training, they have to begin by unlearning inappropriate ways of moving their bodies. Much initiation in Mâori identity is remedial, also physical. Under biculturalism, all this physical initiation is financed on the same footing as mainstream programs. This includes examining bodies like the National School of Ancient Weaponry, of which Pita Sharples is the highest chief.

A third aspect of physical initiation on the *marae* is training troupes of Mâori ballet performers, one of which, Te Rôpu Manutaki, is among the highest rated in the country. Its name suggests the role assigned to it: acting as sentry to the flock of *rôpu*, warding off the snares of crypto-colonialist habit. This effect is achieved partly by the inspiration of theme songs, written by Pita Sharples for each major performance. Full of historical and mythological allusions, they take a bold contemporary view of issues of the day. After a new theme song is presented, the troupe's practices liven up.[24]

This is a delicate role. Ballets often contain movements burlesquing Mâori warfare. One may explain this by the self-derision in Mâori (and most other) folk art. Perhaps religious dread leads them to desacralize what they give Pâkehâ to see. Perhaps, too, some groups sardonically deride the Mâori self-image, to the displeasure of Mâori critics like Pita Sharples. In order to create a positive self-image, Te Rôpu Manutaki plays such passages with classical elegance. Outside Auckland, this reform has not aroused much interest, nor does it always help to win national *haka* competitions.

This emergence of two styles, two strategies (derision versus earnest pedagogy), reveals a basic contrast in Mâori modes of perception of self-identity. The derision strategy is an ironic acknowledgment of inferiority, of savagery, in which neither actors nor spectators seriously believe. It is also a mocking response to Pâkehâ racism, a dramatization of existing Mâori-Pâkehâ relationships. In spite of this derision, performers clearly value their own culture very highly. Pita Sharples, as a social scientist, is less interested in the dramatization of actual relationships than in transforming them by educational methods, which include changing the performers' perception of their self-identity. He wants his *marae rôpu* to be decolonized and to forget their past humiliations and their self-derision.

Non-traditional *whânau* are only one of the institutions where the basic spiritual, social, and aesthetic values of Mâori culture are being refigured today. One of the conditions for maintaining an autonomous Mâori literature is the continuing vigour of institutions like the *whânau*. As Witi Ihimaera notes, it is no longer the primary role of Mâori writing to reproduce a 'collective iwi impulse': 'In the 1990's we may have come to a crossroads of a literature of Mâori writing and a literature of race relations, of a literature of a past and a literature of a present and future and of a Mâori response and an individual response. It may well be that Mâori writing, true to the collective iwi impulse, true to the *mauri*, the *wairua*, the *tinana*, which comes only from living in a predominantly Mâori context, is behind us. The question about what constitutes Mâori writing remains to be engaged' (Ihimaera 1992, 17; 1993b, 17). In his introduction to volume 5 of his great anthology, however, Ihimaera quotes a proverb that exemplifies the Mâori art motif of the double spiral: *Te tôrino haere whakamua, whakamuri* (At the same time it is going forward, it is also going back). Most authors in his anthology (and not only in volume 5) started life at the 'centre' of the Mâori world, then moved out to explore its (bicultural) periphery, but later returned to its source 'as characterised by the *reo, mana* and *kaupapa Mâori; as home, tûrangawaewae* and *wâ kainga.* It acknowledges that we have a *pito* that, whether we like it or not, replenishes us' (Ihimaera 1996, 15–17).

It is certainly true that this double spiral movement accounts for many major works by the best Mâori and Polynesian writers, but the question is whether return of the spiral can, by itself, ensure survival of the 'centre' of Mâori culture, situated in the daily life of the traditional *whânau*. Now, the genesis of non-traditional *whânau* (under discussion here) is precisely in places like Auckland where the traditional *whânau*'s survival is precarious. Although only a small minority of Auckland Mâori (20 per cent is the most optimistic estimate) are in regular contact with a formal, identifiably Mâori institution, many of the others are members of *whânau*, all of which, in Ihimaera's terms, are 'centres' of the Mâori world. If they were to collapse, Mâori artists and those in need of a firm Mâori identity could not physically go back to it. Moreover, *te reo* would have a dubious future if the deep concepts of which it is the carrier no longer had a live social counterpart.

The rise of non-traditional *whânau* is therefore a major event in Mâori culture. Inevitably, however, such *whânau* lack some 'natural' qualities of the traditional ones. A refigured community has to be created to take their place. It is for this purpose that Pita Sharples often talked to me of his plan to set up a Mâori-language 'university,' a university-level *whare wânanga*, at Hoani Waititi Marae. He intended it to be a place for researching and teaching 'Mâori knowledge.' This would include language, history, myths, society, and art as well as medicine and spiritual welfare. When I asked what this last term meant, he spoke of asthma and diabetes. The *whare wânanga* would also study the Mâori people today: praxis, politics, and economics. The focus would be cultural and spiritual. All these were fragments of a *kaupapa* in gestation.

He had called a meeting to present this project to some prominent dignitaries, but on the day they came to Hoani Waititi Marae he was absent, called away to an unavoidable meeting with members of his home tribe, who were visiting Auckland. His absence made little difference. The dignitaries, in unison, advised Hoani Waititi Marae to link up with Massey University at Albany, but Pita was not ready to say yes or no to that.

The idea of a *whare wânanga*, however, is a crucial one. As such an institution has to construct its own system of teaching, it could fruitfully be related to a living laboratory of cultural practice, ensuring continuous dialogue between practice and analysis. Dialogue between *marae* and university may arise even today: a brilliant Mâori student at Auckland University explained to me why the Io religion is an unsuitable foundation for Mâori education. He did not query the content of the courses on the *marae*, but the reasons teachers gave to justify them. If a university is set up for Mâori knowledge, it ought to offer untrammelled debate on such questions. And where would debate be most untrammelled, at Massey or on the *marae*? Are the pressures of a mainstream university system less or more deleterious than traditionalist Māori pressures?

In June 1999 I visited a Basque-language university sponsored by the Mondragon Corporation of Basque cooperatives. The comparison was interesting as Basque culture and language had been suppressed in the past with the same vigour as Māori, but are being as vigorously revived today. This university has four campuses, three of which are oriented to technology and business administration. The fourth one, Eskoriatza campus, caters to the general social needs of Basque society and of industrial enterprise. It trains Basque-language teachers and has an advanced program, with a humanities approach, on the social organization of industrial enterprise. Its courses in the social sciences and humanities have a Basque perspective and provide openings for careers in the corporation.

Both the Basque and the proposed Māori programs claim the right 'to tell our own stories, write our own versions, in our own ways, for our own purposes. Writing is part of theory and writing is part of history' (Smith 1999, 28–9). Both programs are deeply involved in the economic and cultural needs of industry and Indigenous language teaching. Both apprehend that mainstream universities might unwittingly impose scholarly crypto-colonialism. While the Basque curriculum is outwardly structured like that of mainstream Spanish institutions,[25] it offers fundamental criticism of mainstream views, seeks to transform prevailing theories, and transmits authentic 'Basque knowledge.' I do not know how close such a program is to Pita Sharples's idea of a new *whare wānanga*.

Hoani Waititi Marae already presents Māori 'knowledge' of this kind up to the end of secondary school. Its teachers voice critiques of mainstream positions, but as Dr Linda Smith rightly remarks, 'this does not make [those positions] go away ... This means struggling to make sense of our own world while also attempting to transform what counts as important in the world of the powerful' (1999, 38–9). This refers specifically to Western epistemological and methodological presuppositions. A Māori-language university community would help Māori to make sense of their own world in their own language. It would have the formal authority to determine the correctness of 'knowledge' taught in Maori-language schools. It would challenge foreign-language interpretations of Māori concepts and practices with the authority inherent in an academy of Indigenous speakers.

Such considerations seem to support the principles of New Zealand's present biculturalism policy. A cornerstone of this policy, maintaining two viable cultures in one country of four million citizens, has been privatization. Similarly, in the Basque case, the university was sponsored not by the state system but by a group of workers' cooperatives. Although the Basque regional government is even more 'bicultural' than New Zealand,[26] Basques – and Mâori as well – need autonomous academic spaces to which bicultural access remains restricted. Here non-traditional *whânau* have a role to play as they are concerned increasingly with the advancement of 'Mâori knowledge.'

This may seem a strange way to end an essay on modern Mâori culture, but it corresponds well to my perception of Te Whânau o Hoani Waititi Marae. TWHWM is not just a school but also a laboratory for an alternative world of Mâori knowledge and practices. TWHWM is adding another tier, as it feels its program is incomplete. It is not ethnically limited but explores fields beyond the Western mainstream. Pâkehâ participation will be limited,[27] as successful biculturalism requires an autonomous Mâori space. This space is to be neither a copy of mainstream New Zealand thought nor a mirror for fabricating contraries.

This case study means to challenge the fashion of viewing the position of Mâori and other Indigenous Peoples as part of a bicultural or multicultural system. This fashion may have been inspired by theories such as those of Bourdieu or Foucault, but Mâori, Basques, and other Indigenous Peoples do not submit passively to alien power and symbolic capital. They are the authors of their own figured worlds and respond creatively to positional constraints imposed by a dominant group. Such was the response of Te Whânau o Hoani Waititi Marae, which successfully subordinated constraints of urban life and officialdom to their own *kaupapa*. Ranginui Walker (1990) was right, however, in calling such symbiosis a 'struggle without end.'

GLOSSARY

Note: Most entries are copied from glossaries in Walker (1990), Kawharu (1975), and Mead (1997), marked by the initials W, K, and M, respectively, with others taken from Ryan (1995) and Williams (1971), marked R and HWW.

(te) ao hou – (the) new age
aroha – love (M)
haere whakamua, whakamuri – to go forward and backwards (R)
haka – ritual war dance (M/W)

hapû – subtribe, descendants, pregnant (W)
iwi – tribe, bone (W), social unit bound by common genealogical links and, formerly, common residence (M)
kai moana – seafood (W)
kainga – home, place of residence (W), village (M)
kaumatua – male elder (W)
kaupapa – plan, principle, philosophy (W)
kete aronui – basket of knowledge (R)
koha – donation, gift (R)
kôhanga reo – Mâori language nest (M)
kura kaupapa Mâori – Mâori language school (M)
mamau – wrestling (HWW)
mana – authority, power, prestige, psychic force (W), status (M)
manaaki – care for, entertain, show respect, hospitality (R)
marae – courtyard in front of meeting house (W), village meeting ground (K)
matua – parent (W)
matua whângai – foster parent (R)
mauri – life force (W), life principle (M)
môrehu – survivors (W)
motuhake – discrete, separate, independent (W)
ohu – cooperative work group (W)
pâkehâ – white man, European, related to *pakepakehâ* and *pâkehakeha*, imaginary beings with fair skins (W)
patu – club, beat, kill, defeat (W)
pito – navel, umbilical cord (W)
pôwhiri – wave, welcome, opening ceremony (R)
puhi – plumes, virgin chieftainess (W)
(te) reo Mâori – (the) Mâori language
rongoâ – medicine, drug (medicinal), antidote (R)
rôpû – society, group, gang, heap (R), concert party
rûnanga – council, assembly (W)
taha – side
taiaha – longstaff weapon (W)
tangata – man, human, person (W)
tangi – cry, weep, funeral (W), mourning ceremony (M)
tapu – sacred, prohibited, ritually unclean (W/M)
tinana – body (W)
tôrino – spiral
tuatea – terror, pale, anxious (HWW)
tukutuku – decorative wall panels in meeting house (W)

tûrangawaewae – standing in the tribe (W), place for feet to stand (M), domicile derived from *hapû* membership (K)
wâ kâinga – true home (R)
wairua – spirit (M)
waiata – song, chant (W)
wânanga – lore, occult knowledge, learning (W)
whakapapa – genealogy (W/M)
whânau – birth, offspring, extended family (W)
whanaungatanga – relationship (M)
whare wânanga – house of learning (W), teriary institution that caters to Mâori language needs, established under the Education Act of 1990 (M)

NOTES

1 These 'events' are not cited as effective causes, but as part of a 'historically situated, historically unfolding ensemble of signifiers-in-action, signifiers at once material and symbolic, social and aesthetic' (Comaroff and Comaroff 1992, 27). Thus, the passing of the above-mentioned acts of Parliament was an *event sequence* that also led to important new historical *processes*.

2 A glossary of the Mâori terms used appears at the end of this chapter.

3 Eriksen (1998, 18) uses this term to mean 'similarities and shared horizons, or platforms of discourse and interaction.'

4 All these terms, translated in the glossary below, are 'synthetic' and present semantic complications similar to *mana motuhake*, discussed above.

5 Defined by Holland et al. (1998, 52) as 'a socially and culturally constructed realm of interpretation in which particular characters and actors are recognised, significance is assigned to certain acts, and particular outcomes are valued over others.' Bakhtin (1981) calls it a 'chronotope,' Munn (1986) calls it 'spacetime.'

6 See *Pinepine te kura* (Binney 1995, 378–80). This song requires much closer analysis, with reference to Te Kooti's concept of the *kaunoti* (Best 1982, 241–2).

7 Positional identities, as described by Holland et al. (1998, 127), 'have to do with the day-to-day and on-the-ground relations of power, deference and entitlement, social affiliation and distance.'

8 This charter has not been signed by France, Spain, or Britain but is arousing much discussion. Canada has no such charter.

9 Space forbids fully expounding the theory about signs, voices, dialogism, and heterogeneity on which an analysis of culture as semantic space is based, but see Lévi-Strauss (1962), Bakhtin (1981), Lotman (1990), Holquist (1990), and Holland et al. (1998).

10 See his text in Ihimaera (1993a, 241–4).

11 A very influential document at that time was Maori Marsden's 'God, Man and the Universe' (1975), which drew on the Greek terminology of the Gospels.

12 'Foster parents' is a term that describes *iwi*-appointed welfare officers.

13 It differs in all these respects from Mauritius, described in Eriksen (1998, 186).

14 This confirms analyses of Piddington (1968) – ignored too long – and Taylor (1992).

15 The character Potiki identifies, in part, with the demigod Mâui.

16 The same triadic typology, less developed, is present already in *Potiki* under the names of Roimata (=Missy), Tangimoana (=Makareta), and Mary (=Mata).

17 See the Sir Tipene O'Regan interview in Melbourne (1995, chap. 15).

18 Such ambiguities as a political and personal Mâori/Pâkehâ 'partnership' negotiated by setting up 'countercultures' and movements of resistance (Holland et al. 1998, 251).

19 See, for instance, Ihimaera (1986), especially chap. 20 and his use of Italian texts to accentuate the universality of the Matriach's sentiments, *passim*.

20 Salmond (1976, 1–176) describes this custom in detail.

21 Te Toi Huarewa was the suspended ladder climbed by the mythic hero Tawhaki. Today it also refers to a training support agency.

22 See note 14.

23 The *rongoâ* are gifts of the god Rongo who is also god of peace.

24 Pita Sharples keeps no copies of his songs after performance, but one of them survived and was printed in *Te Ao Mârama*, Vol. 5 (Ihimaera 1996, 84).

25 The program *Humanitateak-Enpresa, Lizentziatura* 1999 of Mondragon Unibertsitatea offers courses inter alia on psychology, language, sociology, literature, geography, history, art, philosophy, and social anthropology. These courses will survive only as long as they compete successfully with those offered by mainstream institutions.

26 The Basque country is an autonomous region of Spain under the *Ley organica 3/1979 de 18 de diciembre, de estatuto de autonomia para el Pais Vasco*.

27 Smith (1999) forcefully presents a balanced view on this delicate issue.

272   Eric Schwimmer

REFERENCES

Bakhtin, M.M. 1981. *The Dialogic Imagination: Four Essays by M.M. Bakhtin.* M. Holquist, ed. Austin: University of Texas Press.
– 1986. *Speech Genres and Other Late Essays.* Austin: University of Texas Press.
Barclay, B. 1990. *Our Own Image.* Auckland: Longman Paul.
Best, E. 1976, 1982. *Māori Religion and Mythology.* 2 vols. Wellington: Government Printer.
Binney, J. 1995. *Redemption Songs.* Auckland: Auckland University Press.
Buck, Sir P.T.R. 1949. *The Coming of the Māori.* Wellington: Whitcombe & Tombs.
Comaroff, J., and J. Comaroff. 1992. *Ethnography and the Historical Imagination.* Boulder, CO: Westview.
Curnow, J. 1985. 'Wiremu Maihi Te Rangikaheke: His Life and Work.' *Journal of the Polynesian Society* 94: 97–147.
Deloughrey, E. 1999. 'The Spiral Temporality of Patricia Grace's "Potiki."' *Ariel: A Review of International English Literature* 30 (1): 59–83.
Durie, M.H. 1994. *Whaiora – Māori Health Development.* Auckland: Oxford University Press.
– 1997. 'Whānau, Whanaungatanga and Healthy Māori Development.' In P. Te Whaiti, M. McCarthy, and A. Durie, eds., *Mai i Rangiātea*, 1–24. Auckland: Auckland University Press.
Eriksen, T.H. 1998. *Common Denominators: Ethnicity, Nation-Building and Compromise in Mauritius.* Oxford: Berg.
Government of Spain. 1979. *Ley organica 3/1979 de 18 de diciembre, de estatuto de autonomia el Pais Vasco.* Madrid: Government of Spain.
Grace, P. 1986. *Potiki.* Auckland: Penguin Books.
– 1992. *Cousins.* Auckland: Penguin Books.
Grey, Sir G. 1854. *Ko nga Mahinga ā nga Tūpuna.* London: Willis.
– 1855. *Polynesian Mythology.* London: Murray.
Holland, D., D. Skinner, W. Lachicotte Jr., and C. Cain. 1998. *Identity and Agency in Cultural Worlds.* Cambridge, MA: Harvard University Press.
Holquist, M. 1990. *Dialogism: Bakhtin and His World.* New York: Routledge.
Ihimaera, W. 1986. *The Matriarch.* Auckland: Heinemann.
– 1992. *Te Ao Mārama: Contemporary Māori Writing.* Vol. 1. Auckland: Reed.
– 1993a. *Te Ao Mārama: Contemporary Māori Writing.* Vol. 2. Auckland: Reed.
– 1993b. *Te Ao Mārama: Contemporary Māori Writing.* Vol. 3. Auckland: Reed.
– 1996. *Te Ao Mārama: Contemporary Māori Writing.* Vol. 5. Auckland: Reed.
Kawharu, H. 1975. *Orākei, a Ngāti Whātua Community.* Wellington: Council for Educational Research.

– 1975. *Conflict and Compromise*. Wellington: Reed.

Lévi-Strauss, C. 1962. *La Pensée sauvage*. Paris: Plon.

Lotman, Y.M. 1990. *Universe of the Mind: A Semiotic Theory of Culture*. Bloomington: Indiana University Press.

Marsden, M. 1975. 'God, Man and the Universe: A Māori View.' In M. King, ed., *Te Ao Hurihuri*, 191–219. Wellington: Hicks Smith.

Mead, S.M. 1997. *Landmarks, Bridges and Visions*. Wellington: Victoria University Press.

Melbourne, H. 1995. *Māori Sovereignty: The Māori Perspective*. Auckland: Hodder Moa Beckett.

Mendez, L. 1998. *Os labirintos do corpo*. Vigo, Spain: A Nosa Terra.

Metge, J. 1995. *New Growth from Old: The Whānau in the Modern World*. Wellington: Victoria University Press.

Ministerial Advisory Committee on Māori Health. 1990. *He Ara Tohutohu mō nga Hauora ā Rohe: Guidelines for Area Health Boards*. Wellington: Department of Health.

Mita, M. 1986. *Head and Shoulders*. Auckland: Penguin.

– 1993. 'Head and Shoulders' (extract). In W. Ihimaera, ed., *Te Ao Marama*. 278–82. Auckland: Reed.

Munn, N. 1986. *The Fame of Gawa*. Cambridge: Cambridge University Press.

Piddington, R. 1968. 'Emergent Development and "Integration."' In E. Schwimmer, ed., *The Māori People in the 1960s*, 257–69. Auckland: Blackwood and Janet Paul.

Rangihau, J. 1975. 'Being Māori.' In M. King, ed., *Te Ao Hurihuri*, 221–33. Wellington: Hicks Smith.

Rata, E. 1996. 'Global Capitalism and the Revival of Ethnic Traditionalism in New Zealand.' PhD diss., University of Auckland.

Ryan, P.M. 1995. *The Reed Dictionary of Modern Māori*. Auckland: Reed.

Salmond, A. 1976. *Hui: A Study of Māori Ceremonial Gatherings*. Auckland: Reed Methuen.

Schwimmer, E. 1990. 'The Māori Hapū: A Generative Model.' *Journal of the Polynesian Society* 99: 297–317.

Sharples, P. 1996. 'Hine-ahu-on.' In W. Ihimaera, ed., *Te Ao Mārama*, Vol. 5, 84. Auckland: Reed.

Smith, L.T. 1999. *Decolonising Methodologies: Research and Indigenous Peoples*. London: Zed Books.

Smith, S.P. 1913, 1915. *The Lore of the Whare Wānanga*. Vols. 1 and 2. New Plymouth, NZ: Avery.

Suzuki, D.T. 1959. *Zen and Japanese Culture*. Princeton: Princeton University Press.

Taylor, C. 1992. *Multiculturalism and 'The Politics of Recognition.'* Princeton: Princeton University Press.

Tuhoto-ariki. 1907. 'An Ancient Mâori Poem.' *Journal of the Polynesian Society* 16: 44.

Walker, R. 1990. *Ka Whawhai Tonu Mâtou: Struggle without End.* Auckland: Penguin.

Williams, H.W. 1971. *Dictionary of the Mâori Language.* Wellington: GP Publications.

Epilogue

ERIC SCHWIMMER

New fields in anthropology cannot be established outside the flow of conceptual changes permeating the general culture. We could enumerate many reference points on which new fields could be founded, ranging from Nietzsche and Heidegger to Marxism, psychoanalysis, and evolution, but even after this, as Sloterdijk (1999, 52) has suggested, our lives are confused answers to questions that were asked we know not where. This may well apply also to the works in the present volume, whose authors are not philosophers, and who necessarily borrowed existing anthropological frameworks. So, if these papers can begin to set up a new scholarly field, this field existed intuitively at the outset of the project, and it can be further specified only now that all the material is in.

Irrespective of when and where we were trained in anthropology, our professional careers were marked by a long series of conceptual bubbles that burst, from Cartesianism to colonialism to Western phenomenology and, more particularly, empiricism, which preached that there was objective truth to be discovered and mystification to be exposed. It was often during our fieldwork period, due to the philo-- sophical expertise of Indigenous mentors, that we discarded our naive self-image as seekers of truth.

I give my own case as an example. The house of an old Orokaiva (Papua New Guinea) villager burnt down, killing a child, and I was told the old man had carelessly left his fire burning, which explained the mishap. I gave him some clothes. A few days later, I was told a different story. The child had died as a result of sorcery practised by the lover of the child's mother. It was also this lover who burnt down the old man's house, because the old man had criticized his adulterous relationship with the child's mother. I expressed surprise that the plausible first explanation of the cause of the fire had been totally discarded. Did people no longer think the old man had been careless? No, they no longer thought so. Given that the child was dead, and the house burnt down, their only concern was to stop the lover from coming to the village again. They even started a law case against him. The Australian magistrate did not convict the lover of either sorcery or arson, but ruled that he could no longer visit the village. The only person querying that trumped-up ruling was I, impersonating the objective scientist.

I thought it was useful to know, and to state, what had *really* happened. I could see the practical wisdom of the actions of villagers and magistrate, but still thought we should *know* whether or not there had been sorcery and arson. The magistrate had sidestepped the question, but the villagers were satisfied as long as the lover did not come back. My anthropological report suggested that Orokaiva justice was based on fictions and that these fictions were a necessary part of their social system. However, I am no longer sure I can state the 'real truth' about this or any other incident. Perhaps the old man had been careless because of his anguish at the adultery; perhaps the child died because the lover distracted the mother from looking after it properly. The number of possibilities is endless and terms like 'arson' and 'adultery' are much less precise than they seem.

In any case, when do we need to know whether an interpretation of events is 'really true'? It was only during a later field trip that I learned the Orokaiva rules about the value of 'truth.' My friend André had joined a party that had gone out to kill a supposedly dangerous stray bull in the forest. I joined him there briefly and returned to the village. People asked me how the hunt was going and I deliberately fabricated a juicy hunting yarn instead of reporting the (so far) dreary reality. They laughed, knowing my story was invented, just like some of their own stories. People sometimes find it more agreeable or comforting to tell fictions rather than the debilitating or unverifiable bare truth. Ethnographic apprenticeship teaches what these situations are.

I thus learned by trivial examples what Parkin (in this volume) shows with rarer, substantial evidence: precise factual data (like violence suffered by victims) could be ascribed to a non-human, mythical agent like Popobawa. Parkin also describes the unbearable reality of actual political events, implying that people left it to Popobawa to convey sentiments it would be too dangerous for them to express otherwise. Samson and Tanner similarly show that there were unbearable realities Innu were unable to present to the outside world as they had no 'solid evidence' and would not be believed. If suicides are frequent among Innu, one reason could be that those who commit them are showing indisputable evidence that, for them, reality is unbearable. Suicides are like Popobawa signals: they state a mythical reality whose truth cannot be disputed, unlike a claim to find truth by empirical enquiry that can never be conclusive. The contemporary world is coming increasingly closer to Nietzsche's view that 'truth' is a kind of fiction. The fact that the United States keeps prisoners of war in cages thus illustrates the truth or fiction that we live in a particularly bestial age. Such changes in values do, of course, concern contemporary anthropology. Anthropological theory and method have not yet arrived, however, at a suitable response to such events.

Thus, the return to animism, discussed in this volume, reveals doubts concerning the 'reality' of 'facts' about progress since hominization. Progress has been spectacular in certain domains, but our image of that progress could, in other respects, have been illusory. What Ingold calls the 'poetics of dwelling' could be an ineradicable, ever-present part of the human condition. This could also be the case with what Appadurai (1996) has analysed as our stubborn attachment to 'locality.' If this is no more than a theoretical starting point, Poirier's notion of 'apprenticeship' carries the study of such patterns to the level of scholarly method. The religious pattern that Clammer calls animism is flourishing in highly industrial civilizations as much as among hunters and gatherers, but it has likewise so far escaped detailed scholarly attention.

It is in that framework that Parts II to IV of this book should also be understood. If there have thus been several notable gaps in mankind's social evolution, then there has perhaps never been a rational basis for colonialism or the superiority of majority over minority peoples. By such reasoning, furthermore, there is no room either for ideas of regression, but some domains of life have to be treated as unalterable, even though we do not yet know their biological foundation. The emphasis on ontologies in this volume expresses a need for anthropologists to ask questions about what is supposed to exist. Here, the ontological 'proof' is not to determine, as in earlier years, whether God exists, but is more like 'dismantling a clock to demonstrate how its parts work together.'[1] This is the major preoccupation of every chapter.

It is risky to formulate in overall terms what binds together the constituent chapters of this book. Perhaps the best point of entry is the debate with Maurice Bloch in Adrian Tanner's chapter. This is part of the endless argument within the humanist heritage that goes back to Spinoza's critique of Descartes. In a programmatic book such as this, it is useful to recall the many points on which Spinoza was in agreement with Descartes and on which Tanner and Bloch are likewise in agreement, for instance, the cardinal importance of clear and distinct universal concepts and propositions, and of rigorous logical sequences. Moreover, Descartes's *cogito* was not always aridly cognitive – he even wrote a treatise on the passions of the soul. Disagreement between Cartesian foundations and the anthropological methods of this book mostly arises in specific fields, in a framework of sociocultural pathologies for which remedies are sought in cosmocentric ontologies. Although, in these fields, we are concerned less with universals than with 'actual systems of real people' (as Tanner suggests), this is justifiable in terms consistent with the Cartesian foundation of the modern scientific attitude. We can illustrate this conveniently by making a brief reference to Michel Foucault's Collège de France seminars of the 1980s, reflecting on the history of the relationship between truth and subjectivity and, in particular, on the notion of 'taking care of oneself.'

This issue preoccupied the philosophers of classical antiquity, from Plato to the fifth century AD. It dealt not only with how to behave, how to take action, and how to have relations with others, but also with turning one's gaze from the outside, the others, and the world to internal self-reflection. Above all, the notion of taking care of oneself meant to take charge of oneself, to change, purify, transform, and transfigure oneself. The question arises why, especially since the Renaissance, all this was excluded from the field of modern philosophic thought. Foucault's answer was that Descartes's *cogito ergo sum* made knowledge beyond any possible doubt into a necessary condition of access to being. This principle was substituted for the older Socratic one of *gnôthi seauton*, and effectively disqualified it. As Foucault writes, 'l'histoire de la vérité est entrée dans sa période moderne le jour où on a admis que ce qui donne accès à la vérité, les conditions selon lesquelles le sujet peut avoir accès à la vérité, c'est la connaissance, et la connaissance seulement. Il me semble que c'est là où ce que j'ai appelé le "moment cartésien" prend sa place et son sens' (2001, 19).

This is also Bloch's heritage, but then Bloch is interested exclusively in what Foucault calls 'les conditions internes de l'acte de connaissance.' There are many other conditions but all those are 'extrinsic.' Those are the kinds of conditions Tanner and Samson are concerned with – and, long before them, Spinoza:

Prenez les neuf premiers paragraphes de la *Réforme de l'entendement* de Spinoza. Et là vous verrez ... comment chez Spinoza le problème de l'accès à la vérité était lié, dans sa formulation même, à une série d'exigences qui concernaient l'être même du sujet : en quoi et comment dois-je transformer mon être même de sujet? Quelles conditions est-ce que je dois lui imposer pour pouvoir avoir accès à la vérité, et dans quelle mesure cet accès à la vérité me donnera-t-il ce que je cherche, c'est à dire le bien souverain, le souverain bien? ... je crois que le thème de la réforme de l'entendement au XVIIE siècle est tout à fait caractéristique des liens encore très stricts, très étroits, très serrés entre, disons, une philosophie de la connaissance et une spiritualité de la transformation de l'être du sujet par lui-même.' (Foucault 2001, 29).

The excuse for these long quotations is that they give a sort of summary of the framework of the healing movement described in various chapters of this book, especially Tanner's. We are introduced to all the extrinsic conditions of knowledge Cree and Innu had to impose on themselves in order to have access to the truth that, as subjects, they needed to attain to the good they were seeking. Tanner systematically reviews the long list of conditions: religious concepts, ritual actions, ceremonial performances, and, above all, reconstitution of their habitus of relations to landscape, animals, narratives, dreams, visions, social system, as well as many affects, aroused by images provided by such experiences, that may transform Cree and Innu subjects into active agents of human progress.

Bloch's idea is that none of this is knowledge, because none of these concepts are universals causally connected to other universals. They are, according to Cartesian logic, extrinsic to knowledge, but as Foucault points out, they may be part of a process of self-empowerment. They may help distressed subjects in need of care-of-the-self, as a precondition to recover a capacity of attaining to knowledge. It should be noted, however, that Foucault's analysis of Spinoza is placed in a historical framework and not as a kind of general law. As far as today's Cree and Innu are concerned, Tanner's paper shows evidence that the subjects in question, once their care-of-the-self is restored, turn to the resolution of what he calls practical questions. This is what I also show in my paper about the Mâori. There also, the first step of the healing program was for the group to provide communality to new members, by sharing knowledge and practices. It was only on the basis of this communality that members became able to acquire what Bloch or

Descartes would qualify as knowledge. But in Foucault's theory, this is happening because the peoples in question are in a particular state of philosophical transition. Yet that is the state we happen to be studying.

It does not need demonstrating that the peoples we studied, and many others, are now in need of this care-of-the-self and this communality. What does need attention is the question of what role anthropology is to play in this, and the reason why we set up the present cosmocentric schema as the basis of our method. It is in dealing with that question that we are apt to meet with opposition like Bloch's. There is, of course, first of all, the point that we are describing healing methods we observed amongst peoples we have actually studied, but why should that be relevant? The more basic point is that these methods involve the asking and answering of ontological questions of the type 'Who are you?' and 'Who am I?'

When I did fieldwork in Whangaruru, New Zealand, I inquired into the class of Māori deities called animal guardians, a form of animism that still survived into the 1960s and perhaps even today. The most frightening of these animal guardians was the one that took the form of a large bird called *kawau*. It would swoop down on its victim screaming *kawau*. And the victim would become hysterical and very sick. But what the victim heard in that cry was '*Ko wai ahau?*' (Who am I?),' a question that would horrify any person unable to answer it. An anthropologist could as easily be the victim of that kind of ordeal as an informant.

Such experiences clarify what is ultimately involved in taking the 'non-human persons' seriously. Could this dangerous bird be addressing an anthropologist? Well, some anthropologists do take the same question seriously, when, for instance, it was asked by Socrates and reported by Plato. Other anthropologists, for the sake of scientific rigour, prefer to set it aside.

Finally, the issue remains ambiguous. One part of me takes it seriously, whether the question is asked by Socrates or a fabulous bird, while another part of me still poses a further, professional question: why do *these* people tell *this* story? But if I ask and answer it (for such professional questions always do have an answer), do I become any wiser? The Mormons say that *kawau* was the devil. The person to whom the bird was said to have appeared became a Mormon convert. By force of professional habit, I noted a sort of symbolic equation between Socrates and the devil. So did the judges who condemned Socrates to death. Ah, but we become no wiser if we take up that inquiry. Perhaps the bird's question was still the right one.

NOTE

1 Mason (1997, 35) uses this phrase to describe Spinoza's ontology.

REFERENCES

Appadurai, A. 1996. *Modernity at Large.* Minneapolis: University of Minnesota Press.
Foucault, M. 2001. *L'herméneutique du sujet. Cours au collège de France, 1981–1982.* Paris: Gallimard, Seuil.
Mason, R. 1997. *The God of Spinoza: A Philosophical Study.* Cambridge: Cambridge University Press.
Sloterdijk, P. 1999. *Règles pour le parc humain.* Paris: Mille et une nuits.

Contributors

John Clammer is Professor of Comparative Sociology and Asian Studies at Sophia University, Tokyo. He is trained as an anthropologist, and his work encompasses economic anthropology, ethnicity, development studies, and the anthropology of religion with a focus on Japan and Southeast Asia.

Tim Ingold is Professor of Social Anthropology at the University of Aberdeen. He has carried out fieldwork in Finnish Lapland and has written on comparative questions of environment, technology, and social organization in the circumpolar North, evolutionary theory in anthropology, biology, and history, the role of animals in human society, and issues in human ecology. His current research is in the anthropology of technology and environmental perception.

Bjarne Melkevik, DDL (Paris), is Professor of Law at the Faculty of Law, Université Laval. His main domains of research are legal philosophy and legal epistemology, international legal protection of Indigenous Peoples, and political Indigenous legal affairs. He is the author of *Horizons de la philosophie du droit* 1998); *Réflexions sur la philosophie du droit* 2000); *Rawls ou Habermas. Une question de philosophie du droit* (Quebec: PUL; Brussels, Bruylant, 2002); and co-author of *Peuples autochtones et normes internationales* (1996).

David Parkin is Head of the School of Anthropology, University of Oxford. His research interests include religious transformation with special reference to Muslims in East Africa, Indian Ocean diasporas, healing systems, language use, and the politics of objects and artefacts.

His recent books include *Sacred Void* (1991). He is co-editor of *Islamic Prayer across the Indian Ocean* (2001).

Sylvie Poirier is Professor of Anthropology at Université Laval. Her main domains of research include the anthropology of dreams, anthropology of religion, contemporary hunters and gatherers, and indigenous political and territorial claims in Australia and Canada, with a focus on Western Desert Aborigines (Australia) and the Atikamekw (north-central Quebec). She is the author of a number of articles and a monograph, *Les jardins du nomade. Cosmologie, territoire et personne dans le désert ocidental australien* (1996) (with a support from the CNRS).

Colin Samson is Senior Lecturer in Sociology and Director of American Studies at the University of Essex in England. He is the author of *A Way of Life That Does Not Exist: Canada and the Extinguishment of the Innu* (2003). He maintains interests in the areas of Native American history, politics, and art, as well as medical anthropology and environmental studies.

Eric Schwimmer was Professor of Anthropology at Université Laval until his retirement in 1992. He taught at the University of Toronto from 1968 to 1974. He specialized in the Mâori (New Zealand) and Orokaiva (Papua New Guinea). His latest books are *Le syndrome des Plaines d'Abraham* (1995) (with Michel Chartier); *Parle et je t'écouterai* (1996) (with André Iteanu).

Adrian Tanner is Honorary Research Professor of Anthropology at Memorial University of Newfoundland. His current research deals with Moose Cree (Ontario) knowledge of their forest environment. He also conducts research in Fiji. Recent publications include 'The Double Bind of Aboriginal Self-Government,' in Colin Scott (ed.), *Aboriginal Autonomy and Development in Northern Quebec and Labrador* (2001) and *Bringing Home Animals*, a book on Cree hunting rituals.

Sylvie Vincent, an independent researcher, has focused mainly on the oral tradition of the Quebec Innu, while working in a variety of other fields. She has been particularly interested in collecting stories told by the elders of events and phenomena from the past, which help us to understand how elderly Innu view their history.

Index

Aboriginal rights, 231–8
Aboriginal treatment centres, 195
Abuse, domestic, 152
Action, hunters', 70–3. *See also* Ancestors
Adelson, Naomi, 195, 206
Aesthetic forms, 5, 74–8, 106–7, 228, 231, 260, 265
Ainu, 103
Akaneshau. *See* Euro-Canadian
Akasaka N., 101
Alcohol, 152, 179–80, 195; expresses Innu experience, 180
Alienation, collective, 162–72, 180; of hunting land, 195; and reckless dependence, 172
Alliance, 136–8; economic aid, 137; irreconcilable interpretations, 138; territory, 137
Anadabijou, 136
Ancestors, 64, 67–8, 87, 103, 245–6; as actors, 62–3, 72–3; as agencies, 59–60, 64, 70; as connections, 61–4, 68, 75–6, 87, 92, 100; embodiment of, 68–9, 74, 77, 87; exchange with, 71, 87; by genealogy, by life-world, 53; mediators of, 75

Ancestral order, 60, 65–8, 74, 88, 90; consubstantial, 66; encounters with, 67; essence, 62, 65, 69; female deities in, 77; immanent, 65; law, 76; time of, 139–41
Ancestral rights, 231–8; droits ancestraux, 232; fixed, 232; inherent, 231; social test of refused, 232–4
Anderson, C., and F. Dussart, 76
Andrew, Ben, and Peter Sarsfield, 174–5
Animacy, 34–8, 97–8
Animals: encounters, 198, 206; family groups and leaders, 207; homeland of (*nôcimîc*), 207–8; as liberation, 103; masters (gods), 141, 174–6, 203, 209; in narratives, 30, 141; non-anthropomorphic, 29–30; rules of respect, 165, 174, 197–8, 204–8; spirits, 204–8; as spirits of the dead, 31; as spiritual beings, 204–5, 210, 280. *See also* Anthropomorphism
Animism, x, 7–9, 50–3, 83–107, 141; in alternative medicine, 103–4; alternative social analysis, 84; and

263–4; suffering, 116–18; unity of –
and mind, 98, 103, 106
Bolle, Kees, 86
Boundaries, 101, 216
Bourdieu, Pierre, 12, 17, 247, 268
Brightman, Robert, 203
Brøsted, J., 238
Brody, Hugh, 193
Brosseau, James, 173
Buck, Sir Peter Te Rangihiroa, 263
Buddhism, x, 14, 88, 90, 98–100

Cartesianism, 275
Ceremonials, 17, 36, 39, 196
Certeau, Michel de, 61, 75, 77, 142
Champlain, Samuel de, 135–6, 138
Child (protection, abuse), 168
Chomsky, Noam, 215
Christianity, Japanese, 7–8
Clammer, John, x, 3–20, 83–109, 277
Clark, Bruce, 231
Clifford, James, 4
Clinics, 124, 127
Code, 12, 144, 217; code switching,
13, 165, 217
Co-development, 91–102, 257–68,
271n18
Coexistence, 132; of people in
territory, 132; of versions of
history, 132
Cognitive barriers to intercultural
understanding, 6, 20, 189–94, 213–
14, 217; differences, 49; incompat-
ible metaphysics, 189–91; practical
misunderstandings, 191–4; practi-
cal problems of, 189–94
Colonialism, 20, 162–9, 182, 267, 275
Common denominators, 226, 244, 252
Communality, 101, 103–5, 164, 168,

229, 245, 260, 279–80
Communication, 189, 205, 215–17.
Community (larger): 157, 161;
localities of sedentary indigenes,
151–5, 160–1, 164, 172, 181, 189;
settler (Euro-Canadian), 155–6,
161; trustee of Great Law of Na-
ture, 229. *See also* Settlement;
Village
Conception, 66–9
Conflict resolution, 168
Consciousness, 102–3, 215
Constitutional Act (1982), 231
Constructivism and culturalism,
9–10, 12–13, 19–20, 102
Consubstantiality, 60, 64–6
Continuous birth, 37–8, 62, 66, 73
Contradiction, 153; biologists/
hunters, 176; double binds, 165–6.
See also Meaning
Control, 93, 115
Cosmology, cosmic, 89, 98, 104, 189;
communion, 230; human relation-
ships with, 89, 97; law, 228; of
nature, 204, 208–12, 227; order,
204, 208, 211–12, 218
Cosmocentric/anthropocentric, 5,
46, 89, 91–4, 100–1
Counter-discourse, 87, 95–6, 271n18
Creation spirituality, 103–4, 227
Cree, of Quebec, 194; northern and
eastern, compared, 203
Cultural incompatibilities, 191–5,
213–14, 216–17
Culturalism/constructionism, 10,
20
Culture, 213; boundaries, 213;
ordering principles, 214
Culture camp, 18, 201

Eriksen, Thomas H., 3, 244, 252
Essentialism, 10, 100, 117–18, 129;
  essence of aboriginalism, 233
Ethnicity, 3, 5, 14, 19–20; ethnocentric judgments, 189
Euro-Canadian, 152–3, 180; authority, 161–2; idea of Innu goals,
  167–8; professional codes, 173–4
Events, in history, 132–41; conceptual framework, 138–43; fore-
  grounds and backgrounds,
  118–19; interpretation, 135–8;
  models, characteristic situations,
  140; narration, 133–5; reconciling
  accounts, 129, 137, 144; relativity,
  fluidity, analogy, 143–5
Evil, as imperfection of human
  choice, 116, 128
Evolution, 85–6, 167, 277; poetics of
  dwelling, 55, 61; of species in
  nature, 53–5
Exclusion, 101–2
Exodus, 136
Experience, 35–42, 58–9; Indigenous
  concept of, 39–41, 142; mythico-
  ritual, 64–6, 73–5; ontological level
  of, 151, 16; and ritual thought,
  214–15; sensory involvement, 39–
  40; truth, authenticity, 40; Western
  concept of, 39–41. See also Alcohol;
  Alienation

Fair, L., 122
Fanon, Franz, 162, 182
Farley, M., 162
Farnell, Linda, 75
Figured worlds, ix, 3–5, 9–12, 17,
  270n5; authoring selves, 248–54,
  268; characters, meanings, values,
  246; complementary, ix; conflict-

ing, ix; Mâori, 245–7; positional
  identity, 12–15, 17, 247–9, 252–4,
  270n7; relational logic, 9, 11, 12;
  remaking, by reinterpretation, 257;
  sites of cultural production, 254;
  types of, in Mâori fiction, 253–4.
  See also Persons; Identity; Voices;
  Dialogism; Co-development;
  Cosmocentric; Kaupapa Mâori
Foreigners, 140–1
Foucault, Michel, 94, 117, 247, 268,
  278–80
Fouillard, Camille, 195
Fox, M., 103, 105
Framework, conceptual, 133, 138–44;
  Nechi vs Innu, 177–9; time, 138–9
Freud, Sigmund, 86
Frideres, James S., 219n3
Fujisawa C., 104

Gatherings, 191, 197–202. See
  also Culture camps
Gaventa, John, 185n17
Geertz, Clifford, 58, 142–3
Genealogical model, 52–3
Gennep, Arnold van, 85
Girard, Camil, and Édith Gagné,
  136–7
Glowczewski, Barbara, 79n7
Gluck, Carol, 91
Goehring, Brian, 238
Goody, Jack, 11
Gordon, Milton, 235
Grace, Patricia, 253–4, 256, 262
Grandfathers, other-than-human,
  31–2, 39; as guardians, 32. See also
  under Person
Great Law of Nature, 227–9
Grey, Sir George, 245
Guardian spirits, 30, 40, 203

Anthropological Horizons

Editor: Michael Lambek, University of Toronto

Published to date: